Communism
and
Communist Systems

Communism
and
Communist Systems

Robert G. Wesson

Professor of Political Science
University of California at Santa Barbara

Prentice-Hall, Inc., *Englewood Cliffs, New Jersey 07632*

Library of Congress Cataloging in Publication Date
WESSON, ROBERT G
     Communism and communist systems.

     Includes bibliographical references and index.
     1. Communism.   I. Title.
HX56.W47   320.9'171'7   77-24378
ISBN   0-13-153437-8

© 1978 by Prentice-Hall, Inc.
Englewood Cliffs, New Jersey 07632

10 9 8 7 6 5 4 3 2 1

Printed in the United States of America

PRENTICE-HALL INTERNATIONAL, INC., *London*
PRENTICE-HALL OF AUSTRALIA PTY. LIMITED, *Sydney*
PRENTICE-HALL OF CANADA, LTD., *Toronto*
PRENTICE-HALL OF INDIA PRIVATE LIMITED, *New Delhi*
PRENTICE-HALL OF JAPAN, INC., *Tokyo*
PRENTICE-HALL OF SOUTHEAST ASIA PTE. LTD., *Singapore*
WHITEHALL BOOKS LIMITED, *Wellington, New Zealand*

KM
3-1-82

Contents

Preface

The most striking political phenomenon of our times is the rise and growth of Communism. The Russian Revolution, from its inception, was the political sensation of the century and the focus of an enormous volume of political controversy. It became even more influential after Fascism, a reaction to Communism and in some ways its reflection, was vanquished in the Second World War. Fourteen or fifteen states, including two of the biggest and most important and comprising a third of humanity, have turned sharply away from what once seemed the clearcut road of historical development, and have challenged, materially and morally, the basic Western tradition. Some—including numerous non-Communists—regard this as essentially progressive, pointing to the commitment of Communist states to modernization and social justice. Others consider it regressive, pointing to repressive practices and un- or antilibertarian political structures erected in the name of revolutionary liberation. There is, however, no doubt of its importance. The simpler nineteenth century viewed civilization as single and unilinear; Lenin and his followers divided it politically with consequences yet to be fully grasped.

For these reasons, Communism has evoked an enormous outpour of literature, propagandistic, polemical, and scholarly. But it mostly concerns itself with particular countries particularly those with the greatest capacity for upsetting world affairs such as Russia-Soviet Union and China. There are also many treatments of the ideology and practices of Communism as a revolutionary movement, especially in the Western world, a subject beyond the purview of the present work. Comparative analyses of Communist states are few, even of the two hostile but in many ways kindred giants.[1] Studies of the Communist countries together, considered as a political genus, are remarkable for their non-existence. Books on comparative Communism are ordinarily collections of articles on various Communist states.[2] It is my hope in this book to step into this somewhat forbidding gap and to attempt a broad summary of the entire Communist system of government, somewhat as a zoologist might attempt an introductory monograph on cats.

This study consequently includes the obvious kinds of information, plus generalizations and surmises, which a student would expect regarding a genus or family under examination. This includes first a survey of the general character-istics of the Communist states to make clear what we are talking about and why we consider these states to form a group apart. Next to be studied are the general conditions giving rise to this political phenomenon and related forms. This leads to more specific considerations of how individual Communist regimes have come into existence; that is, the genesis of the Bolshevik state in Russia, of Mao's China, Castro's Cuba, etc. Then individual Communist states are sur-veyed, the most important in some detail, others hastily, to establish some of the ways in which Communist states may vary within the common parameters. Finally, there are some observations of evolutionary trends of Communist states and societies, which may yield some conjectures as to the future course of Communist systems.

It is a pleasure to acknowledge indebtedness to many persons who have been helpful in the preparation of this book, especially those who read all or part of the manuscript and offered criticisms and suggestions. Among these, the following should noted: Alvin Z. Rubinstein, Alan P. Liu, Arpad Kadarky, John S. Reshetar Jr., Milorad Drachkovitch, Alexander Dallin, and John N. Hazard. Their comments have made it possible to eliminate misconceptions and tighten the argument whether or not they fully agreed with it.

ROBERT G. WESSON

---

[1] Donald W. Treadgold, ed., *Soviet and Chinese Communism* (Seattle: University of Washington Press, 1973), is an outstanding example.

[2] Such as, for example, Gary K. Bertsch and Thomas W. Ganschow, *Comparative Com-munism: The Soviet, Chinese, and Yugoslav Models* (San Francisco: W.H. Freeman, 1976), Lenard J. Cohen and Jane P. Shapiro, *Communist Systems in Comparative Perspective* (Garden City: Doubleday, 1974), or Alvin Z. Rubinstein, *Communist Political Systems* (Englewood Cliffs: Prentice-Hall, 1966); Chalmers A. Johnson, ed., *Change in Communist Systems* (Stanford: Stanford University Press, 1970) contains more comparative material but attempts no overall description or analysis.

Communism
and
Communist Systems

Chapter one

Nature of Communist States

It may be questioned whether the states commonly called Communist or Marxist-Leninist—the Soviet Union, its six East European allies (Bulgaria, Czechoslovakia, East Germany, Hungary, Poland, and Romania), Mongolia, Yugoslavia, Albania, Cuba, China, North Korea, and Vietnam with its sister states of Indochina—form a coherent object of study.[1] They include some relatively advanced and fairly affluent societies, such as the German Democratic Republic and the Soviet Union, along with some feebly modernized economies, such as Albania and Vietnam. From the Marxist viewpoint of historical materialism it would be absurd to lump such disparate entities together. A cultural or social historian could not contemplate treating together countries with cultural traditions so different as those of Confucius and Leibniz. They are joined by no friendship; China and the Soviet Union, one another's worst enemies and strongest critics, certainly do not admit a familial relation. Yet, the utility of the classification can hardly be doubted—few political labels are so consistently applied. It may be uncertain whether an individual is properly to be called Communist, but our listing of states is hardly open to dispute except as some might be inclined to increase it by adding a few radical leftist governments. Parisians celebrating the 1975 victory of Communists in Vietnam did not doubt that this was much more significant than the replacement of one authoritarian regime by another.

There is no generally accepted analytical category, however, for states designated as "Communist." It was formerly the mode to characterize them as "totalitarian," but this, if satisfactory in Stalin's time, has become much less so.

---

[1] Concerning the study of Communist systems, see "Symposium" by John A. Armstrong, Alfred G. Meyer, John H. Kautsky, Dan N. Jacobs, and Robert S. Sharlet, in *Slavic Review*, 26, no. 1 (March 1967), 1-28.

The correspondence of "Communist" and "totalitarian" has never been exact; the latter designation, in fact, belonged to fascist states rather than to Communist ones, having been invented as a description of Mussolini's Italy. Moreover, to characterize Communist states as totalitarian by no means exhausts their qualities. This term, originally connoting praise for the would-be thoroughness of fascist regimes, later came to be associated with the cold war and terror, which many persons feel no longer applies to the majority of Communist states. There is likewise an implication of fixity frequently (and unjustifiably) read into the totalitarian model which is belied by visible change in the Communist states. Perhaps partly from the desire to encourage such change, writers hesitate to apply the pejorative adjective.

Another conceptual framework for consideration of Communist states is as mobilizing-developmental regimes. This is perhaps as valid as the totalitarian approach, but the two are not necessarily contradictory except in an emotional sense, the one stressing the positive, the other the negative aspects of a regime which sets about forcefully and more or less brutally to reshape a society. The mobilizing-developmental model is certainly valid to the extent that it points to an important generality, the fact that Communist revolutions have been victorious only where there has been a strong drive to modernization, be it for welfare or, perhaps more intensely, for national security, strength, and pride. Thus, in and after World War II, Communist movements came to power in Europe not only where the Soviet occupation so decreed but in areas most in need of economic development, Albania and Yugoslavia. However, the developmental approach fails to differentiate Communist from non-Communist states concerned with rapid economic growth; the Communist road is certainly not the only one, perhaps not usually the best, to industrialization. Moreover, the developmental approach tells little about Communist ways and forms.

The only generally recognized categorization of the Communist states is that they are Communist. This is no empty tautology. Communist states in effect are self-defined. They call themselves such with insistent pride and boast of their moral and political superiority over the non-Communist world. Although only seven of these nations' ruling parties are actually labelled "Communist," the others being "workers'" or "labor" parties,[2] they all recognize their equivalence to the Communist Party as exemplified by the Soviet party, Lenin's party. More significantly, non-Soviet parties maintain doctrinal adherence to Marxism-Leninism—although the Yugoslavs usually simply call themselves Marxists. This ideology is variously interpreted and applied, but it is quite remarkable that non-Russian, even anti-Russian independent states should insist upon the authority of a long-dead Russian; that peoples as diverse as Chinese, Romanians, and Cubans do so is a tribute to the usefulness of Lenin's ideas.

---

[2] Michael Waller, *The Language of Communism* (London: Bodley Head, 1972), p. 8.

The group of states ordinarily called Communist also has unity of historical origin; all, in one way or another, have come out of the Russian Revolution. Not only were Communist governments in most East European countries, Mongolia, and North Korea put in place under the overseeing eye of Soviet occupation authorities; revolutions in China, Vietnam, and Yugoslavia were carried out by parties formed by or actual members of the Comintern, founded by Lenin and always dominated by the Soviet Union. Fidel Castro made his own non-Communist revolution; but he put it into the organizational framework of the old Cuban Communist party, of onetime Comintern discipline, and sought support and accepted guidance from the Soviet state. It may be noted, incidentally, that non-Soviet Communisms are of Stalinist rather than Leninist imprint, although Stalin has been set aside as a prophet in countries following the Soviet line.

The Communist genus has thus been defined in a de facto fashion. Nonetheless the degree of similarity of institutions, policies, and ideals of the fifteen or sixteen states considered Communist is in fact quite remarkable and not easily accounted for in the face of their diversity of conditions and background. The similarity of institutions from East Germany to Vietnam to Cuba, for example, is an extraordinary refutation of economic or cultural determinism and an affirmation of the power of politics. Compared to the varied structures and outlooks of states conventionally called democratic, the Communist ones are extraordinarily alike despite their differing emphases. This does not mean that statements made about them necessarily apply to all in anything like the same degree. Humans after all deviate endlessly, yet they form a class quite distinct from non-human organisms. A one-legged man is human, just as Yugoslavia is Communist despite the delegation of some powers to workers' councils.

It is at the same time true that the line between Communist and non-Communist is somewhat indistinct. A number of African states take or have taken a leftist-radical stance in world affairs, have used much of the Marxist-Leninist vocabulary, and have imitated Soviet Communist institutions. These include Congo (Brazzaville), Tanzania, Mozambique,[3] Angola, Guinea-Bissau, Somalia, Guinea, Burundi, and Equatorial Guinea. It might well be instructive to consider some of these together with longer-recognized Communist states; the chief reason for not doing so in the present work is the great difference between their economic and social conditions and those of European or even Asiatic Communist countries. Various other nations, including Algeria and Iraq, have also claimed socialism as their goal or condition and used more or less

---

[3] Mozambique has perhaps come closest to the Communist model. It carried out an extensive purge of "reactionaries," imposed the military discipline of the "people's democracies" and a political party organized in the name of Marxism-Leninism, nationalized even private homes, and decreed work without pay for some people. *New York Times*, February 4, 1976, p. 5.

Communist political language, while displaying political traits ordinarily associated with Communism—strong leadership, single ruling party, close control of communications, free use of force, and monopoly management of a large part of the economy, especially banking and foreign trade. It is quite probable that the boundary between Communist and non-Communist will continue to become more blurred in the Third World.

Despite these qualifying remarks, there are many strong and usually fairly clear distinguishing characteristics of Communist regimes. More numerous than commonly realized, they may be grouped in two broad but interrelated categories, the political–organizational and the ideological–psychological.

Political Morphology

Marxism vs. Leninism. Marx was concerned with theory, Lenin with organization. Although the Communist states claim to draw inspiration from Marx (and Engels), they are in fact more Leninist than Marxist. Thus the role of the political party, as emphasized in writings and practice by Lenin, is more essential than class consideration in the Marxist sense. However often Communist revolutions have invoked the name and idea of the proletariat, they have never yielded real power to the workers. Several Communist revolutions, especially in Asia, have leaned, usually frankly, on the peasantry, even while talking of the proletariat in Marxist fashion; but the Leninist party has always been the mover and director of first the revolution and then the state.

Communist countries are more Leninist than Marxist because Lenin speaks to them in the language of organization and power. Marx is vague, more or less philosophical, and concerned primarily with revolution in an industrialized society. Lenin is direct and concerned with securing power in a relatively unindustrialized country—Russia, and by extension anywhere. The revolutionary party as adapted by Lenin is central to Communist governments. It acquires a mystic value through its mystic relation to the proletariat and historical destiny; and people should be, and often are, loyal to it for its own sake, as to a church. One belongs to it as to an enveloping brotherhood. For the true believer, the party is not a means but the end, the way and meaning of life.[4]

Communist Party. The influence of Lenin (and Stalin) is the more striking because Communist states not only maintain the general principle of the supremacy of the party as vanguard of the proletariat; they follow similar patterns. Membership is somewhat elitist, elected supposedly from the best of the working classes, ranging from about two to three percent of the total population in Cuba and China to six percent in East Germany and North Korea. In non-Communist states, political parties, even those of one-party states, are ordinarily open to all those interested; in the Communist world the party is a self-selected elite.

---

[4] Robert V. Daniels, *The Conscience of the Revolution: Communist Opposition in Soviet Russia* (Cambridge: Harvard University Press, 1960), p. 16.

The parties that form the core of Communist states are also similar in structure. They have cells or primary membership groups, and elected local, district, and/or regional and national conferences or congresses, which at the higher levels meet quite infrequently. More operative are the committees or bureaus and secretaries at all levels except perhaps the very lowest. At each level, party committees have more or less administrative staff (called "departments" in the Soviet Union and most other states) to manage party affairs, exercise control over governmental and other organizations at their level, and to cooperate in indoctrinating and mobilizing the people.

At the top there is a Central Committee of a few score to a few hundred individuals, which is at least in theory the most authoritative arm of the party meeting with any frequency. A more effective leadership group is the Secretariat of the Central Committee, typically composed of six to ten Secretaries, headed by a General Secretary or First Secretary, who is the leader of the party and at least primus inter pares of the political system.[5] The most powerful organ of all is the top governing committee, usually called the Political Bureau or Politburo (termed "Presidium" in the Soviet Union from 1952 to 1966 and in the present regimes of Czechoslovakia, Romania, and Yugoslavia), composed ordinarily of twelve to fifteen men. There is substantial overlap between Secretariat and Politburo, many or most of the Secretaries being members of the Politburo.

This degree of institutional uniformity in countries large and small, primitive-rural and urban-industrialized is accountable by imitation of the powerful motherland of Communism, by the fact that Communist parties have been founded by Comintern, i.e., Soviet agents or affiliated persons, and by the fact that Leninist organizational forms have been found very effective for the exercise of power.

There is considerable resemblance in de facto as well as in formal organizational principles. At each level, the elite within the elite are the apparatusmen, principally the secretaries. Decision making is strongly centralized; maximum attainable concentration of decision making and loyalty to higher authority are practically the essence of Communism. Analogous to the party's assertion of absolute supremacy over society is the concentration of authority in ever narrower circles within the party. The unity of the party is held sacrosanct, an indefeasible principle to which everything else must yield.

Unity generally means unity around a leader, a central personage with the modest title of "First Secretary" or "General Secretary" (except in Yugoslavia and China, where the grand figure is "President" and "Chairman" respectively). Although neither ideology nor party rules furnish a basis of monarchy, the leader has usually been strong if not monarchic. The history of the movement has been made primarily by powerful individuals—Lenin, Stalin, Khrushchev,

---

[5] The central Secretariat in China was dissolved in the Cultural Revolution beginning in 1966.

Mao, Tito, Castro, Hoxha, Kim Il Song, among others—excercising monocratic if not despotic powers. The leader has also been virtually irremovable in the independent Communist countries, the ouster of Khrushchev in 1964 having been the notable exception. A Tito or Mao remains the respected, even un-challenged authority into advanced age, in true monarchic fashion, and ordi-narily survives failures that would topple rulers in less firmly organized lands. Thus Stalin came through the early 1930s, despite the disasters of collectiviza-tion and a sharply reduced standard of living. Mao survived the Great Leap Forward (1959-1961) falling flat, although he was more respected than obeyed prior to his Cultural Revolution. Castro was unbowed by the ignominious shortfall of his planned 10 million-ton sugar harvest of 1970, although he had to retreat from his style of personal government.

There has been some feeling for the propriety of collective leadership; after the demise of Lenin, Stalin, and Khrushchev the superiority of shared power has been taken for granted, and a fairly equal oligarchy has taken the reins. In each case, however, an individual has been able to make himself clearly superior to his fellows. Possibly the only real collective leadership in the Com-munist world today is that of Vietnam.

Whether or not they are truly dictatorial, Communist leaders are rarely removed except by death (as Stalin) or infirmity (as Ulbricht). By way of com-pensation, however, they (except founding fathers) are usually deprecated by their successors. Thus Khrushchev denounced Stalin; Brezhnev and company, Khrushchev. In East Germany, Honecker in charge found his former mentor and boss, the grand old man of that Communist state, to have been unworthy. In Romania, Ceausescu similarly condemned his predecessor. In the past, in-security of subordinates, or purge, has seemed a frequent feature of the Com-munist way. It has receded in the maturer Communist societies, and a good deal of security of tenure seems to be the rule in most. But the stakes of polit-ical struggle are still morally equivalent to death, because there is no career to be made outside the party-centered system. The apparatus is not a bureaucracy in the Weberian sense, since it lacks regular rules for entry, promotion and permanence.

The Party-State. It is another consequence of Leninism and a major dis-tinguishing trait of Communist societies that the party, ceasing to be a mere party in the Western sense, keeps to itself major decision making and policy direction. It does not organize and staff a government in the framework of which policy is consulted and decided, as in Western political systems, but sets itself up as supreme authority, a sort of supergovernment for which the official state serves as administrative agency. This peculiar and historically novel scheme, which merits the appellation "party-state," seems to be necessary for the prestige of the party and in order to facilitate arbitrary action so far as deemed politically desirable. The state, as a legitimate and accepted master that functions on the basis of regularity and legality, serves as a predictable backdrop for economic activity; the party is free to move in any direction. It is logical, moreover, if the party incorporates the will of the forward section of society, that it should be responsible for guidance, and not the government, which is to some extent representative of the whole of society. The rule of law must be kept subordinate to the will of the working class, that is, of the party. This accords with the Marxist view of the state as a mere instrument of the ruling class.

Party-centered decision making is also useful for maintaining the monopolistic position of the party. If decision making were in the government, the Communist party would have less special status, while the government, with its specialized functions, would be more subject to pressures of interested parties and organizations. It seems suitable if not indispensable to keep authority within the party framework in order to maintain a coherent, organized elite group bound by self-interest and ideological purpose to control and supervise the state and ensure the necessary unity of movement. Very strong rulers, such as Stalin, Castro, and at times Mao have taken decision making more to themselves and their immediate entourage. But after Stalin, it seemed necessary to restore party primacy; and Mao, having shattered the party in his Cultural Revolution, permitted it to be revived in order to govern the country. In Cuba, the maturation of the system in the 1970s has seen greater use of party mechanisms. In the case of Yugoslavia, substantial powers of decision making were devolved to the republics of the federation and other organs, but the early 1970s brought the restoration of party primacy in order to prevent loss of power.

A related principle is the party's monopoly of political organization. To forestall challenges to its authority, the potential opposition must remain isolated and unorganized, hence impotent. In the Communist state, not only is there no competing political party—the shadow parties permitted to exist in China, Poland, Czechoslovakia, Vietnam, and elsewhere are mostly de facto adjuncts of the Communist party—but any independent organization is perceived as a potential threat likely to take on political meaning and is hence undesirable or inadmissible. Literary societies, for example, are likely to become foci for dissent. By the same token, no autonomous subsystems, or local or partial powers are to be permitted to blemish the fullness of central authority (with the partial exception of Yugoslavia, which has permitted some substance to flow into the formal rights of workers' councils, communes, and constituent republics).[6] It is even dangerous for a leader (except the highest) to be independently popular; authority should flow only from the party and by its sanction.

The Democratic Facade. The political party in the West is integral to the electoral process, and Communist one-party states are characterized by democratic forms with authoritarian content. Although some mobilization regimes of less developed countries share this tendency, it is especially characteristic of Communist states; and it particularly distinguishes them from the fascist states which were otherwise in many ways similar. The democratic facade serves to prove the state modern and progressive at home and abroad and also presumably helps the self-satisfaction of the elite. It also is to assist maximum mobilization of human resources promoting "voluntary compulsion" (in L. A. Unger's phrase) by showing how the state is responsible to the people and sanctified by their overwhelming approval. One aspect of what may be called pseudo-democracy is the intensive participation of the citizenry in local administration, even to the extent of low-level decision making within the limits of party policy. This is a general boast of Communist states; the Chinese have doubtless gone farthest, following the Maoist slogan "From the masses, to the masses." Democracy is also equated with social–economic justice, supposedly furnished automatically by the workers' party.

The democratic facade also includes extensive rights and freedoms written into the constitution but without effect against police powers, arbitrary laws, and illegal measures. Communist states, moreover, claim to be ruled by elections and theoretically sovereign elected councils and congresses. All Communist states have paid some deference to the principle of elections, but in China they have been dropped, even in form, since the late 1950s, when China began diverging

---

[6] Although the single-party regime is characteristic of Communist states, it is by no means their exclusive creation. Many states of the less developed world have virtual or complete monopolies of a governing party, and the fascist states of Europe have displayed the same phenomenon. These may be considered reflections of, or at least greatly influenced by, the Leninist pattern. But there have been pre-Leninist examples. Mexican one-party rule, an autochthonous development, emerged in the 1920s, like the Soviet system a product of social revolution with equalitarian drives in a less developed country. As in Russia, it answers to the desire of an elite to preserve power while observing democratic forms. Another single-party system, that of Liberia, is much older, the dominance of the True Whig Party having been complete since 1883. Here there was no social revolution but a need for an outwardly democratic system whereby the Americo-Liberians could assure their supremacy over the Afro-Liberians, who constitute 90 percent of the population. The results have been similar to those in the Soviet system: elaborate electoral campaigns without opposing candidates and virtually unanimous victories; an elaborate constitution, formally observed but of no practical effect; the predominance of politics over economics and the channeling of ambitions into party standing; religious organizations controlled by the rulership; few and weak independent organizations of any kind; a rubberstamp legislature; cult of personality of the president; and harassment of critics. J. Gus Liebenow, *Liberia: The Evolution of Privilege* (Ithaca: Cornell University Press, 1969), pp. 63, 81, 83, 85, 91, 96–97, 112, 153–154, 159.

from the Soviet model. Fidel Castro has generally contended that the popular will as expressed in mass meetings was an adequate substitute for elections, but Cuba has recently moved toward regularizing the rulership by electoral or pseudo-electoral processes. In the face of inequality of power and rulership by a self-selected elite, it is important to uphold appearance of popular participation and consent, although Communist leaders, from Lenin on, have known very well that real democracy would mean loss of power.[7]

Within the party, elections serve an additional purpose of control, providing opportunities to check on the performance of lower party officials and to weed out those undesirable either because of incompetence or politics. The practice of electing party leaders is everywhere obscure on the higher levels; and some parties, such as the Chinese and Cuban, have paid little or no heed to the principle at any level. But in theory elections are an integral part of the Leninist doctrine of Democratic Centralism, in effect centralism reinforced by a democratic facade. The member of the Leninist party should have no opinions, conscience, or interests at odds with the party, and his subordination is legalized by the theory of democratic control.

Closely related to pseudo-democracy is the use of formally democratic mass organizations as "transmission belts" for the party, in Stalin's apt phrase, multiple harnesses to integrate people into a party-directed system, organizing them without inviting them to share power to the limited extent that lower party members do. Transmission belts include principally trade unions, women's groups, paramilitary associations, and youth leagues. They are "preemptive organizations"[8] in the sense that they stand in the way of independent organizations. A host of party-controlled organizations, from recreation clubs for schoolchildren to societies for pensioners, are supposed to fill all social needs. The regime finds it the more necessary to stress these "mass organizations" to the extent it feels insecure.[9] Such an approach is not definitively Communist; many other authoritarian regimes make use of officially sponsored economic, recreational, and political organizations; but their full flowering to the exclusion of competitors is a Communist specialty. In the result, Communist societies are exceptionally highly structured and generally effective for the purpose of concentrating power in the leadership and transmitting the central will to the population.

Control of Information. The political monopoly must be supported by other monopolies. One is the control of information, whereby attitudes should be so far as possible purposefully shaped. This means not only censorship of

---

[7] Moshe Lewin, *Lenin's Last Struggle* (New York: Vintage Press, 1970), p. 123.

[8] Chalmers A. Johnson, ed., *Change in Communist Systems* (Stanford: Stanford University Press, 1970), p. 19.

[9] As noted by S. Huntington in Samuel P. Huntington and Clement H. Moore, *Authoritarian Politics in Modern Society* (New York: Basic Books, 1970), p. 38.

criticism, a common practice in a majority of the world's states, but the use of all means of communication positively for political and civic edification, wherein the Communist states must outdo their rivals. Only the Communist states try to fix the beliefs of everyone about almost everything, from politics to morality and aesthetics. Writers are told what message they should convey, either broadly, as in the present-day Soviet system, or specifically, as when Stalin commanded the writing of scores of plays glorifying the Baltic-White Sea canal. There are some concessions to pure entertainment, but these go against the grain of principled Communism; the sterner regimes, as the Asian, have very little room for frivolity. After a day's work in the rice fields, peasants should relax with thoughts of the leader.

A correlate of the policy of furnishing only suitable information is the practice of secrecy. All governments have a penchant for screening potentially embarrassing realities, but there seems to be an inverse relation between the freedom of information in a state and the use of coercion.[10] Secrecy is a special fetish of the thoroughly controlled states. To admit differences of opinion among the leadership is to admit fallibility, and to inform is to suggest a right to information if not participation. Among Communist systems, relatively relaxed and mildly coercive Yugoslavia stands out, but even here very little is publicized of the political process. In the U.S.S.R., not only is all decision making veiled so far as possible, but many nonpolitical matters are considered unfit for publication, for example, mishaps or the private lives of political personalities. The leading cadres, so far as the public knows, have no private lives. Even weather injurious to crops is likely to be publicized only long after the event. Secrecy is still more absolute in such countries as China and North Korea. China publishes very little solid statistical information of any kind, however favorable; and the very existence of high organs of government and party has at times been screened from public knowledge. That the formally supreme legislative body met to adopt a new constitution in January 1975 was admitted only in retrospect.

Centralized Economic Control. The control of the economy is another adjunct of the political monopoly. Not only is collective ownership of some kind mandated by Marxist theory and tradition, but centralized control of the economy removes any possible material support for opposition. It is claimed to be essential for economic development that the state be able to allocate resources and plan investment. A poor country, it is felt, cannot afford individual luxury. Socialization of the economy also means that everyone works for the state and is hence psychologically as well as economically bound. Moreover, rewards are given more in terms of position and perquisite than money, so it is very difficult to acquire independence or individual security, while centralized economic control means that a great many persons in authoritative posts have a stake in the system.

---

[10] Johnson, *Change in Communist Systems*, p. 21.

For such reasons, Communist states have gone very far toward excluding private enterprise on principle even where the state is unable to fill needs effectively. Practical considerations require some compromises; peasants, in particular, are allowed small private plots for gardening and stockraising. In the Soviet Union a good deal of private trading is tolerated, and repair services and much small construction are done by private entrepreneurs. But these are all illegal so far as done for gain, and even individual handicrafts are much circumscribed. There is more latitude for small-scale private business, such as taxis and restaurants, in Eastern Europe, especially Yugoslavia, less so in China and Cuba. In the latter, even shoeshine boys and street vendors were nationalized in the interests of socialist purity.

Socialism is a generally accepted virtue in most of the world, and nationalization is common doctrine from Peru to Egypt to India. Latin American dictators have sometimes virtually taken possession of their countries; for example, 65 to 85 percent of the economy of the Dominican Republic was in the hands of the Trujillos.[11] But the Communist state differs from competitors in making political ownership and management of the economy a matter not of convenience but of principle and in insisting that it should be as total as feasible.

Introversion. Monopolistic control and concentration of authority in a single center make the Communist states tend to be introverted and nationalistic —a paradox for societies supposedly guided by an internationalist ideology that regards boundaries between nations as artificial and outworn and looks to the eventual liquidation ("withering away") of the state. This inwardness has many aspects: severe restrictions on travel out of the country (except Yugoslavia and to some extent other East European countries), prohibition or strong limitation of foreign periodicals and the like; efforts toward economic autarky, with a relatively small part of the national product entering foreign trade. The foreign trade of Taiwan, for example, is larger than that of Communist China with fifty times the population. The countries of the Soviet bloc are responsible for about one-third of the world's industrial production but conduct only a tenth of world trade, this mostly within the bloc.[12]

Even among Communist states, regimes that highly propagandize their proletarian brotherhood, movement is unfree and largely limited to officially sponsored and managed tours. There are barbed wire fences with watchtowers and plowed strips between East European countries and the Soviet Union, just as exist between these satellites and the West. There have been experiments in freedom. Poland and Hungary opened borders for their citizens in 1958, and

---

[11] Eric R. Wolf and Edward C. Hansen, *The Human Condition in Latin America* (New York: Oxford University Press, 1972), p. 267.

[12] Josef Wilczynski, *Profit, Risk and Incentives under Socialist Planning* (London: Macmillan, 1973), p. 203.

Poland and East Germany in 1971; in both cases, however, the experiment was curtailed after a few months. When substantial numbers of citizens of one Communist state live on the territory of another, as Soviets in East Germany and Cuba, there is little mixing or fraternization.[13] The planners like to plan without looking to the world market and the propagandists want no interference from competitive messages, even from friendly sources. The fanatical Communists, moreover, distrust all, friend or foe, who do not belong to the brotherhood.[14]

Despite many variations, the Communist states thus reveal a basic set of distinguishing political forms and practices; it is not imaginary that "going Communist" represents a real lurch into a different political universe, from the more loosely framed pluralistic Western or traditional authoritarian societies to a system modernly designed for maximization of power over society, with all its consequences.

Ideals and Ideology

If the political structures of Communist states are distinctive, it is equally true that their peoples live and are educated in another intellectual world from the pluralistic societies of the West or even the looser dictatorships of the Third World. It is a shock for the person formed in the rigid lines of the Communist mental universe to be set loose in Western society, antagonistic to the regime and skeptical of its assertions as he may be.

In part, the psychological–cultural specialties of the Communist states are those of authoritarianism in general, shared with other strongly ruled, totalitarian or mobilization governments. For example, there is much emphasis on sports and physical culture, from the regular calisthenics of Chinese workers to the specialized Soviet boarding schools for children with talent for swimming, hockey, etc., from the promotion of athletics in Cuba to the Olympic excellence of the professional amateur sportsmen of East Germany. The athletic bent, along with fondness for parades, for muscular marching men and maids and mass demonstrations, was shared by the Nazi and fascist regimes; in part it stems from the desire to occupy leisure time in a wholesome and at the same time invigorating manner.[15] Caesars long ago saw the virtue of circuses.

It is also notable that Communist societies are exceptionally militaristic. Relatively long periods of military duty, paramilitary activities, popular militias (notably in China and Cuba), glorification of military heroism, cult of leadership and of violence, and emphasis on will and character on a scale reached or ex-

---

[13] Cf. Mohammed A. Rauf, *Cuban Journal* (New York: Thomas Y. Crowell, 1964), p. 87.

[14] Renzo Sereno, *The Rulers* (New York: Praeger, 1962), p. 110.

[15] As noted, for example, for Yugoslavia by Nenad D. Popovic, *Yugoslavia: The New Class in Crisis* (Syracuse: Syracuse University Press, 1968), p. 57; for Romania, by Julian Hale, *Ceausescu's Romania* (London: Harrap, 1971), p. 140.

celled only by the Nazi-fascist states, are characteristic. Loyalty is the basic virtue, as always in authoritarianisms. Doubts, neutrality, and division are threatening and bad in principle; and political imperatives prevail over economic. The approach is more moralistic than in looser societies, and judgments are typically extreme, either black or white.

Marxism-Leninism. Beyond these typical traits shared by nearly all authoritarian or imperial regimes, Communist states claim to be guided by a specific canon of interpretations and goals—Marxism-Leninism. As Shafarevich wrote, "socialism is not just an economic system, as is capitalism, but also—perhaps above all—an ideology." [16] Various States have somewhat diverged from the original Bolshevik ideology, the Chinese most widely. However, the ideas of Marxism-Leninism continue to motivate all the Communist states and, with it, a special vocabulary of politics, stressing "proletariat" or "workers," "class," "capitalist" or "bourgeois," "imperialist," "contradictions," "feudal," etc.

Marxism-Leninism in its details and ramifications is an elaborate scholastic edifice; [17] but the fundamentals are suitably simple for mass indoctrination. The basic proposition is that political history derives from an economic basis, the class struggle. Society proceeds through stages dependent on ownership of means of production, from the feudal order dominated by landholders to the capitalist order dominated by greedy owners of industry, which is destined to be overthrown by the workers. Becoming owners of the means of production, the workers establish a new and higher form of society, socialism, which is to grow into the perfect order of communism, a society of free and voluntary labor, sharing material goods and living in perfect harmony, the climax of history and redemption of mankind. The agent of progress is thus the proletariat, an ill-defined group, basically manual workers in the ordinary understanding. But the mass of proletariat is ill equipped to act; hence, in Lenin's interpretation, its responsibilities and rights are assumed by the party, consisting of persons imbued with the infallible philosophy and devoted to the interests of the workers—that is, the interests of society as a whole.

The broad appeal of Communism, however, is to the ideal of equality. The cheated, the misused, the scorned, and the exploited are to receive justice. This is a pervasive modern idea, widely associated with freedom, democracy, and human progress; it is also an ancient ideal ("Blessed are the poor") based on timeless sympathy for suffering and hatred for successful cheaters in the game of riches and power. It assumes the virtues of poverty, both of the deprived masses and of the poorer nations. It has two sides: the attack on the traditional society as the bulwark of privilege and inequality; and the promise of a new order of brotherhood, compassion for the formerly despised, and welfare for all.

---

[16] Igor Shafarevich, "Socialism in our Past and Future," in *From Under the Rubble,* Alexander Solzhenitsyn et al., eds. (Boston: Little, Brown, 1975), p. 29.

[17] Cf. Gustav A. Wetter, *Soviet Ideology Today* (New York: Praeger, 1962).

The original function of the ideology was to make possible the Communist revolution. It gave a group of rootless agitators the coherence to form an effective organization and the self-confidence to assert national leadership, seize power, and beat off their enemies. Power having been secured, Marxism-Leninism becomes the basis for the transformation of society, the justification for social and institutional changes that will fulfill the revolutionary program and make irreversible the shift of power. Thus it was ideology that enabled the Bolsheviks to carry out their coup of October 1917 and to win the ensuing civil war. Ideology also bolstered Stalin's *Gleichschaltung* of the peasantry ("socialization of agriculture"), his rapid industrialization program, and the purges supposedly in defense of the revolution.

Maintenance of Marxism. After the transformation has been completed and the interest of the party changes from revolution and social change to the maintenance and enjoyment of power, Marxism-Leninism must obviously evolve to meet these new goals. It is, after all, a revolutionary creed when revolutions are no longer desired, perhaps not even abroad. It is equalitarian when equality has ceased to be desirable for the new privileged class; it is internationalist when the state is nationalistic. It must turn into the opposite of what it was, a defense of the established order.

Yet the substance of the main propositions and even the pre-revolutionary language in which they are couched have been retained to the present day. It is never admitted that ideology is being revised; this would imply errors, or at least inadequate knowledge in the past. "Revisionist" is a term of contempt; leaders admit only to "creative development" of Marxism. A basically outdated dogma is to be sustained indefinitely.

It is sustained with great effort, the intensity of which is perhaps inversely proportional to the waning of revolutionary enthusiasm. Millions in the Soviet Union, tens of millions in China, spend much of their time propagating it, while the ordinary citizen is expected to give a substantial part of his waking life, from kindergarten on, to absorbing the message. The political costs are enormous; to propagate the message is one of the chief tasks of both party and state. Communism may be called government by propaganda; Castroism has been labelled "government by television." [18] No non-Communist states are closely competitive in this respect; even Hitler's Reich lagged well behind Soviet and ordinary Communist standards of organized opinion making.

Ideology in the Service of Nationalism. The role of ideology is only to a slight extent the result of inertia, the fact that leaders are accustomed to the message and would feel lost without it. The originally revolutionary ideology continues to have manifold utility for the stable Communist state. One of its functions is to promote a mission throughout the world. Although only a minority of Communist regimes, notably North Korea and Cuba, show much evidence

---

[18] Herbert L. Matthews, *Fidel Castro* (New York: Simon and Schuster, 1969), p. 148.

of the urge to spread revolution, the mission of supporting socialism, the working class, and the oppressed masses is still apropos. Communist governments claim to act not in the national interest but in the name of universalistic values, promoting patterns of a higher order. Thus, in the invasion of Czechoslovakia, in supporting Arabs against Israelis, as well as in organizing Communist parties against Maoist China, the Soviet state allegedly acts on behalf of sacred causes. The appeal to equalitarian justice makes the military-patriotic stance and concomitant sacrifices more acceptable. Since ideology assures that imperialism is the result of capitalism, Communist forces in effect can do no wrong. If there is peace, it can only be because of the strength and good will of the naturally peaceful Communist side. It is not certain that the adherence of foreign Communist parties has been valuable to the Soviet Union in strictly foreign policy terms, because these parties have raised the level of distrust and antagonism. But the applause of the world movement bolsters Soviet pride and confidence in ultimate success.

There is little evidence that Soviet or other Communist foreign policy of recent years has been shaped by ideology rather than a more conventional national interest. Theoretically there is no real conflict: underlying Marxist-Leninist goals coincide with state goals, the maximization of the influence of the Fatherland of the Workers; means are flexible. But if Marxism-Leninism does not appreciably restrict Communist options, it has confused many abroad who have been disposed to overrate the linkage between words and intentions. How is one to judge a state that purports to represent the cause of socialism and the workers of the world?

There is a convenient ambiguity in the picture. In Communist thinking as reflected in the press, the enemies, capitalist or imperialist countries or forces, are decadent, divided, and doomed; yet it is necessary to keep the guard up because they are clever and dangerous. The capitalists are in league against us, but we are to use their divisions, as Lenin taught,[19] and ally ourselves with those we would destroy. If a Western state does something right, it is because of the pressure of the popular or progressive forces supporting the Communist position. Since all politically important events are explainable according to Marxist-Leninist analysis, there are no accidents;[20] and the phrase, "It was not accidental that . . ." is recurrent in Soviet discussion of sinister affairs. For example, the appearance in 1973 of an exceptional number of books on Hitler could only be the result of a Nazi plot.

Legitimation by Ideology. A stronger use of ideology is to sustain the legitimacy of the ruling party and government; as Rousseau said, ideology

---

[19] Especially in *"Left-Wing" Communism—An Infantile Disorder,* written in April-May, 1920. Selected *Works in three Volumes* (Moscow: Progress Publishers, 1971), vol. 3, pp. 345-418.

[20] Nathan Leites, *The Operational Code of the Politburo* (New York: McGraw-Hill, 1951), p. 1.

transforms might into right and obedience into duty. All governments have something that may be called an ideological basis, a myth (not necessarily untrue) supporting the exercise of authority; but the Communist regime has a triple need. It exacts much more of its citizens than do other governments and imposes tighter controls. It not only expects that people pay taxes and cooperate so far as needed in the national defense but limits severely their expressions, activities, and movement, while demanding total loyalty and the production of ever more grain or steel. Such sternness has to be benevolent, or to seem so. Moreover, the Communist state lacks an electoral basis for its claims of popular support. Undiluted rule by a self-selected and self-perpetuating elite needs highly developed rationalization.

The party asserts its right to rule as representative of the working class, maker of the socialist revolution, and consecrated heir of the future by Marx's analysis—the "wisdom, honor, and conscience of the people," in the current Soviet slogan. All government, by Marxist thinking, is class dictatorship; hence the virtuous government is that which rules in the name of the virtuous and historically sanctioned proletariat, the future majority. In the Marxist-Leninist picture of class struggle, the revolution is never finished (at least, not so long as there remain capitalists in the world), hence opposition is always execrable as counterrevolutionary. The "bourgeoisie" and greedy capitalists were overthrown by the common people; since the capitalist class was removed, it follows by Marxist logic that the new rulers are the proletariat, whose rule is fully realized by the party. Since the proletariat is a selfless class, the party necessarily governs for the benefit of the people; the socialist state, unlike capitalism, cannot possibly be exploitative but strives only for human happiness, in the name of which all means are good. The leadership represents the will of the workers because the party, composed of the "best" workers, stands for all. To fail to follow its directives wholeheartedly is treason to a sacred cause, the building of a better future for mankind.[21]

The Communist citizen is told that, whatever the superficial appearances, he is working for himself. Factories produce not to make a profit but to serve the people. Workers can't strike against *their* plants, just as they must be happy to serve *their* state. Since Marxism sanctions total control of trade, industry, agriculture, and communications, it removes any economic basis for competitive groups and permits a total junction of political and economic power. In practice this has meant that a small group enjoys the prerogatives of both capitalist ownership and of state control. Ideologically, however, there can be no legitimate class division or class struggle, because class is a function of ownership

---

[21] Trotsky expressed this sentiment as he was being squeezed out of power in 1924: "Comrades, none of us wishes to be or can be right against the party. In the last instance the party is always right because it is the only historic instrument the working class possesses for the solution of its fundamental tasks." Cited by Merle Fainsod, *How Russia is Ruled,* rev. ed. (Cambridge: Harvard University Press, 1964), p. 149.

or non-ownership of means of production, and ownership is legally vested in the people. Indeed, there can be no legitimate political contest, because political conflict is a reflection of class interests. Any opposition must be motivated by alien interests, usually attributed to foreign "bourgeois" powers.

The position of the ruling party is intellectually reinforced by the scholastic side of Marxism, dialectical materialism, which appropriates the prestige of modern science. The key to penetrating political realities is "scientific socialism," which furnishes verbal answers decipherable only by the initiated, sees issues as clearly decidable in terms of right and wrong, and enables the Communist leadership to profess certainty about many uncertain things. Only party leaders, trained in this supreme blend of art and science, can grasp the true political essence. Since society and politics are capable of being fully interpreted by dialectical materialism and Marxism-Leninism, or its national variant, disparate ideas are "bourgeois," "reactionary," or anti-state. They may be regarded as a symptom of schizophrenia in the Soviet Union or as indicative of a need for reeducation in China; everywhere they are reprehensible, even in relatively relaxed Yugoslavia. No moral claim can be raised against the party, because morality subsists only within the system—is in fact a product of class position, class struggle, and class interests.[22] "Morality was always a class morality."[23]

Ideology also serves to regularize and strengthen relations within the elite. It gives leaders self-confidence by explaining their status in moral terms, and furnishes a language of self-justification. Useless except for a political career, its mastery implies dedication to the party. It gives coherence as all are assiduously educated to common values, modes of thought, discourse, and euphemisms. The fellowship of the old school tie in Western societies is a very feeble counterpart. The shared understanding based on ideology, training, and commitment is also to some extent a surrogate constitution, more effective in allocating power than the regime's written constitution, which has largely formal application. Ideological understanding is the basis on which men with a legal claim to power on their own accept the supremacy of the party. And, most importantly, when there is no institutional means of resolving differences between various agencies and interests, e.g., ministries, armed forces, trade unions, Soviet Republics, and so forth, community of belief—reinforced by awareness of common interests in maintenance of the system—enables the party to hold the entirety together without overt political struggle.

Moral Insulation. The Communist claim to rulership is buttressed by moral isolation from the nonbelieving world. The Marxist-Leninist analysis sets progressive socialism off from backward capitalism, the faithful from the heathen, and glorifies the defense of Communism against the nefarious influences of individualism, democracy, and (especially in the Soviet case) "bourgeois

[22] As observed by Leites, *ibid* p. 7.
[23] Friedrich Engels, *Anti-Dühring* (New York: International Publishers, 1939), pp. 109-110.

nationalism." Polarizing the universe between good and evil, Communism always exalts its moral superiority. Opponents are external or externally inspired, and in sharp contrast to the good citizens of the Communist state, who are united behind their party and government.[24] A line is drawn between the controlled, hence virtuous society and the uncontrolled, sinful outside. A critic can be placed outside the pale by calling him "bourgeois." Deviants are also damned by the accusation that they are bought by the capitalists; the imputation of greed seems appropriate for those who directly or indirectly support a society based on private gain. The feeling that the heathen world is bad extends to a broad range of manifestations of foreign culture, from modern art to jazz; only in such semi-religious terms is it understandable that political leaderships should find it necessary to exclude not only decadent popular music but twelve-tone symphonies.

Marxism-Leninism is thus a rationalization for censorship. It is more—a positive inspiration for the censors and a guide in helping them (and writers and editors) to sense the limits of the permissible. The doctrine acts as a sieve to keep out undesirable ideas while permitting the importation of technology. This comes directly from Marx, who found Western industrial society ("capitalism") mechanically productive but socially rotten. From the days of Ivan the Terrible Russia has been in the dilemma of having continually to borrow technology while fearing Western political and philosophic ideas, and the dilemma has only grown worse with the steady advance of the West. The Russian state might well have foundered on this rock of perplexity if Lenin had not engineered a solution in the shape of Marxism-Leninism.

The Marxian dialectical idea of quantitative difference becoming qualitative contributes to depicting the antithesis as total and unbridgeable. There can be no ideological peaceful coexistence, the Soviets and other Communists reiterate, even while pursuing commercial relations, seeking credits, and promoting technological cooperation. For all their good will, the Soviets say, they cannot change the class relations which dictate hostility; the onward march of socialism and the consequent aggressive behavior of the capitalist-imperialists are not to be set aside.

The two-world antithesis makes more credible the blackening of Western society and institutions and by implication the praise of everything on the "socialist" side. The capitalist West, the theory dictates, is moved by blind self-seeking; and the people are mercilessly exploited, as Marx showed to be inherent in capitalism. The bleak picture of poverty and oppression in the rich industrial states presented by the Communist press becomes more convincing because it is fitted into a philosophic framework. Racism, energy crisis, inflation, unemployment, drug addiction, corruption, and pornography

---

[24] John Kautsky, *Political Consequences of Modernization* (New York: John Wiley and Sons, 1972), p. 175.

are all explainable in terms of capitalistic abuses. This has been effective; in Stalin's day, when the standard of living had been depressed far below tsarist levels, Russians felt sorry for American workers.[25]

More academically, Marxism-Leninism gives the Communists, especially the intellectuals, the pleasing word that they have nothing of philosophic substance to learn from the West, that they are really in the lead as the West reels backward. This is no longer so convincing as in the nineteenth century, when Marxism was a daring innovation; but it has the advantage of lifelong impregnation. One must rehearse and show understanding of the approved system of thought through years of schooling and demonstrate excellence in it to rise through higher education. The personality usually becomes incapacitated for striking out alone in unapproved directions; to avoid dissonance one must believe. Simple enough for the ordinary person yet capable of indefinite elaboration and embroidery, Communist ideology is a broad philosophical system with many ramifications fleshed out with semi- and pseudo-scientific arguments. Those soaked in it through their formative years are structured to function in the politically proper fashion and immunized to Western liberal, empirical-positivist thinking. They can apply only Marxist-Leninist tools to the analysis of society, and these help to give Marxist-Leninist answers.

Ideology as Unifier. Marxism-Leninism not only excludes poisonous ideas but more directly provides a single creed which, although drier than a religion, can be taught to people of any creed or nationality as a science, backed by an array of facts and supposed facts, like physics or geography. "Scientific socialism" is simply correct thinking, which is required as part of education.

This is most important for states troubled by ethnic divisions, including Vietnam, Czechoslovakia, Romania, Yugoslavia, and above all the Soviet Union with its approximately 50 percent minority population. As proved by Marxism, nationalism is a deceitful "bourgeois" creation, a device to divide and weaken the workers. The workers have "proletarian internationalism," by which the interests of all nationalities are merged into the common cause headed by the Soviet Fatherland of the Workers. Class interests, as beginners in Marxism know, are inestimably superior to national interests. The imperative of "proletarian internationalism" is particularly useful as a tenet underlying the Soviet obligation to preserve socialism in the satellite countries of Eastern Europe.

Marxism-Leninism improves coherence by supporting collectivism. It is a basic Communist idea that persons should consider themselves members of "collectives," from the primary school classroom to the factory unit, groups from which they can expect support and help and to which they owe loyalty. "The basis of our life, as we all know, is collectivism. The collective upraises the personality and aids in the development of its best capacities. Without

---

[25] Cf. John Scott, *Behind the Urals* (New York: Arno Press reprint, 1971, original 1942), p. 119.

the collective there is not and cannot be a worthy individual.[26] The organization or collective is always entitled to demand an accounting of its members; even if they are abroad (or especially when so exposed), Soviet citizens should remember their collective and behave honorably. No organized group at all is considered licit (except for some tolerated churches) unless it is guided and controlled by the party.

Much the same is true of the economy. Socialism is taken to mean control by the people as a whole, that is, the state. If factories and other enterprises were owned by independent cooperatives or local administrations, they might look to their own disparate interests. The vesting of all property in the center assures that no section or economic interest is in a position to challenge the predominance of the party.

The Break with the Past. The centralized controls of the Communist state at once make possible and are justified by a program of fundamental change within society. A marked break from the past is practically a defining characteristic of Communist as against other authoritarian states. Although respect for and interest in the national past may grow, as it has in the Soviet Union since mid-1930s and in Romania and other countries of Eastern Europe in recent years, time is still divided into before and after the Revolution. In China, the repudiation of the traditional culture has been very strong, presumably because Confucian philosophy is closely associated with national weakness. Although the vigor of rejection of the traditional society varies, this is still another distinctive mark of the Communist state.

A concomitant of casting out old ways and competing philosophies is the anti-church stance that distinguishes Communist governments. Although policies differ from the toleration of Poland, where the party would like to do away with religion but is not in a position to do so, to the heavy-handed atheism of Albania, all Communist states strive to convert the citizenry to the official faith. This aim is deeply entwined in the movement; Marx was an atheist before he was a socialist, and both he and Lenin pushed atheism beyond the logical requirements of Marxist theory. In 1932, Stalin promoted an anti-religious Five-Year Plan to abolish worship entirely by 1937.[27] The means employed in the 1970's are more subtle, and the timetable is forgotten, but the purpose remains. Communists are philosophical materialists, although they call upon idealism with exceptional fervor.

Standing in theoretical opposition to traditional ways, the Communist states place emphasis on the liberation of women, both in order to break down old social structures and to gain recruits for the labor force. This is a strong point of the movement, since it represents an attack on outmoded forms and

---

[26] A. Protopopova, *Pravda*, February 27, 1971.

[27] Igor Shafarevich, "Socialism in our Past and Future," p. 49.

discriminations; and there is gratitude for the opening of professional opportunities to women, although women have been as much excluded from power in Communist as in other societies.

Dedication to the Future. The other side of rejection of the past is future orientation. Communist states are outstandingly goal-oriented, holding up a utopia as the reward for present sacrifices and the motivation for faithful service to the bringers of utopia, the party. One aspect of this orientation is investment in economic construction, much less in the production of consumer goods than heavy industry, a fixation shared with some other developing countries but especially strong among the Communist states. The graph of an economic plan is taken as equivalent to progress, proof of modernization, power and prestige. Education is also a vital means of future building. It at once removes the youth from traditional influences, inculcates appropriate values, teaches loyalty to the party (and its leader), and raises skills and productivity. It also, as much as any Communist achievement, reaps gratitude for turning peasant youngsters into engineers and doctors.

While educating, the Communist states seek to remake character, to make the New Man. Calling for people to work, study, fight, and if necessary die for the cause, they consecrate loyalty and dedication to the service of the collectivity or the people as defined by the leadership. Communist idealism replaces friendship (a personal relationship of mutual trust) with comradeship (helpfulness in the context of party directives).[28] It upholds a work ethic; one should toil diligently with little thought of material reward—"to serve the people" is the maxim not only of Chinese but of all Communisms. The faith makes people into disciples (or heretics) and makes feasible the use of moral incentives, such as tributes, diplomas, medals, etc., in the economy—a policy which recommends itself not only because symbolic rewards are inexpensive but because they accord with the anti-capitalist and antimonetary spirit.

This also helps to raise the spiritual value of labor, the true glory of man in the Marxist view—an attitude very appropriate in countries, as the Communist are, of aristocratic tradition, and also a means of attacking intellectual individualism. Bourgeois values, on the other hand, are little esteemed; monetary calculation is mean and unworthy in the Communist view. Casting aside the religiously-based morality of the older society, the Communist state badly needs a rationale for officials to refrain from using their positions to enrich themselves, for checking personal material enjoyment or at least keeping it inconspicuous. A tightly controlled economy in the West is feasible only in wartime; in the Communist state it requires an ideological underpinning strong enough to persuade enough people to relinquish their own self-interest for the common good.

---

[28] For the Chinese case, see Ezra F. Vogel, "From Friendship to Comradeship: The Change in Personal Relations in Communist China," *The China Quarterly,* 21 (January-March 1965), 46-60.

Dedicated to the collective, the good Communist should be an ascetic with little thought of personal pleasure, and the Communist movement (contrary to the free-love impulses of early Bolshevism) has substantiated such a marked puritanical bent. Sex is individualistic, hedonistic, and competitive with state enterprises, something hardly to be denied (Soviet policy has been natalist, sometimes strongly so, and there have been many indications that the Russians are anything but puritanic in practice)[29] but to be kept out of sight and mind. Communist art and literature are chaste. For many decades, no kiss sullied Soviet screens, and boy and girl loved tractor. In the aftermath of the Cultural Revolution, Chinese youth seems to have been phenomenally restrained. If a couple had lunch together, they were considered engaged.[30] A partial exception is Cuba; it has not apparently been possible to ban eroticism on that tropical isle, and Cuban movies may be lewd by Soviet, not to speak of Chinese standards. The state even operated a network of love-making sites.[31] Nonetheless Cuba has moved far from the older libertinage and takes much pride in the abolition of the former industry of prostitution. Homosexuals are barred from the party and otherwise penalized,[32] and fornication among students is frowned upon.[33] Men wearing sandals or shorts were hounded as presumptive homosexuals.[34]

The Utopian Vision. Central to this "idea world" of Communism is the utopian vision, seen by some as the special distinguishing feature of Communist societies.[35] The more repressive the system, the more grandiose its promises of future bliss. The reward of present sacrifice is to be a society so well ordered that its people will be perfect, not only morally but, it is sometimes supposed, physically, as was suggested in Khrushchev's 1961 Party Program, which promises "spiritual richness, moral cleanness, and physical perfection" (not, however, intellectual prowess). The utopian vision is as old as the *Communist Manifesto*; it is now imbued with a reality and power beyond ever recurrent peasant visions of the land of milk and honey. It is based on a systematic and allegedly scientific analysis, the laws of social development propounded by Marxism-Leninism.

Importance of Ideology. The utopian-directed ideology of future peace and present struggle is one of the three main pillars of the Communist system, along with the political monopoly of the party and the centralized control of

---

[29] As graphically depicted by Yuri Brokhin, *Hustling on Gorky Street* (New York: Dial Press, 1975).

[30] Edgar Snow, *The Long Revolution* (New York: Vintage Books, 1971), p. 46.

[31] Herbert L. Matthews, *Fidel Castro,* p. 252.

[32] Lee Lockwood, *Castro's Cuba, Cuba's Fidel* (New York: Macmillan, 1971), p. 124.

[33] Arlie Hochschild, "Student Power in Action," in Irving L. Horowitz, ed., *Cuban Communism* (Chicago: Aldine, 1970), p. 58.

[34] David Caute, *Cuba, Yes?* (New York: McGraw-Hill, 1974), p. 23.

[35] As, for example, R. Lowenthal, "Development vs. Utopia in Communist Politics," in *Change in Communist Systems,* Chalmers A. Johnson, ed. (Stanford: Stanford University Press, 1970), pp. 33-116.

the economy; lacking one element, the other two would surely break down. The ideology, although never very systematically put together, has enviable strength. With long-term conviction, it has tactical flexibility, a quality often apparent in the Communists' ability to retreat in good order where necessary, as, for example, in the turn to moderation after Soviet War Communism (1921) and the Chinese Great Leap (1960). Firm conviction in ultimate rightness permits concessions to the needs of the day without much loss of morale. Stated somewhat differently, the ideology has enabled Communist leaders to act unscrupulously without being cynical. They have been able to maneuver, to disregard promises, to give words unaccustomed meaning, and to eliminate opponents for no other sin than opposing, all, it would seem, with a feeling of acting in a good cause.

Although outlook and ideology differ somewhat among Communist societies, some stressing certain aspects more than others, a rather coherent moral-philosophical universe emerges. Some states are more strongly dedicated to the ideals, others less so; North Korea might be placed at one end of the spectrum, Yugoslavia at the other. But all are recognizably Communist because of this philosophical basis. Its utility is evidently great, because those elites which have adopted it have not let it go. Hungary in 1956 and possibly Czechoslovakia in 1968 seemed on the brink of doing so, but the Communist system has shown great firmness and stability over many tumultuous decades; and when it has wavered, as in China's Cultural Revolution of 1966–1968, it has rebounded.

Perhaps Communism's greatest source of strength is that the ideology has much to offer both masses and leaders. To the former, it offers respect, formal equality, and a role in the cause. It may be that Communism uses people, but they may be happier for being used as parts of the great collective. And in contributing to the cause they are invited to feel superior to the people of the non-Communist world, who are not only oppressed but adrift.

Equality is a difficult and somewhat artificial concept in a world of unequal humans, but in the Communist state there are at least theoretical dignity for the poor, usually a concern for subsistence welfare, and opportunities to rise in skill, responsibility, and authority. The revolution is a great leveller, casting down the proud and elevating new leadership, at least when the movement is fresh from the ranks of the people. Often the most trusted young activists and new recruits to the elite are children of the poor, who may be expected to be most grateful for their opportunities and hence most loyal. For this reason, most Communist states have favored the entry of children of workers or peasants to higher education and discriminated against "bourgeois" elements.[36] Mao and Tito shared the troubles and dangers of war;

---

[36] For the Soviet case, see Dimitri Pospielovsky, "Education and Ideology in the USSR," *Survey*, 21 (Autumn 1975), 24-25.

Lenin dressed simply and occasionally participated in manual labor even during his tenure as chief of state. Castro and his cabinet cut sugar cane at least two weeks each harvest.[37]

The elite, on the other hand, enjoys inequality of power, which is less offensive than inequality of wealth and more satisfying. Meanwhile the ideology would make them responsible to the class which is most manipulable. The best way to require that workers serve the leadership is to demand that they serve the people. Similarly, while the Communist utopia promises future equality and happiness to the masses, to the elite it spells the perfectly governable society. In the utopia no one has any independence or private standing, all are harmoniously dedicated to the collective, and all strive joyously for the goals of the community (i.e., of the leadership), displaying all the virtues of perfect servants. It then becomes unnecessary to ask whether the leadership believes in the ideology for its own sake or because it supports the status of the elite. The ideal inspires the ruler, justifying in his mind the sacrifices accepted or imposed; and the ideal is the excuse for his holding and using power. The two aspects are inseparable. The rulers are at once the masters and the servants of the cause. Communism welds inseparably together the most selfless idealism and the most unscrupulous self-seeking.

Historical Precedents

Present-day Communism, with its remarkable joining of ideology and organization, is a modern invention, like the internal combustion engine. The political party holding all power in the name of progress and social betterment, planning the economy in detail, prescribing a social and political philosophy, and requiring the participation of all the people while calling itself democratic, is a new thing. Not only those who greet it as an answer to modern problems but most of those who disapprove have treated it as an innovation in the ageless art of government. The former consider it a discovery, an application of scientific thinking to society. The latter regard it, together with fascism, as a qualitatively new form of despotism, a regrettable by-product of the age of the machine and mass man.

---

[37] Matthews, *Fidel Castro*, p. 251. At least nominal egalitarianism comes easily to strong authoritarian regimes, from ancient empires to tsarist Russia and modern fascism. Thus, of the Nazis it appears that

> The status revolution that accompanies this [opening of opportunities for advancement] was not a matter of elitism, even in the form of technocracy, but the triumph of egalitarianism, the reward and consummation of the *Volksbewegung* that had brought Hitler to power.... [T]he man without diploma, family, or independent economic position laid cornerstones, greeted foreign visitors at the station, claimed the royal box at the theater. [David Schoenbaum, *Hitler's Social Revolution: Class and Status in Nazi Germany 1933-1939* (Garden City, N.Y.: Doubleday & Co., 1967), p. 273.]

It is well to remember, although history shows nothing quite like the modern Communist state, that many societies have shown kindred characteristics. If the central idea of Communism is considered to be communism, or holding of property in common, this is age-old; and very strongly controlled societies with an ideological (or religious) basis abound in the historical record. Many primitive societies have regarded private property as only a conditional right, subject to the requirements of others. This has probably been true especially of those living in inhospitable environments, such as the Bushmen or the Eskimos. A feeling of need inclines to communal or communistic arrangements. Pioneering communities inevitably share extensively their limited goods and probably join to perform the necessary labor for the safety and welfare of the community. For example, the Plymouth colony was at first communistically organized; it went over to private enterprise after a few years when the emergency was past.[38] The besieged city, likewise, will find it natural both to allocate provisions and to direct labor for the general cause according to the mandates of an incontestable leadership.

For different reasons religious orders have oftentimes been in effect small communistic societies, with common ownership of all or nearly all property, anticommercial mentality, anti-individualism, and strict discipline, all in the name of a higher truth. This holds both of contemplative societies, such as the Trappists, and of militant ones, such as the Knights-Templar or the Teutonic Knights. It seems to be felt that individual property stands in the way of total dedication to a higher cause. Something of the same spirit prevailed in classic Sparta, whose men ate at a common mess.

Those philosophers who have tried to envision the ideal society have agreed that ownership is an impediment to moral perfections, and their utopias have generally been communistic. Plato wished to keep the elite of his *Republic* propertyless so that they should suffer no distractions from perfect rulership; inferior beings might be allowed possessions. The guardians, that is, should be like higher officials in a Communist state who possess nothing of importance but whose wants and luxuries are supplied by the state. In Tommaso Campanella's *City of the Sun*, the needs of all were to be provided from the common stores. Similarly, in Sir Thomas Moore's *Utopia,* as in Marx's state of the future, each was to receive according to his needs.

These various elements come together, to some degree, in modern Communism. All independent Communist states have been relatively backward, at least in their inception; and it seems obvious that a complex industrial society presents severer problems for Communist management. The element of need or emergency has been strong in the struggles of Communist states against military enemies and in the sometimes frantic drives for industrialization.

---

[38] William Bradford, *Of Plymouth Plantation*, ed. S. E. Morison (New York: Knopf, 1952), pp. 120-121.

And in the Communist order, semi-religious drives for moral purity are mixed with philosophic utopianism.

There is also a timeless populist element in the modern Communist movement, to which leaders, however exalted, from Stalin or Mao downward, always pay at least verbal tribute. Chinese peasant revolts, of which there have been hundreds, regularly demanded a sharing of the land or of the ill-gotten wealth of the court parasites; and equality of status or property was the demand of many a jacquerie in medieval Europe. The abolition of privileges is an ever popular cry, especially in times of distress and breakdown of old institutions. For example, rather modern-sounding theories of utopian sharing were current in the declining Hellenistic world of the third and second centuries B.C. Visions of universal equality and a better society without private property or conflict encouraged various "proletarian" insurgencies of the poor and slaves. Such ideas helped inspire the revolt of Corinth (a "national liberation movement") against Rome in the middle of the second century. In the rebellion of Pergamum, 133-132 B.C., national liberation from Roman imperialism was mingled with the call for a "Kingdom of the Sun," without rich or poor, high or low.[39]

Imperial Precedents. Modern Communism also reveals something of the spirit of empires from time immemorial. All autonomous Communist states have a background of authoritarianism, wherein great power was vested in the ruler and little or nothing was known of democracy, human rights, or freedom. It is also a commonplace of history that revolutions destroy only superstructures and build on old foundations. It might be expected, therefore, that a Communist movement would appeal more strongly and function more effectively where people take conformity for granted and accept the right of their betters to govern without restraint. Revolution is appropriate to societies where there is no provision for peaceful change of government, where a large majority of the people are permanently excluded from the political process, and where leaders of dissent are schooled by jail or violence. In these traditionally autocratic societies, Communism rather than democracy seems the logical answer to need for change. Thus for a Chinese in 1930 or a Vietnamese in 1960 to expose democracy was more radical than for either to brand himself a Communist.

The great empires of the past, at least in their times of strength and glory, have exhibited the same general characteristics prominent in Communist systems: a large part of the property of the realm, theoretically perhaps all of it, held by the emperor as representative of the community (or at least subject to his requisition); anticommercial attitudes and economic controls; government without legal restraints; a bureaucratic rather than a hereditary elite; strongly hierarchic structures; universalistic claims of the state; xenophobia and introversion; and a more or less obligatory creed supporting unity under the ruler.

---

[39] W.W. Tarn, *Hellenistic Civilization* (London: Edward Arnold, 1936), pp. 113-515.

Imperial regimes of the past[40] have, of course, generally not espoused such an explicit ideological basis or mission of transformation as Marxism-Leninism. Confucianism in the old China provides an interesting parallel, however, by according the supreme power a place in the natural order of the universe and helping to articulate society. The position of the emperor was like that of the Communist Party or Chairman Mao; the people owed him obedience and he was bound to care for their welfare. In moralism, stress on rectitude and the ethical basis of authority, and government by indoctrination, Mao was closer to Confucius than to Marx.[41] Something analogous to ideology has always seemed essential to the maintenance of a great empire. Imperial power, deifying a few to the exclusion of all others, needs to justify itself, to create for itself a rationale that sets the cumbersome structure in motion and supplements compulsion with consent, for the satisfaction of high and low alike. Lacking common purpose in its noncompetitive universe, it needs a cement of faith and mystic significance. The more total the empire, the more necessary to prove its ordainment by heaven, and the easier, in universality and self-righteousness, to do so.

Exalting rulership as infinitely good, the empire inculcates discipline, fosters ideals of loyalty and obedience, and encourages the subjugation of the individual will to the higher will and the larger order of the universe. Sacredness is an essentially imperial, authoritarian concept, whereby the politics is transformed into morality and goodness is redefined as those organizational virtues and that spirit of dedication which facilitate the empire's functioning. The imperial regime turns to its own use basic human sentiments, especially those rising in the family, the loyalty of brothers, perhaps the love of men and women, certainly the respect of children for fathers, sublimating these to lofty generalities. It creates the ultimate vision of lordship: something essentially human yet boundlessly great; omnipotent yet somehow needing the devotion of subjects; caring and tender of its charges yet fierce in anger; devoted to justice but accountable to no one. It gives the blessings of dependence and service to a supreme cause, and simultaneously lowers and uplifts that which is human.[42] It is the spirit of order and the promise of universal peace.

Empires characteristically create large and highly structured bureaucracies to carry out the imperial will; a similar development among Communist states entrusts the implementation of the communal will to a bureaucratic political party. The empire is anti-individualistic, suspicious of particularism of any kind, ideally a great collectivism. It, like the Communist state, is preoccupied with right conduct—the basic political question—and loyalty or faith is its supreme virtue. It is anti-mercantile because private riches are a threat to the

---

[40] Reference is here made to the continental despotic empires, of which the Roman and Chinese were typical; overseas empires, such as the British or French, were of another genus.

[41] Lucian Pye, *China: An Introduction* (Boston: Little, Brown, 1972), pp. 343, 346, 350.

[42] Cf. R. G. Wesson, *The Imperial Order* (Berkeley: University of California Press, 1967), pp. 174-190.

wholeness of power. Private wealth, because insecure, must ally itself with corruption; its very existence hangs by the thread of political favor. The empire, hierarchic and politically self-sufficient, despises the spirit of the free marketplace.[43]

The empire also breathes a spirit of equality, or pseudo-equality. No individual has any fixed rights against the supreme rulership; all are theoretically equal in submission to the all-highest. Equality is thus not only the simplest and readiest criterion of justice but a bar to privileges which might detract from the absoluteness of imperial political power. The only distinctions are those created by the rulership for its own purposes, rewards for service. Theoretical equality serves another purpose, too: it enables the successful to congratulate themselves (i.e., rationalize) that their station has been earned. Also, ideologies, almost without exceptions, imply equality of the believers; when all are called upon to serve, all must be granted potentially equal status. Great emperors, from Hammurabi of Babylonia to Peter of Russia, have referred to the commonfolk as their children and assumed the duty of protecting the weak and aiding the needy. It is with reason, too, that a despotic ruler uplifts the humble, raising the poor, even ex-slaves to his side; these individuals then owe everything to his favor and become his most reliable and least threatening servants.[44] Communist leaderships, usually of middle-class origin, apply the same techniques when they elevate uncritical proletarians to positions as helpmates and supporters.

Thus strong rulership with all its implications—weakness of private property, rationalization by faith, and a pseudo-equalitarianism—is a hallmark of both the ideal universal empire and the Communist state. Historically, empires have lacked the dual aspects of modernization and social change and, of course, have usually fallen far short of the ideal. Especially as empires age, the purity of central power is clouded by local powers and bureaucratic independence; the ability of the rulership to control the economy fades, while fortunate men accumulate vast personal wealth; and the faith becomes a sham, drained of most of its content. Equalitarianism becomes a mockery as both extreme poverty and exaggerated privilege emerge.[44a]

Under these circumstances, in sundry decadent empires there have been attempts to set things right and restore the lost virtues in a communistic society.[45] In a desperate response to the failed promise, people look to a new, better, and stronger authority to restore order. Since wealth has been ill-gained, it should be taken from the parasitic possessors and handed over to those who

---

[43] *Ibid.*, pp. 93-103.

[44] Cf. *ibid.*, pp. 145-153.

[44a] Some such evolution is apparent in modern Communist societies, as detailed in Chap. 4.

[45] Cf. *ibid.*, pp. 425-442.

have been cheated. Since some of the children of the emperor, or of God, starve while others feast, there must be a purge of the bloodsuckers and a new dispensation of plenty for all. Since the great peace has been disturbed by selfish local powers and given way to insecurity and fear, there must be restored the harmony of a single law. Then verily the kingdom of God, or the new Jerusalem, will come, quarrels will be laid aside, and all will work together with good will and together earn the joyous fruits of the earth. This vision of communism has been the cherished dream of intellectuals and peasants of various crumbling empires, Rome and Persia as well as China and Russia—the vision of refurbished authority fulfilling its promise, bringing the happiness and justice it should be capable of bringing—the vision of communism and of Communism.

Communism as Anti-Westernism

In modern times, traditional authoritarian societies have suffered blows to their integrity not merely from internal decadence but also from the cultural, economic, and political intrusion of foreign powers. These inroads have been especially injurious because the more potent and dynamic intruders have drawn their capacities precisely from those values scorned by the imperial or authoritarian society—competition, individualism, pluralism, and commercialism. Consequently the revolutionaries have been faced in modern times with the problem not only of reinvigorating decadent societies but of erecting a defense against the capitalist-industrialist West. This has meant fighting back by borrowing from the enemy.

The Restorative Role of Communism. One means of accomplishing this complex task of reestablishing authority while adopting Western ways and forms to the rulership's own advantage has been Communism. This manipulative device, of course, applies only to countries of authoritarian background injured by the impact of technologically more advanced neighbors, primarily to those big, proud empires, Russia and China, where the old state proved inadequate. In other words, Communism is part of the reaction of traditional societies to the outspreading of modern scientific, industrial power.[46]

The resentment of traditional societies generally stems not so much from material exploitation by powerful industrial states as from social dissolution and injured pride. Poverty gives rise to desire for change not so much because it represents lack of economic goods as because it represents weakness and humiliation, and the Marxist-Leninist drive for unity and power seems to answer this need perfectly. Western influences disrupt a stable, familiar, and consecrated society, interlocked by kinship and traditional bonds, and cause

---

[46] As stressed by Kautsky in *Political Consequences of Modernization*, pp. 240-41.

uncertainty and galling new inequalities. Hence people demand new answers, preferably promises of utopian bliss.[47]

Along the same line, but perhaps psychologically more important, is the need to succor the pride of a nation—and its intelligentsia. Poverty represents not only deprivation but weakness and humiliation. The theme of insult is prominent in radicalism. It was, for example, probably the leading reason for the acceptance of Nazism. Germans accustomed to believing their country the best in the world were forced to accept formally the blame for the First World War as well as the shame of defeat. The Nazis told them to reject this as a slander and to vindicate themselves by building a new strength; when Hitler seemed, by his territorial conquests, to have turned the tables on the former victors, he earned the enthusiastic support of a large majority. Mussolini had a similar appeal for Italians who felt themselves, the heirs of Rome, to have been treated shabbily by the Allies.[48] Perón was the product of an Argentina which, having regarded itself as a leading regional power in the world, found itself after the Second World War relegated to tertiary status.

Communist revolutions have also gained impetus from a desire to restore self-esteem. For Russian intellectuals of the latter nineteenth century, it was bitter that immense Russia amounted to far less in the world than tiny Britain, that its people were so much poorer and its technical capacities so much less. The confrontation with the West was still more distressing for the Chinese; having for ages believed all other peoples to be "barbarians," in the nineteenth century they found themselves impotent as children in the face of Western gunboats. A major initiative of the Communists was the expulsion of foreigners, even medical personnel and nuns caring for orphans, in order to end the humiliation of China.[49] On the other hand, countries less aggrieved by Western imperialism, for example, Liberia and Thailand, have been much less prone to socialist radicalisms.[50]

Inferiority of power and rewards becomes more traumatic because of general expectations of equality. Human beings are equal, that is, endowed with equal rights, so runs a worldwide truism in this latter half of the twentieth century. That the Chinese, or Latin Americans, should have so much less and

---

[47] Eric J. Hobsbawm, *Primitive Rebels: Archaic Forms of Social Movement in the 19th and 20th Centuries* (New York: Praeger, 1963), pp. 4-5.

[48] Nazism and fascism, as has been frequently noted, shared many characteristics with Communism. Similarities of background included not only injured pride but native authoritarian tradition, discredit of the regnant political order, and economic breakdown. Nonetheless fascism pertains to relatively wealthy countries. Poorer cultures are less inspired to raise up racial and national pride but appeal rather to universal standards of justice and human values which should assign them a better lot.

[49] Ezra F. Vogel, *Canton under Communism* (New York: Harper & Row, 1971), pp. 69-71.

[50] Fred R. von der Mehden, *Politics of the Developing Nations*, 2nd ed. (Englewood Cliffs, N.J.: Prentice-Hall, Inc., 1969), p. 115.

be so much less powerful and respected in the world than Europeans or North Americans generates defiant extremism and bitterness among the proud and arrogant inferiors. Violence in thought, language, and action so far as feasible is the only recourse, as revealed in the teachings of revolutionaries from Lenin to Frantz Fanon and beyond. Mao was given to nationalism before he turned to Communism; the latter was simply a stronger expression (vis-a-vis the West) of the former. To this day, self-reliance in contradistinction to the degeneracy of "bourgeois" culture has been an eternally reiterated thesis of Chinese Communism; even Western musical instruments are symbolic of degradation.[51] Likewise, Fidel Castro's primary theme was not the welfare of the workers but sovereignty and independence. Within days after taking power in 1959 he was bitterly attacking the U.S. and in effect calling upon Latin America to join the Cuban revolution—nearly three years before he declared himself a Marxist-Leninist. In 1962, a Cuban official, deprecating the suggestion that the end of the missile crisis would open up economic opportunities, commented, "Security and material goods are not all that important to us. Honor, dignity, trustworthiness, and independence—without these neither economic growth nor socialism mean a damn."[52]

The lament of the beleaguered society becomes a political program of change, a counterattack against the West and those elements of the native society which seem to be in league with it (especially a Westernized "bourgeoisie"). Thus viewed, Communism is a rebellion against the Western liberal tradition that excuses violent expression of emotions. Revolution itself becomes a passion that is fed by associating national liberation with the liberation of the suffering masses of the world—that is, the destruction of the proud elite of the industrialist-imperialist West, the emancipation of humanity from the evils of the capitalist order. This aspect of Communist ideology, its primary concern with moral redemption rather than economic improvement, functions as a compensation for weakness and a means of turning Western values against the West.

Emulation of the West. The West, however, has represented not only aggressive intruders and decadent vices but also a new world of science and technology. As a young Chinese wrote about the turn of the century concerning Europeans in Shanghai, "The foreigner appeared to my mind half divine and half devilish, doublefaced and many-handed like Vishnu, holding an electric light, a steamboat, and a pretty doll in one set of hands, a policeman's club, revolver, and a handful of opium in the other."[53] Modernization represents power, achievement, and prestige on the world stage. These are rewards the

---

[51] Vogel, *Canton under Communism*, p. 84.

[52] Maurice Halperin, *The Rise and Decline of Fidel Castro* (Berkeley: University of California Press, 1972), p. 190.

[53] Michael Gasster, *China's Struggle to Modernize* (New York: Knopf, 1972), p. 18.

developing countries have seldom been willing to forgo. Modernization, including industrialization, becomes a prime aim and justification of state, party, or personal power. However the leaders of the non-Western countries resent the arrogant West and would like to eradicate its influence, they must invariably measure themselves to some extent by its estimate of them.

The Communists, too, congratulate themselves as succeeding by Western standards. Lenin, Stalin, and Mao looked up to the West and cherished its applause; they, like Brezhnev and Castro, have spoken more familiarly to Western reporters than to their own people. Lenin, desiring respectability by Western standards, named a former engineer and corporate executive as negotiator with Western firms. "See," he said, "for the outside world Krassin will be one more proof that we are not exactly a bunch of visionaries, bookworms, and sans-culottes."[54] In Khrushchev's memoirs, it appears again and again that he is striving above all to overtake the capitalist West, whose superior technical capacities he could not comprehend. He was fearful of being treated as an inferior by Eisenhower in 1959, and the height of self-realization was to be received as an equal by the American President.[55]

The West, particularly America, remains the standard by which Russians measure themselves; they find it intolerable to be inferior in anything, from missiles and naval power to sports. Hence they build up strategic forces at an apparently excessive cost, and they feel that they must excel in such "bourgeois" and un-Russian activities as equitation. They even establish special schools for training promising youngsters to be tennis stars although they do not manufacture good balls and rackets.[56] As in the nineteenth century, intellectuals are especially prone to look West. An intellectual in a Stalinist play lamented,

> What is this loathsome tradition that thirty years of the Soviet regime have not enabled us to get rid of, this tradition so common among us intellectuals, this tradition that makes us poor relations of the foreigners and obliges us to go running to them to get our honorary diplomas?[57]

There is a corresponding sensitivity to imputations of inferiority. Khrushchev's claims to be a world statesman did not let the Russians forget his uncultivated manners, which came painfully to the fore in the shoebanging episode at the United Nations.[58] Regardless of party, even in the 1970s Russians are angered at tourists taking pictures of things that seem quaint to the visitor but

---

[54] Simon Liberman, *Building Lenin's Russia* (Chicago: University of Chicago Press, 1945), p. 60.

[55] *Khrushchev Remembers: The Last Testament* (Boston: Little, Brown, 1974), pp. 372, 415.

[56] *New York Times*, March 15, 1976, p. 43.

[57] Michael Gordey, *Visa to Moscow* (New York: Knopf, 1952), p. 166.

[58] Georgie Anne Geyer, *The Young Russians* (Homewood, Ill.: ETC Publishers, 1975), p. 27.

imply backwardness to the Russians. They bristle too at suggestions that Soviet morals may be imperfect.[59] The official policy of masking Russian failures while exaggerating those of the West is doubltless approved by a large majority of the population.

Responses to the West. Within this general framework of anti-Westernism, rulership styles have been diverse and multiform, varying in the mixture of utopianism, bitterness, and extremism. Some leaders have always been more pragmatic–managerial, others more idealistic and revolutionary;[60] some are gradualists while others demand a leap from despair into utopia. Many, especially in the decades before World War I, viewed Russia's problem as simply one of backwardness, to be overcome by the simple substitution of Western ideas and techniques for ancient practices no longer suitable for the modern contest of nations. The Westernizers in tsarist Russia, including a growing party of liberals and constitutionalists shortly before World War I, subscribed to this solution, as did a small sector of Chinese intellectuals about the same time.

This approach seldom met with much success, however. Intellectuals were asked to repudiate their nations' culture, to reeducate themselves to think in ways that were often antithetical to long cherished values. They were asked to replace ascriptive with achievement values, familial with contractual bonds, superstition with rationality. A high receptivity to change was demanded, and rigid social structures were expected suddenly to become loose.[61] Antithetical life styles could not be quickly and easily assimilated, however, a fact that has usually seemed obvious. Where democratic forms were tried in non-industrial countries they quickly failed for a variety of reasons. For example, hopes for the embryonic Chinese republic established in 1912 after the fall of the Manchu dynasty were dashed as it rapidly degenerated to dictatorship and warlordism. Harassment by Western powers concerned only with their own interests was also a contributing factor. As Mao put it, "Imperialist aggression shattered the fond dream of the Chinese about learning from the West," and "All other ways [than Marxism-Leninism] have been tried and failed."[62]

Most nations afflicted by the impact of the industrial West have taken the emotionally sounder course of seeking new bases of belief in their future. One reaction, for example, was the messianic movements based on Christian myth that arose in the relatively backward areas of nineteenth-century Italy and Spain. The early stages of modernization have seen numerous religious

---

[59] *Ibid.*, p. 62.

[60] A point discussed extensively by John Kautsky, *Communism and the Politics of Development* (New York: John Wiley and Sons, 1968).

[61] As outlined by Monte Palmer, *Dilemmas of Development* (Itasca, Ill.: Peacock Publishers, 1973).

[62] Mao Tse-tung, *Selected Readings from the Works of Mao Tse-tung* (Peking: Foreign Languages Press, 1971), pp. 373, 375.

protest movements, especially against money lenders and capitalists.[63] Concomitant with this is the exaltation of native values; the basic theme of the materially beleaguered society is its moral superiority. Slavophils of nineteenth-century Russia found the profoundest virtues in the simple and unspoiled Russian peasantry, just as Africans find the black "soul" ineffably superior to the shallow and commercialized European. Even Marxists find glories in traditional institutions, ascribing to them a harmony and justice erased by artificial Western ways. Nkhrumah, for example, saw socialism as an extension of traditional African communalism.[64] Libya's strong man, Kadaffy, restored Moslem law, including the stoning of adulterers, and banned the metric system as a "vestige of colonialism."

Leninism as Anti-Imperialism. Lenin's genius is revealed in the way he used Western ideas to promote anti-Westernism. Alienated intellectuals were encouraged to assume the rightful destiny of the proletariat, the peasant majority was incorporated into the political scheme, and the injustice of imperialism was stressed. Marxism-Leninism seemed indeed suited to less developed countries; it bespoke something of the power and progress of the industrial West without being associated with the sins of Western imperialism. Before Lenin's adaptations, Marxism was a dogma respected by many persons in leading countries; in particular, it was the creed of the German Labor movement, the world's largest. Since the Russian Revolution, however, Marxism has enjoyed the unique standing of a creed that inspired a world-shaking revolution, and best of all, an anti-Western one. Subsequent decades have seen the big Marxist-Leninist state rise to enviable heights of power. Meanwhile, the Soviets with all means at their command have been pressing others to follow their example. The message is fairly plausible, at least for those countries too poor to be much concerned with the human cost of Soviet progress and for which freedom or democracy has little meaning.

The movement profits greatly from being anti-capitalistic. The imperialists, colonialists, or neo-colonialists are states and enterprises based on privately owned and profit-making enterprise. Thus where there is no overt political aggression against less developed countries, Marxists can claim that the attack is carried on by private businesses, through money and market mechanisms, that is, by capitalism. But if the problems are caused by capitalism, they should be cured by the alternative, socialism. It is here that the idea of socialism merges with national liberation and the defense of the native personality. Add to this the observation that Marxism is *the* powerful, modern attack on capitalism, slashing at its evils and weaknesses in a systematic way. It is the sophisticated damnation of the detested bourgeoisie; no rival comes close in cogency.

---

[63] Gerald A. Heeger, *The Politics of Underdevelopment* (New York: St. Martin's Press, 1974), p. 30.

[64] K. Nkrumah, *Consciencism: Philosophy and Ideology for Decolonization* (New York: Monthly Review Press, 1970), p. 78.

Socialism, certified as the coming form of society by Marxism, promises technological improvement without the humiliation of following in the footsteps of the enemy or risking the traumas of capitalistic industrialization. Glory to the proletariat, was thus translated into glory to the poor nation, to whom, as to the workers, the future must belong. Poverty became an advantage in the eyes of Russian Slavophils, of early Bolsheviks, and of Maoists, who held that the "poverty and blankness" of China made possible an early leap to the higher society.[65]

The ideals of Marxism-Leninism fulfill the needs of the injured societies. Communism's fundamental ambivalence toward the West consists not only in accepting technology while rejecting liberal politics ("We take your tools but throw back your ideas"); but in accepting some Western values, at least nominally, and putting them at the service of anti-Westernism. The strictly Western belief in reason and progress promises amelioration of suffering and degradation, a belief without which it is impossible to be properly radical.[66] The sophisticated and scientific-sounding Marxist doctrines are token and promise of the knowledge which has made the West powerful; they are at the same time a substitute for the genuine science and scholarship in which less developed states are deficient.[67]

Goals such as improving the welfare of the masses, achieving racial nondiscrimination, upholding the rights of women, and raising the standard of living of the peasants are part and parcel of any movement of social renewal. Simple and persuasive, the ideal of equality appeals to the elite as vindication against the undeserving rich at home and abroad. The doctrine engages the intellectuals and at the same time binds them to the people with assurances of a decent life with equality and democracy—fraudulent pillars of capitalist society—only realizable under socialism.

Marxism-Leninism as a Vehicle for Unity. Such utilities might seem ample to recommend Marxism-Leninism, but it promises much more. Most non-Western countries suffer or have suffered severely from disunity—among ethnic, racial, sectional, cultural, and class minorities—virtually requiring dictatorship to override the disparities. Marxism-Leninism provides a rationale for unity, the cause of socialism and the working class, and simultaneously a new ethos of integration. Marxism's original scope was internationalist; for non-Western states it has become instead an aid to nationalism. Blaming imperialism or capitalism for disunity, Marxism-Leninism would expel the alien influence and promises not only wholeness of the state but a higher degree of harmony than ever known before.

---

[65] Benjamin Schwartz, "Modernization and the Maoist Vision," in *China under Mao: Politics Takes Command*, Roderick MacFarquhar, ed. (Cambridge: MIT Press, 1966), p. 15.

[66] Zevedi Barbu, *Democracy and Dictatorship* (New York: Grove Press, 1956), p. 173.

[67] As observed by Edward Shils, *The Intellectuals and the Powers, and Other Essays* (Chicago: University of Chicago Press, 1972), p. 479.

The promise of unity through Marxism-Leninism is more effective because much of its theory and practice harmonizes with political realities of the non-Western world. As characterized by Lucian Pye, the sphere of government among these nations is not sharply bounded; a political party represents a total way of life, and the political process is irregular and dominated by cliques. Parties are expected to maximize the interests of their members, and opposition to the ruling party appears revolutionary. Moreover, people feel little need actually to participate in politics, the few organized groups that exist are feeble, and leadership is usually charismatic.[68] From this perspective, Marxist-Leninist organizational doctrine and practice offer no innovation, only systematization and reinforcement.

Democratic and equalitarian rhetoric in basically authoritarian societies serves the interests of the rulership and the state by setting aside the older institutions and traditions and the limitations they set upon political power. The masses are flattered and indoctrinated to believe that only the new system can save them from imperialism and exploitation; only the trusted leader, consulting democratically with the masses, can unite and protect them.[69]

Socialism and the theory that the party and government are synonymous with the collectivity or the working class—that is, essentially the people—make it possible to demand not only passive conformity but active support. There is no room for strikes against the workers' own enterprises. Socialism implies an obligation to work in the present with a promise of reward in the future.[70] It promises an end to unemployment, the scourge of the non-Western world. At the same time, socialism makes democracy impossible by raising the values at issue in politics, legitimizing the appropriation of wealth,[71] and further blurring the shadowy boundaries of the sphere of government.

There is no need to tolerate an opposition when imperialism is the enemy; as Julius Nyerere of Tanzania said, a multiparty system would make no sense because "to us 'the other party' is the colonial power."[72] Symbols of struggle, revolution, and change are invoked to induce quiescence and acceptance of new authority. The exaltation of the people in theory means in practice that the benighted masses have to be saved and guided despite themselves, while the enlightened elite, entitled by their knowledge of the theory to act as vanguard,

---

[68] Lucian W. Pye, "The Non-Western Political Process," in *Politics in Transitional Societies*, 2nd ed., Harvey G. Kebschull, ed. (New York: Appleton-Century-Crofts, 1973), pp. 22-30.

[69] Palmer, *Dilemmas of Development*, pp. 98-99.

[70] G. Arrighi and John S. Saul, "The Theory and Practice of African Socialism," in *Politics in Transitional Societies*, 2nd ed., Harvey G. Kebschull, ed. (New York: Appleton-Century-Crofts, 1973), p. 133.

[71] Heeger, *The Politics of Underdevelopment*, p. 61.

[72] Cited by C. Andrain, in *Ideology and Discontent*, David Apter, ed. (New York: Free Press, 1964), p. 165.

are free to remake social structures as sanctioned by theory and practice of the movement. Marxism-Leninism thus lays the groundwork for a democratic-populist type of elitism, in effect a dictatorship, since there is no provision for limiting power within the elite.

To great masses of people beleaguered by seemingly insurmountable problems, Marxism-Leninism promises a shining future — and the means of getting there. Offering guidance and comfort to questioning and insecure people, it restores a sense of identity and a role in the world. It reassures that the enemy is really weak even though he may appear strong (a "paper tiger" in the Maoist phrase). It promises mastery of history, a shortcut to freedom and prosperity, turning backwardness into an asset. By recasting of institutions, collective efforts, rational planning of the economy instead of capitalist anarchy, the formation of a dedicated elite of innovators, and modernization through ideological drives,[73] the Marxists promise progress independent of and superior to that of the West, quick modernization by political act. It is only remarkable that Marxism-Leninism has not been still more successful in a world largely unhappy and disturbed in its relations with Western industrial civilization.

The Basis of Marxist Anti-Westernism. Marxism was not originally intended for less developed countries. Marx and Engels spent most of their lives in England, wrote with English conditions in mind, and regarded imperialism as a spreader of civilization to the backward. Their class of the future was not the peasantry but the factory proletariat. Yet Marxism in simplified form has always appealed to the deprived; one easily distills from it the simple dichotomy of exploited masses against rich masters. And the grievances of the less developed countries are close to Marx's basic theme. He was champion of those aggrieved by industrialization and the powers of industry, and he was a rebel before he took up the factory workers as the new class destined to destroy the bourgeois order. He charged that "The bourgeoisie, wherever it has got the upper hand, has put an end to all feudal, patriarchal, idyllic relations. It ... left no other nexus between man and man than naked self-interest ..." and promised that the future would bring back long lost brotherhood and noncommercial harmony.[74]

It is easily forgotten that for Marx and Engels their native Germany was something of a less developed country and its relationship to England might nowadays be called neocolonialism. Engels, for example, wrote that "The ancient manufactures of Germany had been destroyed by the introduction of steam, and the rapidly extending supremacy of English manufactures ...."[75]

---

[73] I. R. Sinai, "The Case for Authoritarianism" in *The Developing Nations: What Path to Modernization?* Frank Tachau, ed. (New York: Dodd, Mead, 1972), p. 146.

[74] Karl Marx and Friedrich Engels, *Manifesto of the Communist Party,* in *Selected Works* (Moscow: Progress Publishers, 1973), Vol. I, p. 111.

[75] Frederick Engels, *Germany: Revolution and Counter-Revolution* (New York: International Publishers, 1968), pp. 11-12.

An article in a German paper published under the name of Marx but composed by Engels goes farther, saying, "the German states were the best market for English goods and served only to enrich the English bourgeoisie"; England fought Napoleon only to open Continental markets and did so "with such success that the profits made from Germany alone since the peace would suffice to cover the costs at least six times over," while Germany is "held in handcuffs by a few English capitalists."[76]

The Marxian attack on capitalism was in effect an attack on Britain, the then richest power in the world. Hence, to place injured countries and the downtrodden peasantry in the place of factory workers as a revolutionary force does violence rather to the letter than the spirit of Marxism. It is an adaptation of which Marx would in all probability have approved. He was in fact elastic enough to look with glee upon any genuine revolution no matter how discordant with his dialectic.

But Marxism was framed in terms of the dialectic and succession of economic ruling classes and it became the theory of proletarian revolution. It was so understood by Lenin. Although he modified both theory and practice to suit the conditions of his feebly industrialized homeland, Lenin saw his revolution as international rather than national and expected salvation from revolution in the West, especially Germany.[77]

But revolution did not catch on in the West, and the Bolsheviks perceived to their surprise that ferment was more promising in Asia. Moreover, according to Lenin's theory of imperialism, if the leading European powers could be deprived of their colonies and the loot therefrom, they would no longer be able to bribe their working classes to betray the working class under the leadership of the Social Democrats. Hence, by 1920, at the Baku Congress of Peoples of the East, dogma was mostly forgotten in the enthusiasm for war against England. Karl Radek called upon Eastern peoples to emulate their conquering ancestors who "marched against Europe under the leadership of their conquerors."[78] Lenin subsequently expressed the conviction that peasants, like workers, could establish a soviet form of government and proceed to socialism under a Marxist party. Near the end of his life, January 1923, he ventured that a country might start toward socialism by expelling landlords and capitalists regardless of economic level or lack of a factory proletariat.[79]

Despite this flexibility of Lenin, the Comintern struggled in vain to accommodate the disparate ideas of class war and national liberation. The idea of

---

[76] Karl Marx and Friedrich Engels, *Über Deutschland und die deutsche Arbeitsbewegung* (Berlin: Dietz, 1970), Vol. II, pp. 42-43.

[77] As outlined by Lucio Colletti, "The Question of Stalin," *New Left Review,* no. 6 (May–June, 1970), pp. 61-70.

[78] Cited by Roger E. Kanet, *The Soviet Union and the Developing Countries* (Baltimore: Johns Hopkins University Press, 1974), p. 8.

[79] *Selected Works* (Moscow, 1971), Vol. III, p. 770.

action by factory workers was too strong in the Marxist outlook to be set aside. Moreover, the Comintern guided the movement in the interests primarily of the Soviet Union as conceived by an increasingly narrow group, eventually by Stalin. Consequently, Communist parties in the less developed countries, then mostly European colonies, made very little progress prior to World War II. The single exception was in China, where national weakness was most keenly felt and desire to restore proper authority was particularly acute.[80] There the Communist Party, having failed painfully in following the Comintern line, turned to the peasants and emancipated itself from Muscovite direction,[81] gaining power in the tumult of the Japanese invasion and world war.

Communism Turns National. After World War II, the proletarian–internationalist freight of Marxism-Leninism was lightened and to a great extent replaced by nationalism. This form of the dogma is more palatable in countries without a consequential proletariat and whose interests are primarily in their own redemption rather than in general social revolution, countries whose immediate vision is liberation, not a socialist utopia which becomes less believable as the Soviet Union failed to achieve it. As Djilas said, Communism had to turn national.[82]

As nationalists, sometimes supernationalists, Marxist-Leninist parties of the non-Western world have woven together the potent themes of equality, nationalism, and modernization. Studying much less Marx than Lenin's Marxism, they have given the peasantry the revolutionary role which Marx assigned to the proletariat and have cried much more anti-imperialism—of late anti-Americanism—than anti-capitalism. Undertaking the dual and related purposes of national independence and economic development to catch up with the West, Communism should do for countries like China, Korea, Albania, Yugoslavia, and Cuba—not to speak of Russia itself—what historic nationalism had done for countries like Britain and France.

The mission of nationalistic Communism is to unite, mobilize, free from foreign domination, and modernize, adopting new techniques to save old political values. Its victories have been numerous. The Soviets have found the element of nationalism so much more promising than proletarianism that they have adopted the theory, absurd by Marxist logic, that less developed countries can advance toward "socialism" under "bourgeois" leadership.[83] In contradiction to Marxist internationalism, they espouse the virtues of nationalism (outside their sphere) and the claims of the poorer countries against the West.

---

[80] Pye, *China*, pp. 349-350.

[81] Kautsky, "The Communist Perspective," in *The Developing Nations*, F. Tachau, ed., p. 151.

[82] Milovan Djilas, *The New Class* (New York: Praeger, 1957), p. 174.

[83] Kautsky, *Communism and the Politics of Development*, p. 97.

China makes itself champion of the Third World.[84] The evil of neocolonialism is the only thing all varieties of Communism and radical socialism agree upon. Thus Communism merges into the broad protest of the Third World, and the effect of the merger has been to shift the whole political spectrum of the non-Western majority of the world radically to the left.

Barriers to Communism. Marxism-Leninism is still, however, burdened by irrelevant dogma; the Marxist metaphysics tarnishes the allure of Marxist politics. The Communists cannot admit being merely nationalists, because they would thereby lose both the advantages of attachment to a universal cause and the assurance, promised by dialectical materialism, of riding the wave of history.[85] But the only universalist cause in sight is that of the Marxist class struggle. Hence Communists are unable to free themselves entirely from preoccupation with the battle of a nonexistent proletariat against native capitalists, whose support may be vital for any anti-imperialist struggle.[86] Since the Marxist dialectical edifice also includes philosophical materialism, i.e., atheism, the dogma is at odds with another powerful element of the national tradition nearly everywhere.

Class forces are also opposed, as Marxists would say. Intrinsic to Communism are class violence and social revolution, but especially in less developed countries those who stand to lose are almost always stronger than those who hope to gain. The counterattack on the capitalist West is most attractive to the marginal and unemployed elements or to poverty-stricken intellectuals and students whose hopes for advancement through education are cheated,[87] to people who have been sufficiently Westernized to feel profound dissatisfaction and resentment at the difference between what is and what should be, to those who find the traditional society embarrassing and would do away with it.

But the levers of power are not ordinarily theirs to grasp. It is one thing to transfer the class struggle to the international stage and use the capitalist interests and the governments which allegedly act at their behest as whipping boys for political and economic troubles; it is another to turn over power to a Marxist-Leninist party. The Communists, inevitably a small minority, want total authority for themselves; that is, they wish to deprive everyone else of any authority or autonomy they may have possessed. They are also intransigent

---

[84] Bruce Larkin, "China and the Third World," *Current History*, 69 (September 1975), 75-79.

[85] Chalmers A. Johnson, *Peasant Nationalism and Communist Power* (Stanford: Stanford University Press, 1962), p. 30.

[86] Kautsky, "The Communist Perspective," in *The Developing Nations*, F. Tachau, ed., p. 151.

[87] Robert Scalapino, "Patterns of Asian Communism," *Problems of Communism*, 20, no. 1-2 (January-February 1971), 4.

[88] Barbu, *Democracy and Dictatorship*, p. 188.

and commonly have difficulty working with other parties, hence find themselves isolated. Ruling groups virtually never desire to rush into change.[89] A nationalist party can pull together many local associations and movements; Communists have to supplant them.[90]

Against the Communists stand not only traditionalists and all who fear to upset the social order but those who have been drawn into the web of the Western economy, culture, and philosophy. Modernization of the economy brings not only disruption but increased productivity and, for some, prosperity. Western culture is an intrusion, but it intrudes because it is widely attractive as well as because it is supported by modern commercialization. Inferiority is galling, but most people can ignore it unless it is rubbed in by direct arrogance and violence. People learn to live with the traumas of industrialization; proud old cultures under attack may decay or merge into modern ways, as in the case of Japan, without necessarily generating much violence of deed or even emotion.

Communism consequently seems a practical possibility only where there is a deep sense of grievance, such that many people become willing to accept loss of personal standing for the national cause, and where the magnitude of the storm so opens the floodgates as to permit reshaping of the social landscape.

War and Communism: Genesis in Struggle

Communist revolutions have succeeded only through international conflict or as a result of defeat in war. History shows no peaceful road to Marxist-Leninist dictatorship. It seems impossible to establish the full panoply of Communist controls without the burning and hardening of violent confrontation with powers labelled capitalist. This seems necessary in order to add to the national liberation struggle the Communist theme of social transformation.

A party disqualified by its extremism in ordinary conditions is qualified by its extremism in disturbed conditions. War is not the midwife of revolution, but its mother. The legitimacy of all Communist states has been based first of all upon victory, not merely in a revolutionary coup but in prolonged hostilities, generally against foreigners and representatives of "capitalism." War has supplied both the esprit de corps to all Communist regimes and their future leadership. Until after the death of Lenin, Russia was governed by a coterie of fellow fighters, as are present-day China, Yugoslavia, Albania, Cuba, North Korea, and Vietnam.

This relationship has been slighted in Communist propaganda, as in Western discussions of Communist doctrine and practice; but many Communist pioneers

---

[89] Kebschull, in *Politics in Transitional Societies*, Harvey G. Kebschull, ed., p. 76.
[90] Heeger, *The Politics of Underdevelopment*, p. 38.

were keenly aware of it. Even the prophets, Marx and Engels, thought in such terms, however contrary to the spirit of historical materialism and economic determinism. In 1848 and afterwards, they looked eagerly to a European war to unite and revolutionize Germany.[9][1] On one occasion, Engels wrote to Marx, "Surely the fact is evident that a disorganized army and a complete breakdown of discipline have been the conditions as well as the results of a victorious revolution."[9][2] Engels participated in skirmishes in the disorders of 1848 and saw himself as an officer in the revolutionary war; an expert in military affairs, he earned the nickname of "The General." As the nineteenth century wore on, it became increasingly apparent that economic forces were not bringing the proletarian revolution nearer, while improved weapons made it hopeless for a city crowd to stand against a disciplined military force; hence the philosophers of Communism looked to war to overthrow capitalism.[9][3]

The Russian Case. In the decade prior to 1914, Russia was advancing economically at an unprecedented rate; the standard of living was rising; and the free classes, journalists, teachers, lawyers, engineers, etc., were leavening the stiff imperial society. The tsar was still a theoretical autocrat but his power was in practice substantially restricted. The legislative Duma, introduced under the constitutional reforms of 1905, had slight powers but did serve as a forum of varied opinion and accustomed the country to the idea of popular representation. There was a lively and informative press despite censorship, and intellectual passion for revolution had ebbed since the 1890s. Marxism, de rigueur for would-be progressive thinkers a generation earlier, was by 1914 regarded by many as outmoded. Thus by the beginning of the World War, police repressions plus the changing climate had reduced the revolutionaries to minor sects, more given to doctrinal disputation than political action. The Bolsheviks, a small sectarian group, seemingly on the way to political domestication, were demoralized.

It may be that the tsarist regime was anachronistic, outworn, and incapable of maintaining itself indefinitely. It may also reasonably be assumed that Russia was too big, too backward, and too divided for a liberal–democratic evolution. But if the old order had not been dashed by an external onslaught, breakdown would in all probability have brought a mere dictator or semidictator to power, such as the anti-Bolshevik leaders in the civil war or the rulers of most Third World countries today. It is inconceivable that a movement so alien to Russian tradition as Lenin's could have come to power without the prior destruction of the forces of order.

---

[9][1] Bertram D. Wolfe, *Marxism: A Hundred Years in the Life of a Doctrine* (New York: Dial Press, 1965), Chap. 1; see also, Max Nomad, *Apostles of Revolt* (New York: Bookman Associates, 1959), p. 116.

[9][2] Quoted by Stefan T. Possony, *A Century of Conflict* (Chicago: Henry Regnery Co., 1953), p. 5.

[9][3] See Lewis S. Feuer, *Marx and the Intellectuals* (Garden City, N.Y.: Doubleday & Co., 1969), p. 17.

The Communist movement began, however, in Lenin's brain when the shock of the war and the nationalistic stance of the Social Democrats led him to divorce himself entirely from the moderates.[94] Instead of advocating peace in the humanitarian fashion of most socialists, Lenin called for turning the "imperialist" war into revolutionary war. For many months he could only write bitter articles in Switzerland, but the breakdown of tsardom gave him an opportunity which he was not to pass up.

In March 1917, the Russian generals, despairing in the face of defeats and disorders in the capital, pressed the incompetent Nicholas II to abdicate and thereby decapitated the imperial state. The succeeding Western-oriented Provisional Government, born in a euphoria of liberation, soon began sinking into a morass of anarchy and disillusionment brought on partly by its effort to continue a war beyond its capacities. Concurrently, the best organized of the extremist parties, Lenin's Bolsheviks, swelled rapidly, promising land, bread, peace, a people's regime, and utopia for the suffering masses. The best recruits were refugees from the occupied territories and deserters from the army. Other, even more radical anarchistic parties were also burgeoning. By late September, the Kerensky regime had no firm basis, while the Bolsheviks had become the largest party in all major centers. By the first days of November, the Petrograd garrison, fearful of being sent to the front, was heeding Bolshevik commissars more than the constituted authorities. The soldiers agreed to follow only those orders countersigned by the Military Revolutionary Committee headed by Trotsky and dominated by Bolsheviks along with some assorted radicals. The Committee took charge of distribution of munitions and gave orders for the seizure of communications. Power had thus effectively passed from the Kerensky government several days before Lenin called out the Red Guards of the factories[95]—his was the only party with a military auxiliary.[96] As the 1928 Comintern Congress resolved, for a revolution to succeed, "there must exist a revolutionary situation, i.e., a crisis for the power of the ruling class brought about by military defeat."[97]

Before the revolution, however, Lenin had only the vaguest idea what kind of political order should prevail under "socialism"; in the Marxist view this should take care of itself as a result of changed relations to means of production. The Soviet state was thus forged not from the interminable theorizing and politicking that was prevalent before the Revolution but by the agony,

---

[94] As remarked by Adam B. Ulam, *Stalin: The Man and his Era* (New York: Viking Press, 1974), p. 126.

[95] A. Rabinowitch, "The Petrograd Garrison and the Bolshevik Seizure of Power," in *Revolution and Politics in Russia*, Alexander and Janet Rabinowitch, eds. (Bloomington: Indiana University Press, 1972), p. 189.

[96] On Lenin's military emphasis, see William Kintner, *The Front is Everywhere* (Norman, Okla.: University of Oklahoma Press, 1950).

[97] Quoted by Timothy A. Taracouzio, *War and Peace in Soviet Diplomacy* (New York: Macmillan, 1940), p. 34.

disorder, and passions of war and civil war. The circumstance that Russia was trying to find a way out of the losing war with Germany and needed a government made it possible for Lenin's minority party to obtain a firm grasp of power. And the emergency made it hard to protest the new censorship, the repression of opposition parties, or the reestablishment of the political police. Conditions at the front also made it possible for Lenin to dismiss the elected Constituent Assembly, in January 1918, thereby writing finis to hopes of democracy without audible protest.

In the subsequent civil war the Soviet government took the shape it has essentially retained to this day, and the Leninist party found its soul. It interpreted the struggle, in which defeat several times seemed near, as a duel with the forces of world capitalism—an interpretation made plausible by Entente assistance for anti-Bolsheviks—and was correspondingly exhilarated and vindicated by victory. The party was militarized, and the Leninists equated militarization with communization.[98] Trotsky called the party members, perhaps half of whom were in the army, a "new Communist order of Samurai."[99] Military needs combined with ideology to bring about total control (so far as the government could enforce it) of the economy, originally patterned after the German war mobilization which Lenin admired. With rationing and practically non-monetary distribution of goods, the brotherhood of equal poverty was idealized as socialism on the march toward utopia.

Communist Movements after World War I. There were radical, Communist or near-Communist stirrings in other defeated countries in the 1918-1920 period. For a few months it seemed likely that the Russians' hopes for revolution in Germany might see fruition. In February 1919, a "soviet" republic was proclaimed in the confused and disrupted state of Bavaria, only to be repressed in a few weeks. Desperate Hungarians, led by Bela Kun, established in March of the same year a Communist government that tried to follow in the footsteps of Lenin's Bolsheviks. It lasted only 133 days but at least created a precedent for post-World War II Hungarian Communism. Thereafter Europe quieted down, and economic troubles, even the severest depression of history in the 1930s, brought not Communists but fascists to power.

International violence, however, again favored Communism in the latter 1930s. In Spain, a fascist-supported insurgency brought a previously feeble Communist party to the top on the republican side. And the Japanese attack on China made it possible for a Communist party to assert itself as the defender of the Middle Kingdom against the barbarians.

A Communist Regime Comes to Power in China. After 1923, the Chinese Communist party had expanded greatly in alliance with the Nationalists in the Chinese civil conflict. But Chiang Kai-shek decided in 1927 the Communists

---

[98] Lewin, *Lenin's Last Struggle*, p. 8.

[99] Eric R. Wolf, *Peasant Wars of the Twentieth Century* (New York: Harper & Row, 1969), p. 94.

a liability were, turned against them and destroyed much of the party. In the war against the Japanese, however, the Communists regained power as the Nationalist government was driven far inland to Chungking, and as party members demonstrated an ability to work with the peasants and hence to expand into Japanese-occupied areas. In 1965, Mao credited the Japanese for helping him to power: "They educated the people. ... They created conditions which made it possible for Communist-led guerrillas to increase their troops and expand their territory."[100] The Japanese had driven the peasants to despair by expelling many from their homes; often it was these refugees who became recruits for the guerrilla warfare which was the penchant of Communist leaders. Mao largely set aside the social revolutionary program, seeking to unite the people broadly in the anti-imperialist cause; the peasants' economic troubles were probably secondary in bringing them to Mao's side.[101] War, invasion, and Japanese occupation shattered the traditional framework of life for millions and led them to welcome the security the Communists offered.[102] Many intellectuals, despairing of the corrupt and inefficient nationalist regime, also turned to Communism as perhaps the last hope. The Japanese again inadvertently helped by branding all their enemies "Communists." The Communists seemed the best defenders of China.

In this struggle, the Communist army was almost equivalent to the party, and the army-party was forged into a tight fraternity. Virtually a government, the army was responsible not only for fighting but for keeping order, construction, managing the economy, education and indoctrination. It had the organizational strength, morale, and sense of purpose necessary to occupy the vacuum left by the defeated Japanese at the war's end and to prevail over the much better supplied Nationalist forces. It went on in effect to make itself the government of China, establishing the new administration of the People's Republic. The regime was finally solidified by the Korean war, which raised its pride and facilitated the consolidation of Mao's new government.[103]

Communist Regimes in Eastern Europe in the Wake of World War II. In Europe, the Communists leaped into the resistance struggle when the Nazis attacked the Soviet Union in June, 1941; and they came into leadership in the Eastern European countries by virtue of organization and determination. As German power crumbled, anti-fascist factions everywhere began to contend for supremacy, and where the presence of the Western allies did not impede, the Communists generally had the upper hand. The Yugoslav Communists, for example, were unimportant at the beginning of the war, their numbers having

---

[100] Quoted by Edgar Snow, *The Long Revolution*, pp. 198-199.

[101] Johnson, *Peasant Nationalism and Communist Power*, pp. 16-17.

[102] Lucian W. Pye, "Mass Participation in Communist China," in *China: Management of a Revolutionary Society*, John M. H. Lindbeck, ed. (Seattle: University of Washington Press, 1971), pp. 15-17.

[103] Pye, *China*, p. 170.

shrunk under severe repression from 80,000 in 1921 to 200 in 1932.[104] But Tito looked in 1939 to war to bring about revolution,[105] and his movement did in fact emerge from the collapse of the royal government in 1941. Tito fought diligently—his party paper, founded in 1941, was (and is) called "Borba," or "Struggle"—while his chief rival, the Serbian leader Mihailovic, adopted a passive posture to avoid reprisals, waiting for the front to come to him. Tito consequently became the effective leader of the national movement; Communists were fighters, not Marxists. Of 140,000 members who came out of the war, only 3,000 were of the pre-war revolutionary party.[106] As Tito said, looking back in 1952 on the dual struggle against occupation forces and the old institutions, "If we had pursued only a proletarian revolution, it would not have succeeded."[107] After the war, the national task of reconstruction became the standby of Communist morale.[108]

In Albania, a Communist party was formed only as a result of occupation and war. Under the aegis of the Yugoslav Comrades, the Albanian Communists took the leadership of the liberation struggle and founded the postwar government. The Communists in Greece would have done likewise but for British and American intervention.

In Poland, Hungary, Romania, Bulgaria, and the eastern third of Germany the presence of Soviet armies sufficed to install Communist regimes and carry out social revolution from above; but this task was greatly facilitated by the discredit or removal of the older authorities, hatred for collaborators and war criminals, confiscation of enemy assets, statization of the economy in war, and destruction of independent classes. The fact that industry had either collaborated with the Nazis or had been taken over by them greatly facilitated the socialization of the economy, while wartime violence and passions made Marxism-Leninism seem less extreme. Communist power in Czechoslovakia was at first incomplete, despite profound disillusionment; the Communists who had come to leadership in the resistance gained a plurality but not a majority in the 1946 elections. A Marxist-Leninist dictatorship was set up in 1948 by an essentially military coup. Resistance was ineffectual because of Communist control of the army and police, which in turn armed the workers' militia, all backed by Soviet armies on the borders.[109]

---

[104] Johnson, *Peasant Nationalism and Communist Power*, p. 165.

[105] Phyllis Auty, *Tito, a Biography* (New York: McGraw-Hill, 1970), p. 145.

[106] George W. Hoffmann and Fred W. Neal, *Yugoslavia and the New Communism* (New York: Twentieth Century Fund, 1962), p. 108.

[107] Vladimir Dedijer, *The Battle Stalin Lost* (New York: Viking Press, 1971), p. 299.

[108] Sharon Zukin, *Beyond Marx and Tito: Theory and Practice in Yugoslavia* (New York: Cambridge University Press, 1975), p. 116.

[109] R. V. Burks in *Communist Systems in Comparative Perspective*, Leonard J. Cohen and Jane P. Shapiro, eds. (Garden City, New York: Doubleday & Co., 1974), p. 65.

Post-World War II Victories for Communism in Asia. It is not improbable that the Communist parties of Western Europe, especially those of France and Italy, might have converted domination of the underground into postwar supremacy had the United States not undertaken to furnish economic and political aid for non-Communist forces. In view of the enormous disparity between the American and Soviet capacities to assist, the fact that the outcome of the contest seemed at times in doubt was a tribute to the potentialities of Communism under postwar conditions.

World War II also brought Communism to power in that part of Korea where the Japanese surrendered to the Soviet Union. The tiny Korean Communist movement first acquired some importance among Koreans fighting against the Japanese invaders of China, as guerrillas in Manchuria and as allies of Maoist forces, but in 1940 their only hope was a broader war.[110] The solidification of the Communist government occurred not only as a result of Soviet direction but also because of the confrontation with South Korea and the U.S. in the war of 1950-1953. A million or more persons left North Korea in the course of the disturbances, and the widespread uprooting facilitated collectivization and strict controls.

The removal of French authority by the Japanese and the subsequent surrender of the Japanese in 1945 opened the way for Ho Chi Minh's party to gain power in Vietnam. In 1941 it was feebly organized and very small,[111] but by the end of the war it was the only really organized national political force on the scene, and so was able (as directing element of a liberation front) to set up a government in North Vietnam, where the Chinese (Nationalist) forces delayed French reentry for a few months. During the war against the French (1946-1954), Ho Chi Minh's party was hardened and strengthened, and the government became more strictly Communist. Young warriors, even armed adolescents, took the place of village elders.[112] After 1959, North Vietnam was engaged in the contest in the south, and the seven years of American intervention (1965-1972) stiffened morale and brought popular support to a high pitch.[113] With reason, Hanoi's Museum of the Revolution is a museum of struggle against foreigners.[114] A by-product of the victory against the U. S. and its South Vietnamese protégé in April, 1975, was the establishment of Communist rule in Laos and Cambodia.

---

[110] Robert A. Scalapino and Chong-sik Lee, *Communism in Korea* (Berkeley: University of California Press, 1972), Vol. I, p. 231.

[111] Dennis J. Duncanson, "Vietnam: From Bolshevism to People's War," in *The Anatomy of Communist Takeovers*, Thomas T. Hammond, ed. (New Haven: Yale University Press, 1975), p. 497.

[112] John T. McAlister, *The Vietnamese and their Revolution* (New York: Harper & Row, 1970), p. 74.

[113] Jon M. van Dyke, *North Vietnam's Strategy for Survival* (Palo Alto: Pacific Books, 1972), p. 79.

[114] Harrison Salisbury, *Behind the Lines* (New York: Harper & Row, 1967), pp. 48-49.

Cuban Communism. Cuban Communism owes only a little less to armed struggle. Castro won power by a small-scale but dangerous guerrilla war, during which time his leadership was tempered and tested. Agrarian reform, the only radical item of the movement's program, was a mere adjunct of the fighting, to draw peasants, not a primary reason for it.[115] Shortly after Castro's 1959 victory, he found himself at odds with the U. S. because of criticism of his summary executions and of expropriation of lands and other properties of Americans. When mutual retaliatory actions continued to escalate, Cuban-American relations deteriorated to frank hostility. A growing number of Cubans took refuge in Florida, from where they launched many pinprick attacks—planes dropping a small bomb or two or incendiaries, a few men landing on the coast—beginning at the end of 1959, with more or less support from American authorities. A ship bringing Belgian munitions was blown up in Havana harbor with many casualties in March 1960; Castro blamed the U. S. and thereafter invariably ended speeches with "Patria o muerte, venceremos."[116] The U. S. broke relations, and the expectation of invasion grew to the accompaniment of patriotic enthusiasm. The national militia created soon after Castro's accession soon amounted to several hundred thousand men and women.[117]

Invasion came at the Bay of Pigs in 1961, where Castroite forces scored a glorious victory over the Cuban exiles armed, equipped, and transported by the U. S. On the eve of the landing, Castro declared Cuba socialist in order to qualify for Soviet support. The emergency led to the arrest of all those suspected of anti-Castro activities, probably over 50,000 persons, thereby destroying the basis of the opposition.[118] This traumatic event made it possible to turn Cuba into an authentic Communist state. Not only was it fully exploited propagandistically; there was an apparently genuine conviction that the U. S. would not take defeat but would launch a stronger assault. This was not unwarranted. The Kennedy administration was under some pressure, until the missile crisis, to remove the "cancer of Communism" in this hemisphere. Havana virtually became a city under siege, with omnipresent militia and soldiers and anti-aircraft beacons in the night sky.[119] Much was made of "Cuba, liberated territory of the Americas," and the "imperialist blockade," while the CIA cooperated with a policy of harassment. Castro claimed that until early 1963 Cuba was fighting "a sort of regular war against numerous attacks from the sea,"[120] and there was more or less guerrilla conflict until 1964.[121] Castro

---

[115] Theodore Draper, *Castroism: Theory and Practice* (New York: Praeger, 1965), pp. 66-67.

[116] Halperin, *The Rise and Decline of Fidel Castro*, p. 77.

[117] R. Fagen, in *Cuba in Revolution*, Roland E. Bonachea and Nelson P. Valdéz, eds. (Garden City, N.Y.: Anchor Books, Doubleday & Co., 1972), p. 207.

[118] Halperin, *The Rise and Decline of Fidel Castro*, pp. 97, 130.

[119] Mohammed A. Rauf, *Cuban Journal*, p. 164.

[120] *New York Times*, July 12, 1975, p. 10.

[121] For Castro's comments, see Lockwood, *Castro's Cuba, Cuba's Fidel*, p. 122.

for his part sponsored guerrilla movements against several Latin American governments as a flank attack on the U. S. There developed a variant of Marxist-Leninist ideology, whereby the essence of Communist revolution becomes guerrilla warfare and the guerrilla force takes the place of the political party.[122] The Castroite position was that "Communism stands for peace, but there can be no revolution without war."[123] Under these conditions, Castro set out, after the Bay of Pigs incident, at full speed to establish his state on the Soviet model.[124]

Failed Attempts at Communism. Elsewhere, Communist parties have had only limited success in the relative calm prevailing over most of the world. The Arab-Israeli wars were not sufficiently destructive of the social order in the Mideast to permit a Communist seizure of power, although they may have assisted Nasser's effort to socialize the Egyptian economy. Most countries of Africa achieved independence peacefully, and the new governments, although probably dictatorial and perhaps socialistic, have hardly been Communist. Those coming nearest the Communist model have been Mozambique and Angola, both of which underwent protracted guerrilla warfare.

This warfare also brought the losers, the Portuguese, to the brink of a Communist revolution. Portuguese armed forces were radicalized and inclined to accept a Marxist-Leninist explanation of their defeat. As an admiral explained, "We are both—Frelimo and Portugal—victims of the colonial and capitalist systems. We are now on the same side of the barricades."[125] The Armed Forces Movement took charge of the government, and for many months the power both of the Communist Party—much more Stalinist than any other of Western Europe—and of the non-Communist radical left grew steadily.[126]

But there was no conflict with a capitalist power and no war emergency sufficient to permit the Communists to assert firm control of revolutionary forces. Moreover, while the armed forces were disillusioned by the African war, Portuguese society was not shattered, and many or most persons kept their stake in the status quo and some faith in traditional institutions. In elections of

---

[122]Ernesto Guevara, *Guerrilla Warfare* (New York: Monthly Review Press, 1961); Regis Debray, *Revolution in the Revolution* (New York: Monthly Review Press, 1967), p. 106.

[123]Rauf, *Cuban Journal*, p. 51.

[124]It is possible that, if the Chilean government of Salvador Allende (1970-1973) had been isolated and subjected to chronic but ineffective attack and threats, it would have become as Communist as Castroite Cuba. A violent confrontation with "class-hostile" forces would have permitted Allende to suppress both opposition and constitutional institutions, to gain control over the armed forces, and to unite the parties of the left. In actuality, one of his major assets was propaganda about the misdeeds of American corporations, probably irritating to Chilean patriots but insufficient to galvanize the nation into acceptance of total dictatorship.

[125]*Time,* May 26, 1975, p. 31.

[126]Cf. Arnold Hottinger, "The Rise of Portugal's Communists," *Problems of Communism*, 24 (July–August, 1975), 1-17.

April 1975, the Communist Party received only 12.5 percent of the votes, and a popular reaction led in August to the replacement of the near-Communist premier. From late 1975, the country reverted to ordinary European political patterns.

War and Communist Movements

Many other radical collectivist-equalitarian movements have gained impetus from military conflict. For example, the Israeli kibbutzim, exemplary in dedication to the sharing of material goods, grew up in the struggle against the Arabs.[127] The defeat of Russia by Japan in 1904 led to the Russian semi-revolution of 1905, the radical fringe of which exercised some power briefly through workers' councils ("soviets") in major centers, while peasants rampaged across the countryside, in a curtain raiser for the bigger upheaval to come from a bigger defeat twelve years later. The defeat of France by Prussia in 1870-71 gave birth to the Paris Commune, which Marx adopted (although few Marxists were involved) and analyzed at length as an episode in the "proletarian struggle,"[128] and which Lenin treated as precursor and model for the Soviet state.

In earlier times, wars have likewise brought movements which might be called "communistic" in the sense of stressing communal ownership. Under the strains and tensions of a difficult war, there developed various somewhat communistic tendencies in the French Revolution. In 1796, as the economy was sinking, a young intellectual, Gracchus Babeuf and his "Society of Equals," called upon the French—first of all the army[129]—to make theirs a land of "brotherly communities." The Directory arrested and guillotined this precursor of Lenin; but his followers gave the world the label "Communist" for a radical leftist party. The English civil war of the preceding century evoked the Levellers, who believed that landed property was an alien (Norman) imposition. One Wm. Walwyne wrote, "the world shall never be well until all things be common," thereby ending covetousness and the need for government.[130] The Middle Ages saw a wealth of such communistic or equalitarian movements in situations of plague, famine, religious schism, and above all war, for example, the Hussite Taborites in fifteenth-century Bohemia and the Anabaptists of besieged Münster. The leader of the latter group, John of Leyden, decreed the abolition of private property and ruled by terror and propaganda much like a medieval Stalin.[131]

---

[127]Boris Stern, *The Kibbutz that Was* (Washington: Public Affairs Press, 1965), pp. 16-17, 20-21.

[128]On the commune in Marxist tradition, see Bertram D. Wolfe, *Marxism* (New York: Dial Press, 1965), pp. 105-147.

[129]Kintner, *The Front is Everywhere*, pp. 17-18.

[130]Eduard Bernstein, *Cromwell and Communism: Socialism and Democracy in the Great English Revolution* (London: Allen and Unwin (reprint), 1930), pp. 91 ff.

[131]Norman R. C. Cohn, *The Pursuit of the Millennium* (New York: Harper & Row, 1971), p. 286.

War Removes the Forces of Order. That war should be favorable, perhaps indispensable for the establishment of a radical state is understandable. In the ordinary course even those who might be said to have nothing to lose but their chains are usually distrustful of disruptive change and respectful of the social order, preferring to seek improvement within accustomed channels rather than risking their overthrow. Thus Russian peasants met populist missionaries of the 1870s with incredulity and often turned them over to the police. The much abused and often starving Chinese peasants were mostly deaf to Communist slogans so long as their lives could go on in the old ruts. Routine ways of thought prevail until the old political system ceases to function. Contrary to Lenin, it is not capitalism but Communism which requires wars.[132]

Traditional loyalties are at first strengthened by war, as people almost automatically rally around the leadership for the common defense and the shared cause. The beginning of the First World War brought the supposedly internationalist socialist parties all over Europe to the support of nationalist governments. In Russia a strike wave came to an immediate halt; all parties except the Bolshevik fraction of the Marxists embraced the Russian cause against the Germans. But failure more than undoes the cementing effect of war. In 1914, Nicholas knew that failure would probably cost him his crown, revealing the fundamental corruptness and weakness of his state, just as it later accentuated and exposed the rottenness and incompetence of Chiang's Nationalist party.

War demands the supreme effort of a society; and unsuccessful war more than anything else delegitimizes the government and destabilizes the entire social order, the more so as the government is authoritarian and bases its claim to rule upon its strength. Revolution comes not from misery but from the breakdown of the state, its morale and legitimacy. Defeat is equalitarian, since the upper strata are shown to be incapable and hence unworthy of their status. Repressed hatred boils to the surface, as the privileged can now be openly vilified for having betrayed their responsibilities.

More concretely, the forces upon which the regime counted to maintain the social order are physically consumed by war and disaffected by non-success. The traditional Communist goal of replacing the regular army by a people's militia becomes realistic only when the army is ground down and discredited. A large part of the well-indoctrinated tsarist soldiery and officer corps was lost in battle by 1917, replaced by hastily trained recruits and promoted cadres, men less willing than their predecessors to fire upon rioting civilians. The generals who had sworn fealty to Nicholas II forced him out when they came to see him as a cause of defeat. After his abdication, the famous Order No. 1 of the Petrograd Soviet further undercut the army as the bulwark of order by reducing the authority of officers; of it, a monarchist said, "This is the end of the

---

[132] Adam B. Ulam, *The Rivals* (New York: Viking Press, 1971), p. 394.

army."[133] It was still possible, in July 1917, for Kerensky to activate the army for a major offensive; but the resultant fiasco, after so much exhortation, left it in a state of near collapse. The final blow was dealt by the confusion surrounding General Kornilov's attempted coup. By October, the soldiers' chief, almost sole concern, was to avoid fighting; and deserters and war-dodgers flocked to the Bolsheviks.

War Removes the Underpinnings of Traditional Society. War may remove not only the forces but also the classes of order. The destruction of the middle classes in Russia commenced during the First World War and was completed by the civil war. Through fighting, terror, emigration, starvation, and hardships, the liberal classes were practically eliminated physically and as a political force. Much the same occurred in China, where the small modernized sector of the population was either uprooted or annihilated by the Japanese invasion. In North Korea and North Vietnam, the conflict situation encouraged anti-Communists and potential anti-Communists to remove themselves to the southern part of the country.

War breaks normal rhythms and imposes unaccustomed hardships. In Russia in 1917, as in China in the years up to 1949, inflation was mounting and shortages (conspicuously not shared by the elite) were deepening. Lack of bread, for instance, triggered the riots that led to the end of the Romanov dynasty. Perception of hardships is much augmented by fear and uncertainty, and values become questionable. Feelings of powerlessness and insecurity lead people to seek new bonds.[134] Anxiety of war may induce collective paranoia, mass hysteria, and chiliasm; and displaced hostility seeks scapegoats.[135] Dogmatism becomes a refuge from disquieting facts[136]—the megalomania of utopianism becomes normal under stress.

Since war, especially an unsuccessful war, requires drastic restructuring of life, a party prepared to promise new solutions, stronger certainties, and new leadership unassociated with defeat can offer itself as savior. It is not the hesitant who take the field in the time of troubles but the self-assured; and in Russia in the summer of 1917 hardly anyone but the Bolsheviks was prepared to claim the succession of the tsars. At the April Congress of Soviets, the moderate socialist, Tseretelli, declared, "There is no political party in Russia which would say at the present time, 'Give us power'." Lenin shouted from the

---

[133]William H. Chamberlin, *The Russian Revolution, 1917-1921* (New York: Macmillan, 1935), p. 86.

[134]Cf. Erich Fromm, *Escape from Freedom* (New York: Farrar and Rinehart, 1941).

[135]K. Lang and G. Lang, "Collective Responses to the Threat of Disaster," in *The Threat of Impending Disaster*, George H. Grosser et al., eds. (Cambridge: MIT Press, 1964), pp. 66-67.

[136]L. Grinspoon, "Fallout Shelters and the Unacceptability of Disquieting Facts," *The Threat of Impending Disaster*, pp. 123-124.

audience, "There is such a party!"[137] The exclamation has rightly become enshrined in Soviet Leninolatry.

War Permits Extremism. But defeat is not only uniquely effective in undermining accustomed authority; the experience of war at the same time lays foundations for a more ruthless and more effective regime. It inures to all manner of regulation which would otherwise be felt as excessive and which can function well only when generally supported. Price controls, commodity allocations, etc., were extensively applied almost without protest even in Britain and the United States in the world wars. Lenin's government could socialize the Russian economy by merely extending somewhat the controls already in effect, using some of the bureaucratic apparatus instituted by the tsarist regime. In the civil war the Soviets imposed central direction (so far as feasible under the circumstances) of all transactions and practical phasing out of money in favor of allocation and rationing. As long as the conflict raged, this worked tolerably well, and it may have enabled the Bolsheviks to win. Likewise, the Bolsheviks, after having dissolved authority in the old army, inaugurated unheard of severity of discipline in the new; many a commissar was ordered shot by Trotsky for insufficient vigor in battle. The heat of combat crystallized the theoretical possibilities of Communism into solid reality.

War at once equalizes all strata of society and concentrates power in the hands of a few, in the manner of the Communist revolution. It gives the rulers full command over all aspects of life; Communist discipline goes little beyond martial law. Military necessity excuses all the measures, from censorship to economic mobilization to terrorism, which are appropriate for dictatorship. War makes not only arbitrary command but death and suffering commonplace. War is politically sanctioned mass murder; after millions have been slaughtered on the battlefield, the execution of a few thousand representatives of the old order in the name of the new is small matter. Combat hardens to uninhibited use of power for the general safety, and to discipline for stress; violence justifies violence. The moral ambiguities are forgotten, and private interests are of no account. When so many private interests have been wiped out by the war, there is little protest that the state should take others for its allegedly higher needs.

Destruction and hardships cause people to submit more fully to the overarching authority that claims to protect them. At first glance, it may seem amazing that bombing on a large-scale does not weaken but rather strengthens mobilization regimes. However, it does so precisely because it justifies the overriding of individual desires and rights, while simultaneously demanding sacrifice for a general and distant cause. When the state to which individuals look for safety shows itself incompetent (as the Provisional as well as the tsarist government did), they will listen to the leader who claims to hold the key to the situation, even though his proposals may be ruthless. Few in the Russia

---

[137] Chamberlin, *The Russian Revolution,* p. 159.

of late 1917 felt much revulsion at strong-arm methods for a cause which proclaimed itself holy. Even grand dukes had been willing to murder (namely,
Rasputin) for what they saw as compelling reasons. Ruthlessness is the essence
of totalitarianism, and total war lays the foundation for the total state.[138]

The Holy War. The strong movement requires not only desperation but
faith, which in earlier times would have been religious. More than any other
party, the Communists hold out the security of a strong collective in times of
maximum insecurity; their unqualified and allegedly scientific doctrine mixed
with ageless millenarianism offers new certainties mixed with new hopes. Theirs
is a new and badly needed promise of a better victory, not of small gains for
the failed nation-state but of a new and joyous era under the victorious new
order. The war was going badly, Marxists can say, because the deceived peoples
were fighting the wrong war. Under the leadership of the proletariat and the
party (Lenin and his followers exhorted) the people should strive not for sordid
national aims but for the liberation and happiness of all peoples. Our suffering
is for the release of all humanity. In Lenin's analysis, the entire meaning of the
First World War was greed for markets and colonies, hence it was no shame but
true virtue to turn away from such pursuits. As a Hungarian journalist put it,
"The revolution had to come to usher in those virtues which enabled us to
reconcile ourselves to a lost war."[139]

The Communists can demand greater sacrifices because the victory they
offer, the triumph of the workers over the exploiters, promises pure and permanent happiness; theirs is truly a war to end all wars, unlike Woodrow Wilson's
slogan of 1917-1918. The Communist utopia is like the bliss and ease promised
as reward of victory; Marxism-Leninism makes the fight moral and historically
necessary. The promise of militant Communism is total peace; after the universal victory of the anointed working class, there should be no more conflict
between classes, hence no more conflict between nations, indeed, no more conflict of any kind, so that the state itself should "wither away." In the depths of a
tormented and unsuccessful war, Lenin promised the Russians enchanting de-
liverance, and "Peace" was his most effective byword, especially among soldiers
apprehensive of being sent to the front, who comprised the chief force lifting
the Bolsheviks into power. No other party could pledge so effectively to bring
peace; to be for an immediate end to the "imperialist" war was almost equivalent to being Bolshevik. This theme then and later appealed not only to the un-
sophisticated but to many intellectuals horrified by the stupidity of war, who
would otherwise choke at the logical weaknesses and crudities of Communist
theory and practice.

Yet the Communist call for peace has never resembled Gandhian non-
violence. In theory as well as in deed, the Communists have always energetically

---

[138] The relation of fascism, like Communism, to the decomposition of old values and
institutions combined with political hardening in war is obvious.

[139] Quoted by C. Vermer, in *Political Socialization*, Volgyes, ed., p. 31.

opposed pacifism, just as they refuse to admit conscientious objection to military service. Even in "bourgeois" states, the doctrine has been that workers should not refuse to bear arms but should enter the army and endeavor to take it over.[140] The Communist demand is to improve and elevate the struggle, not to renounce it. Lenin spent the war years prior to April 1917 pleading not for an end to the slaughter but for conversion of the "imperialist" war of nations into a civil war of classes, the only way, he contended, to obtain true victory and enduring peace. Lenin saw a basic necessity for violence; as he wrote in 1905, "So long as there are oppressed and exploited peoples in the world, we must strive not for disarmament but for the universal arming of the people."[141] He did not ask that power fall into his hands but was fully aware of the advantages of snatching it by force. Class warfare is the heart of Marxism-Leninism, the final peace being an ever receding glory for which the party demands present sacrifices.

War, finally, permits the Communists to garb themselves in the jargon of patriotism and to equate their demands with the needs of the state. They can call for and get the collaboration of non-Communist elements without which they could not function—in the Soviet case, for example, tsarist bureaucrats and officers. The Communists, from the Russian civil war onward, have always tried to assume the leadership of a broader patriotic movement. Since Lenin's coup of 1917, when no one had a clear idea what the Bolsheviks might do, no Communist party has ever achieved power in the name of Communist revolution but usually under the banner of a national front for national purposes.

The Militarized State

Similar to the party itself—or indeed a religious order—the model army is hierarchic, anti-individualistic and anti-property, authoritarian and idealistic in spirit, demanding adherence to a creed and sacrifice for a higher good. Both party and army are ideally ascetic, favoring moral over material reward, and essentially political; i.e., it is felt that the government should control the economic sphere.[142] They are collectivistic in that individuals should act and feel primarily as members of the group. They are equalitarian in that differences between individuals are not personal but organizational; and these differences result less from wealth than from power, which is not necessarily conferred on the basis of merit but according to one's status in the hierarchy. The necessities of life are furnished communally in army barracks; the luxuries, in the army as in the party, are mostly obtained as perquisites of rank, not possessions of individuals. Taking the Roman motto of "everything for the fatherland,"

---

[140] Taracouzio, *War and Peace in Soviet Diplomacy*, pp. 37-38.

[141] *Selected Works* (New York: International Publishers, 1943), Vol. III, p. 339.

[142] This holds true even in America. Cf. Morris Janowitz, *The Professional Soldier* (New York: Free Press, 1960), p. 246.

party and army tend toward introversion, disliking competing organizations and
values, offering members emotional and economic security in return for fullness of loyalty.[143]

Thanks to his organizational principles, Lenin created a party model which
has shown itself (along with imitative fascist parties) a capable organizer
and mobilizer of the warring state. The political soldiers excel in battle. Communist parties, having come to power in or through a war situation, have had
greatest success not in bringing justice, equality, abundance of goods, and social
harmony, as they have promised, but in the destruction of their enemies. They
organize an offensive better than they organize production, and they produce
military wares much better than civilian. They give unceasing attention to
morale and indoctrination, and they demand and get more from their people
than their antagonists are usually able to exact. Communist revolutionary war is
revolutionary mostly in that it is wholehearted and total.

The Soviet Military through the Wars. Lenin, however, did not appreciate
so well as many of his successors the potentialities of the fusion of Communism,
militarism, and the national cause. For a few months after the seizure of power,
he continued the demobilization of the exhausted and demoralized armed
forces; and when the Germans presented peace terms in 1918 that even most
Bolsheviks considered quite unacceptable, Lenin forgot his faith in the power of
an ideologically armed people. Instead of conducting a people's revolutionary
war against the invaders, as Mao or Tito would presumably have done, Lenin insisted on accepting the peace of Brest-Litovsk, outraging Russian national feelings and strengthening the widespread impression that he was pro-German if not
in German hire.

However, beginning in March 1918, Lenin and Trotsky proceeded to build
the new Red Army. Compulsory military service was reintroduced in the spring
and summer of 1918, election of officers was ended, and discipline was made
sterner than ever. The backbone of the new army was the party; party members
were sent in to stiffen the otherwise spineless mass by persuasion and example
and to prevent surrender no matter how hopeless the situation appeared to be.
Thanks to the party, the Red Army was able to win out over the better armed
but much divided White forces.

In 1939, the Red Army did poorly against Finland, a nation with a fiftieth
of the population of the Soviet Union. This was partly a result of the purges
which two years earlier had claimed about half the officer corps and nearly all
those in the highest ranks. It was also a result of initial overconfidence, since
Stalin expected an easy victory. Only after months of standoff did he
mobilize the mass of the Soviet army. It may also be surmised that, after
nearly twenty years of peace, the Soviet state had lost most of the élan and

---

[143]On the communal character of military life, see Kurt Lang, "Military Organization"
in *Handbook of Organizations*, James G. March, ed. (Chicago: Rand McNally, 1965),
pp. 848-850.

militancy of revolutionary Communism. In the first three months of war against Germany, likewise, Soviet forces reaped little but disaster. But as the people became convinced of the danger of Nazism, nationalist and Communist ideals fused for the defense of Mother Russia, motherland of the workers. The rejuvenated Soviet state performed miracles of mobilization. It mustered hundreds of new divisions after Hitler thought he had practically destroyed the Soviet army. Despite the loss of much Soviet industry to German occupation, many plants were efficiently transported to eastern regions; and production of some categories of war materials was raised to levels comparable to those of the United States. Hitler found his generals' reports of Soviet production of tanks and planes quite unbelievable. Soviet soldiers marched to the greatest victory of Russian history.

Asian Communist Military Exploits. The military virtuosity of the Chinese Communists has been even more striking. Mao's forces in Kiangsi in the early 1930s had virtually no arms except what they could capture, yet they repulsed repeated Nationalist onslaughts. Finally they broke out of encirclement in the Long March, a 6,000-mile endurance feat. In the Yenan retreat, they performed miracles of improvisation; they were the world's experts in achieving the most with the least.[144] The Nationalists had all the material advantages, control of the cities and means of communication, the governmental apparatus, international recognition, and assistance of the great powers, including the Soviet Union. But the Maoists were able to wear down their enemies and eventually win because they were better able to harness human energies.

In the Korean war, both the North Koreans and the Chinese who came to their rescue displayed military capacities embarrassing to the United States. The attack of June 25, 1950, was not entirely unexpected; and the ability of the Communists to overrun nearly the entire southern section of the peninsula in six weeks was due not only to surprise and superior armaments but to organization, skill, and determination. In November-December, 1950, the Chinese were able to use mobility (on foot), concealment, and surprise to overcome inferiority of firepower, not to speak of airpower, and inflict a severe defeat on the American–U. N. forces, driving them back to the 38th parallel and beyond. The Americans were able to stabilize the front, but their great material superiority did not suffice to push the Communists back.

Communist-led or inspired peasants on several continents, but most prominently in Asian jungles, have demonstrated the skill and will power to stand off and wear down, perhaps defeat, better armed forces ten times as large. Typical have been the opponents of first the French and then the Americans in Vietnam. Massive military and economic assistance for many years was insufficient to give

---

[144]Cf. Edgar Snow, *Red Star over China,* rev. ed. (New York: Grove Press, 1968).

victory to the city-based pro-Western regimes.[145] Until 1965, the Viet Cong received inspiration but little material help from its foreign patrons; what flowed down the jungle trails was less than a hundredth of that which poured into the hands of the Saigon regime. Yet American advisors could hope for nothing better than that Republic of Vietnam forces should learn a fraction of the tenacity and initiative of their enemies. Americans frankly saw North Vietnamese, small, largely untutored Asiatics, in many ways typical of the depressed masses of the less developed countries, as equals of the world's best infantrymen.

At home, meanwhile, North Vietnam, under continual bombardment and supporting a disproportionate military effort, became the model Communist state. Foreign visitors were much impressed by the equalitarianism displayed even by high officials who shared the toil and sufferings of the people; and by the dedication and cooperative will of the people,[146] finding fulfillment in class struggle translated into anticolonialism. Their socialism seemed of a purity and selfless temper that Western leftists might find only in dreams, certainly not in the Soviet sphere. A German journalist called wartime Hanoi the "capital of human dignity."[147]

Summary. The total picture of the Communist state may thus be described as paradoxical. The Communist revolution, to be precipitated according to Marx by economic forces, is generated at any economic level by war. The Leninist revolutionary party, with its theoretical basis in the scholastic philosophy of Marxism, is akin in organization and spirit to any army. The state that promises a pacific utopia excels in combat, and the socialized economy that promises abundance for all is most effective in military production. By corollary, when there is no war, the Communist state is constrained to maintain something of a siege mentality in an atmosphere of continual struggle against a hostile external environment. It remains to be seen whether the war-born Communist state can truly and fully make peace, spiritually as well as de facto, with the alien outside and yet remain Communist.

---

[145]Cf. George K. Tankam, *Communist Revolutionary Warfare: From the Vietminh to the Viet Cong*, rev. ed. (New York: Praeger, 1961).

[146]As seen, for example, by Richard Gott, *Guardian Weekly*, March 14, 1970, p. 6.

[147]*Die Zeit*, December 19, 1972, p. 5.

Chapter two

The Rise of Communism

Russia

The Ambivalent Empire

Communism is a violent reaction to inequality not of classes but of states, a situation caused by the relative creativity and innovative capacity of the pluralistic state system that arose in Western Europe on the wreckage of the Roman Empire. For a thousand years, the West has been improving its technological capacities more rapidly than the other peoples, first slowly catching up with older centers of wealth and power, then surpassing the Near East, India, and China, gathering speed from the fifteenth century and leaping ahead at a rate new to human experience from the beginnings of the industrial revolution at the end of the eighteenth century. From the latter part of the fifteenth century, marked by the voyages of discovery, Western power and influence have thrust out and around the world, dominating if not conquering, humiliating and subverting if not destroying traditional cultures. This Westernization or Europeanization proceeded ever more strongly and without letup until the time of the First World War, and in somewhat changed form but with undiminished intensity it has continued to this day. Communism is one way in which injured states have responded to this Western encroachment upon their independence, social and cultural forms, and self-respect.

That the reaction has taken in part the peculiar form of Marxist-Leninist Communism derives not only from the idiosyncratic thinking of an expatriate German literatus, Karl Marx, but also from the unique nature of the Russian experience. Russia and only Russia was in a position to forge the peculiar political system of Communism, with its imperial–authoritarian essence and Western-derived forms.[1]

The Russian Empire as Predecessor of Communism. The Russians began expansion from the Muscovite center about the same time that maritime European powers were reaching out to found first trading posts, then colonies overseas, in Africa, Asia, and America. But whereas the Western powers acquired properties abroad, the Russians expanded their state into a great continental empire, successor of the Tatars. Russia consequently became a semi-Asiatic despotic empire with a basically European cultural and religious background, much better able to borrow and apply Western technology than the Turks, Arabs, or Chinese. The special Russian success formula was thus to use Western tools (and ideas of administration) in order to rule autocratically an Asian empire. This was coupled with a messianism arising in part from the national struggle against the Tatars, in part from the confidence generated by an expanding empire and the need to justify it morally.

The Russian empire, like the Leninist state, was authoritarian and absolutist in mentality. Autocracy was regarded as necessary to stave off anarchy and hold the empire together. The tsar had to be obeyed as a holy figure; his will, like that of the Leninist party, was equivalent to law. There was no separation of branches of government. The ruling class was a largely self-selected bureaucracy, and the people accepted the dichotomy of rulers and ruled, as they do today. Private property was little respected, and the state intervened freely in the economy. The people were accustomed to all manner of state controls, from censorship to the requirement (still in force today) for a permit to move from the village or reside in the capital. Those who accepted the bureaucratic despotism of the tsars as essential for unity and order did not find unnatural the claim of the party to speak for the workers and the leadership to speak for the party. The Russian state took for granted an unending struggle for self-preservation and expansion; the dynamic drive of Leninism was entirely in its tradition. The Russian empire saw itself as bearer of order and justice, a shining new world; just as later the Marxist-Leninists promised utopia through revolution. The empire, too, was totally confident in its possession of dogmatic truth—Orthodoxy—and was intolerant of heresies.

Living on the fringes of the Western cultural sphere, the Russians owed their superiority over the heathen and weaker peoples of Asia to their willingness to borrow freely and abundantly, a fact that aided greatly in their adoption of the Marxist-Leninist apparatus of Western forms. But borrowing was compensated psychologically by an assertion of moral superiority. The vastness of the Russian empire bespoke its special mission and the excellence of its moral and political values over and against the disorder and amorality of the pluralistic

---

[1] A thesis developed in Robert G. Wesson, *The Russian Dilemma* (New Brunswick, N. J.: Rutgers University Press, 1974).

Western civilization—in fact, the sense of Russian destiny has persisted from the early tsars through Dostoievsky to Lenin and such modern dissidents as Igor Shafarevich.[2] Russia was obviously destined to rule and must be worthy of ruling.

Virtually from its inception, the empire was troubled and ambivalent in its relations to the West. It was necessary for Ivan IV (the Terrible) to import Western technicians, yet to assert the sacred right of autocracy the more forcefully, at least partly as a defensive tactic against the constitutionalism of his Polish neighbor. Peter the Great, the supreme westernizer, compensated for a massive increase in foreign contacts by aggravating the obligations of everyone from peasants to nobles; modernization went hand in hand with reaffirmation of the basic concept of total empire. In the eighteenth century, Russia was becoming superficially more Europeanized—the upper classes taking on Western, mostly French, styles and manners, even language; and hints of intellectual dissent crept into the mentality of the elite.

It was only as the nineteenth century advanced, however, that the problem of reconciling autocracy and westernization-modernization became acute. The industrial revolution was, by comparison with earlier change, an explosion; innovation begat innovation, and Russia was clearly under pressure to keep pace. National power came to require more and more mechanical equipment, plus skilled and highly trained personnel. Russia grew into a complex, differentiated society, and external contacts steadily increased.

Nicholas I, frightened by an attempted constitutionalist coup in 1825 (the "Decembrists"), attempted to isolate Russia for a generation. But expansionist politics led to the most vigorous form of contact with the outside world—war. The Crimean defeat (1854-1856) opened the gates to a wave of reform and a new intensity of intercourse with the industrializing West. Complicating the problem of Russia's attitude toward the West was a steady growth there of those ideas and attitudes most pernicious to the multinational Russian empire: economic and political liberalism, individualism, democracy, and nationalism.

Thus it was that Russia in the second half of the nineteenth century suffered acute philosophical indigestion; what had earlier been a slight malaise became a serious illness. The half-hearted reforms of the 1860s—including unsatisfying liberation of the serfs, establishment of feeble organs of local self-government (*zemstvos*), improvement of the status of the universities, and slackening of censorship—raised expectations that were unfulfillable and increased opportunities for expression of discontent by precisely those growing classes which did not fit into the traditional society. There hence evolved a new social sector crucial for the development of Communism in Russia and its spread to other countries, the discontented intelligentsia, a yeast of social

---

[2] Igor Shafarevich, "Does Russia Have a Future?" in *From Under the Rubble*, Alexander Solzhenitsyn et al., eds. (Boston: Little, Brown, 1975), p. 294.

ferment arising from the interaction of traditional authoritarian society and modern pluralistic civilization.

The Unhappy Intelligentsia. The intelligentsia was composed of persons with sufficient education to feel at odds with the old order and unhappy with their lack of a place in it, mostly students, ex-students, journalists and creative or would-be creative artists, misplaced or unemployed professionals, and the like, including some who might in a later century be classified as hippies or beatniks. Feeling acutely a sense of national humiliation yet suffused with Russian pride, unhappy in the present and hopeful of the future, they were passionate critics, speaking with the more passion for lack of responsibility. Their preoccupation was Russia, its relation to the West, and the ways of modernization. Wishing above all to be up to date and looking for the "last word" from Europe,[3] they laid hopes on science with naiveté beyond the Victorians— an adoration which led some to uncritical acceptance of "scientific socialism." They were also theoretical democrats, a fashionable stance in Western intellectual circles. Their sympathies went out to the poor and deprived because they themselves felt rejected by the power structure. For them, as for Marx, the masses were the potential for attacking the rulership, to be mobilized by ideology, the intelligentsia's chief weapon against a hostile world.[4] Their extremism led them to oppose the "bourgeoisie," who were representative of Western values and subversive of the Russian spirit, rather than the nobility, from which many of them sprang, or the "Little Father" tsar.

Thus the mentality of the radicals was as authoritarian as the medium from which they came, and they inclined to seek salvation from a strong ruler, one who would repudiate any and all evil advisors and be guided by their philosophy to justice. This was the easiest possible salvation, perhaps the only salvation conceivable within a reasonable time. It was indeed close to the salvation the Leninists offered a little later: the enlightened ones would crush the evil and selfish elements of society and guide the people to the new day.

The intellectuals were at the same time strongly inclined toward socialism. This was a vague concept, with connotations of progress, rationalism and science, peace, justice, and the welfare of the people. The word and the idea had become popular in England and France in the first decades of the nineteenth century; and the Russians took it up with uncritical abandon since it rang of old virtues and modern aspirations and well suited the Russian mentality. The writers and debaters could ask for nothing better, however indistinct its contours and however doubtful the road to its Eden; it was much more interesting than freedom, which seemed to mean little in the face of economic inequality and which at best was more of a challenge than a golden promise. Socialism was

---

[3] As noted by Lenin in "Left-Wing Communism, an Infantile Disorder," *Selected Works* (Moscow: Progress Publishers, 1971), Vol. III, p. 353.

[4] M. Malia, in *The Russian Intelligentsia*, Richard Pipes, ed. (New York: Columbia University Press, 1961), p. 15.

also anti-capitalism, and capitalism was irritating not only because it bespoke the power of the West and values discordant with Russian tradition, but also because the greater part of Russian industry was foreign owned or at least foreign organized and managed.

The Russians were happy to observe that they might even have advantages over the West in striving toward the new socialist order. For in Russia private property was politically feeble, and there was among the peasantry a good deal of sharing and equalitarianism—much exaggerated by the enthusiasts. Hence Russia might conceivably skip over the capitalist stage with all its grimy unpleasantness. The humiliating backwardness of Russia might then be considered a positive asset, as many thinkers, from Dmitri Pisarev in the 1860s[5] through Trotsky and Lenin, discerned. Russia was the purer for being poorer and less corrupted than the West, morally superior and readier to leap into the socialism that would surely be a precursor of the millennium.

The promise of socialism also made it easier for the Russians to vindicate their country and their own personalities by damning the West as diseased and fouled by greed, ruthless competition, and the struggle for ill-gotten gain. It was to become ordinary practice for Russians to claim virtues, such as democracy, where they were conspicuously absent, and to deny them to the West, where they were imperfect.[6] Long before Lenin, Russian writers were finding servitude, inequality, and poverty in the West, and seeing freedom, equality, and abundance, or the potential for achieving them, in despotic and impoverished Russia.

The Russian intelligentsia was the more extremist because it was helpless and could do little more than rehash its ideas and spew its passions. Consequently, it moved in frustration from one position to another. In the early 1870s, the great hope was to bring the light to the masses and thereby remake society. When this illusion shattered on ignorance and incomprehension, the Populists turned elitist, hoping perhaps more realistically to overturn the social order by the concerted action of a well-organized revolutionary elite. Perhaps it would suffice for the conspirators to lop off the top of the reactionary structure by terrorism. But the futility of this dream was made clear by the much sterner repression that followed the assassination of Alexander II in 1881. The hope of an easy ride to socialism was undercut by a number of other factors, too, among them the increasing degradation of the peasant commune toward the end of the nineteenth century. Originally a governmental device for fixing responsibility for taxes, it was becoming more repressive and less communal. At the same time, industrialization was advancing with giant steps; it seemed unavoidable that Russia undergo the capitalist development of the West, however morally distasteful. The unfortunate intellectuals were left

---

[5] Theodore Dan, *The Origins of Bolshevism* (New York: Harper & Row, 1964), p. 60.
[6] Cf. Donald M. Wallace, *Russia* (New York: Henry Holt, 1877), pp. 588-589.

with little to hope for—in fact with an expired role in a Russia bypassing their ideas and mocking their aspirations. But haply at this juncture there arrived a new dispensation from the West, the novel and exciting "philosophy-creed-science" of Marxism.

From Marxism to Leninism

Marx was in somewhat the same situation as the Russians. An unemployed intellectual of a relatively unindustrialized country, he was compelled to admire England, the land of the bourgeoisie and triumphant capitalism, while he did not cease to hate it.

Marxism, which raised few waves in England, became the official doctrine of the German labor movement. In Russia it became the new revelation for a generation of intellectuals. Marxism especially thrives on unevenness of development, and Russia above other nations suffered this: failure to keep abreast of the advancing West, the contradiction between social modernization and ancient autocratic ways, and the chasm between the new industrial establishments and the backward peasantry.

Russian intellectuals saw many virtues in Marx. It was appealing that he pointed to the misery not of Russian peasants but of the masses of the most advanced country of the West and that he damned the obnoxious parvenus of capitalism and allowed them a brief span of power. Marx invoked the poor, the factory proletariat, to cast the haughty owners to perdition; penurious Russian students could see the victory as their own. Sharing Marx's insecurity, frustration, and ambivalence toward the industrial West,[7] the Russians were overwhelmed by the learning and systematic thinking with which he confirmed their feelings.

That Marx's attack on capitalism was essentially illiberal did not trouble those of authoritarian mentality. That the Marxian "class struggle" was an invitation to intolerance and persecution and that Marxian truths were dogmatic suited a milieu of intolerance and dogmatism. If Marx's analyses led into morasses of sticky concepts designed not for clarification but political agitation, this mattered little to those who longed not for truth but for change. If Marxism was a blend of mystic faith and scientific world outlook, so much the better for men whose outlook was fundamentally religious but who felt constrained to renounce the old faith in favor of the new science. It was also fitting that Marx's utopia was emotionally retrospective even while replete with progressive terminology. In the face of onrushing change, Marx was, like the Russians, basically nostalgic for simpler and securer days; he promised order, quiet harmony, and freedom from fear and want, from conscription and taxes. In one of the obstetrical metaphors of which Marx was fond, Communism was a social return to the womb.

---

[7] Zevedei Barbu, *Democracy and Dictatorship* (New York: Grove Press, 1956), p. 210.

Marxism also had the advantage of being an ostensibly internationalist creed well suited for an empire suffering from increasing discontent among its non-Russian minorities. It brought together Russians who basically supported the empire and non-Russians who were the bitterest enemies of tsardom, and it mobilized the Balts, Poles, Jews, Caucasians, etc. to relinquish particularistic rights and to unite in the cause of a new social order. Minority peoples furnished the most dedicated of Lenin's recruits. In Lenin's entourage in Switzerland shortly before the overthrow of the tsar there was not a single Russian (except his wife).[8]

The Adaptation of Marxism to Russia. For all such reasons, Marxism became the vogue of those who would consider themselves modernly illuminated, the wave cresting high in the 1890s. Yet there were drawbacks to the Marxist answer. The theoretical picture of feudalism yielding to capitalism, which in turn was to give birth to socialism, seemed inappropriate to the Russian situation. The historical dialectic was an inconvenience, at least when Russian Marxists got down to talking concretely about revolution and the changes it should bring. It was hard to promise anything but an early triumph of the despised capitalist–bourgeois order—many Russian Marxists in the hectic days of 1917, were so enthralled by the historical Marxian scheme that they were hindered from grasping the opportunity for power virtually thrust upon them. Moreover, Marx laid all emphasis on revolutionary factory workers and scorned the peasants; but Russia had forty times as many peasants as industrial workers. It was further inconvenient that Marx, although inclined to violence and of a dogmatic and authoritarian temperament, took for granted the democratic outlook of his age and assumed that the new order would come by the will and action of the large oppressed majority of the population. The Russian radicals had learned that the masses were not prepared to listen to them; to wait until the people would acquire the requisite class consciousness to revolt against their masters would be to relegate revolution to distant generations.

It took the genius of Lenin, far more skilled than Marx as a political leader, to surmount each of these difficulties and in effect to meld Marxism into the Populist creed of the 1880s. Lenin turned the paucity of industrial workers to his advantage. Small numbers were substantially compensated by the fact that these few were easily mobilized, and Lenin took political effect more seriously than any nose count. Russian workers were typically concentrated in large plants, where they were more easily organized and led and where labor-management relations were least patriarchal. Lenin also practically annexed the peasantry to the proletariat.[9] He came near the position subsequently taken by Mao of translating "proletarian" into "propertyless" thereby labeling Russia

---

[8] Michael Heller, "Lenin, Parvus, and Solzhenitsyn," *Survey*, 21 (Autumn 1975), 191.

[9] As in "The Agrarian Program of the Russian Social Democrats," *Collected Works* (Moscow: Foreign Languages Publishing House, 1960), Vol. VI, p. 125.

a land eighty percent proletarian.[10] All this was contrary to Marx's scholastic philosophy but quite in accord with the Marxian revolutionary spirit. Marx was first of all a rebel, and he was willing to applaud revolution by anyone anywhere—witness his reactions to uprisings in Ireland, Italy, and even China— regardless of how few industrial proletarians were involved. It was hardly more un-Marxist for Lenin to look for socialist revolution in Russia in 1917 than for Marx to have hoped for a proletarian revolution in Germany in 1848.[11] As the *Communist Manifesto* proclaimed, "the bourgeois revolution in Germany will be but the prelude to an immediately following proletarian revolution."[12]

Lenin seemed the more deviant because in the interim Marx had settled down, from the radicalism of the *Communist Manifesto* to the scholasticism of *Capital*; Engels had helped to systematize and attenuate the teachings to make them more palatable in Europe, and Social Democratic parties had espoused the view that the socialist revolution was still distant even for an industrially much advanced Germany. Lenin's adaptation of Marxism, whether a revision or a return to basics, was essential in order to apply Marxism to the non-Western world where peasants have provided much, in some places nearly all, of the steam for revolutions alleged to bring about the "dictatorship of the proletariat."

Lenin had the consistency to try to put a theoretical foundation under the revolution he wanted for Russia by his theory of imperialism. In logic, this was profoundly un-Marxist, since he made the exploitation of nation by nation as important as the exploitation of class by class and set a political explanation alongside, at times above, strictly economic causation. Marx had realistically considered capitalism, in a world of warring monarchs and semifeudal powers, to be essentially pacific; but Lenin, in an age of colony-grabbing, saw capital as predatory and war-making. He thereby appropriated for his own use a new catalyst, war, for the socialist revolution which had ingloriously failed to arrive— a logical step of no great originality in a world torn by war but a doctrine eminently suited for political action in 1917. At the same time Lenin solved the old problem of finding a destiny for Russia within the Marxist scheme. If Russia was exploited by the imperialist powers (Russia itself was a most successful imperialist nation) and capitalism was weak there, Russia might well have the honor of breaking the capitalist front and leading the way to the grand socialist revolution.

The Party as Vanguard to the Revolution. Lenin thus explicitly adapted Marxist doctrines insofar as they were emotionally congenial to the Russian

---

[10] Louise Bryant, *Six Red Months in Russia* (New York: Arno Press reprint, 1970), p. 84.

[11] I. Getzler, "Marxist Revolutionaries and the Dilemma of Power," in *Revolution and Politics in Russia*, Alexander and Janet Rabinowitch, eds. (Bloomington: Indiana University Press, 1972), p. 93.

[12] Marx and Engels, *Selected Works* (Moscow: Progress Publishers, 1973), Vol. 1, p. 137.

situation. This is further evident in his approach to the making of the revolution which his theory sanctioned for Russia. The Russian masses, largely apathetic if not loyal to the traditional regime, showed no signs of making a revolution from below, so Lenin rationalized revolution from above. Without guidance, as he stressed in his seminal *What is to Be Done* (1902), the workers developed only short-sighted trade union consciousness, not political consciousness, struggling for extra kopecks rather than the new order of society. Some Marxists concluded that the revolution consequently had to wait; Lenin gave the less patient answer that it was the duty of dedicated revolutionaries of whatever class (with an almost entirely middle-class leadership, in fact) to apply their knowledge of "scientific socialism" to guide the workers. This was again contrary to Marxist theory and the basic belief that social "existence determines consciousness"; that is, that proletarians and bourgeoisie are historically predetermined to have proletarian and bourgeois outlooks, respectively. Lenin may have felt this to be un-Marxist, as he conspicuously left out any quotes from Marx in expounding the idea. He might, however, have cited numerous statements of Marx revealing a firm conviction that he, Marx, whatever his class origins, knew much better than mere factory workers what the latter should desire. He might also have cited the *Communist Manifesto*: "The Communists therefore are . . . . the most advanced and resolute section of the working class parties of every country, that section which pushes forward all the others; on the other hand, theoretically, they have over the great mass of the proletariat the advantage of clearly understanding the line of march. . . ."[13]

The identification of the Bolsheviks with the true interests of the workers was mystical but useful. As the vanguard of the workers, they were purported to be the true Marxists, harbingers of the future majority, however few their present adherents. The party, an umbrella sheltering the proletariat, could also bring in non-proletarian elements—the peasants or dissident minority nationalists, for example. As such it became something of a superclass, against which no dissent could be licit, because by definition the will of the proletariat was monolithic. Further, the party served as a catalyst in overcoming the difficulties posed by Russia's backwardness. If the party could guide by its cognitive will, there was no need to rely on any spontaneous historical development—and Lenin rejected "spontaneity" with a fervor unseemly in a believer in economic determinism. The party could in effect spark Russia to leap ahead of the West.

Theoretically, the party's role should end with maturity of the proletariat, but Lenin recognized that Russia was not merely to be liberated but to be governed, and the party as instrument of governance enabled him to insist on the "dictatorship of the proletariat," a new state whose character should be determined not by the actual proletariat but by its self-selected vanguard.[14]

---

[13] Karl Marx and Friedrich Engels, *Selected Works*, Vol. 1, p. 120.
[14] Moshe Lewin, *Lenin's Last Struggle* (New York: Vintage Books, 1970), p. 123.

This inversion of thought became practically the essence of Marxism-Leninism, although Marxists such as Bukharin took more seriously the promise of the "withering away" of the state.[15] The promise of total and lasting power was essential to Lenin's politics; he could hardly demand total obedience and self-subordination of his band unless he could promise the highest reward.

A further corollary of the Leninist ideology was personal leadership. It was often pointed out that the superiority of the party over the proletariat implied the superiority of a few, or of a single individual over the party. The Bolshevik party before the Revolution was peculiarly Lenin's party. He formed it around himself, and being a Bolshevik meant adherence not to a doctrine but to Lenin. Occasionally Lenin had to yield to the feelings of his followers, but the Bolshevik party remained unique in having a single leader who made the major decisions.[16] This style of leadership, following not in the path of Western social democracy but of Bakunin and Nechaev, made it possible to combine opportunistic policies with ideological determination, justifying strong authority by the promise of great destinies.

Lenin thus adapted Marxism, with scant regard for what had been understood as Marxian dogma but quite in harmony with the spirit of Marx's attack, to the needs of revolution in Russia. It might better be said that he took up the old themes of Russian radicals, the Populists of the 1870s and 1880s, and put them into a Marxist framework. Like them, he saw Russia injured by the West and gave it compensating moral superiority and a special role in the salvation of mankind. He galvanized his movement, as a consistent Marxist could not, by looking to revolution by violence as soon as possible.

Lenin's Victory

Lenin's adaptations of the then current Social Democratic Marxism seem in retrospect a work of high political genius, but prior to 1917 this was not evident. Lenin never attracted to his side leading Russian Marxist intellectuals or theoreticians; not a charismatic leader, Lenin perhaps preferred his one-man party. Among the activist Marxists, members of the Russian Social Democratic Workers' Party, Lenin was usually clearly in a minority. In the 1905 revolution neither Lenin nor his party garnered laurels; and after it their fortunes sank very low. Membership declined to perhaps a tenth of the previous high under police repression and a change of atmosphere. Revolution lost allure and Marxism ceased to be the wave of the hour. Russian intellectuals were finding more of a place for themselves in the rapidly developing, modernizing, and differentiating society. Those who remained faithful to the party were turning more philosophical and for the most part less violent. Lenin himself shortly before World

---

[15] Stephen F. Cohen, *Bukharin and the Bolshevik Revolution: A Political Biography* (New York: Knopf, 1973), p. 39.

[16] David Anin, "Lenin and Malinovsky," *Survey*, 21 (Autumn 1975), p. 146.

War I was talking more like a Social Democratic politician than a revolutionary. Leninism was becoming anachronistic.[17] The obvious danger for the tsarist government was not from the radicals, perhaps least of all from the Leninists, but from the constitutionalists.

Leninism was unsuccessful in normal times because it meant espousing the attitudes and ideas of an earlier generation (the Populists of the 1870s and 1880s). It became successful only when Russia was thrust back, economically, politically, and socially, to a previous age by the great war. The conflict largely isolated Russia from the West, the Western frontier being sealed by battle, and trade and communications with the Allies being limited to long, roundabout routes. Morally, Russia was on its own as it had not been for generations, enemy of its nearest Western neighbors and increasingly at odds with its distant allies. The strain was excessive for the feeble Russian industrial economy, inflation was rampant, and breakdown was on the way by early 1917. The liberal classes were abraded in the stress and conflict, and what little of the bourgeois mentality had crept into the imperial system was largely set aside under the pressure of emergency. The political system reverted to an earlier stage, semidemocratic institutions were disregarded, the tsar and tsarina tried to take charge, and the monarchy was narrowed and corrupted. Insecurity, the delegitimation of authority, fluidity of relations, growing anarchy and despair all put a premium on extreme, revolutionary solutions. The worse conditions became, the more in order Lenin's modernized primitivism.

The departure of the tsar, capstone of Russian society, left a void which the Provisional Government could not fill. There was at first a deceptive euphoria in the new-found freedom and supposed movement toward modern Western democracy; all parties, including Lenin's Bolsheviks, for the first weeks thought in terms of cooperation in prosecution of the war and building the new Russia. The radical April Theses Lenin propounded shortly after his return were widely regarded as a revival of Bakuninism which was current nearly a half century earlier; the Bolshevik Petrograd Committee rejected them by a vote of thirteen to two.[18] But Russia at war was not governable in a liberal manner. The fighting went badly, shifting blame for defeat from the tsarist to the Provisional regime. The economy continued to deteriorate. Socialism in the air—almost all parties considered themselves socialist—caused uncertainty and confusion without the mobilization that might have allowed true socialism to be effective. Workers made it difficult or impossible for owners to manage factories although the government was not prepared to take charge. Anarchy swept across the countryside as peasants saw no reason to restrain their land hunger. The freedom-oriented Provisional government had no political means

---

[17] Malia in *The Russian Intelligentsia*, p. 17.

[18] Alexander Rabinowitch, *Prelude to Revolution: The Bolsheviks and the July, 1917, Uprising* (Bloomington: Indiana University Press, 1968), p. 40.

of checking aspirations of minorities to autonomy or perhaps independence, and had to allow some of them to have their own military formations. It seemed as though the empire was breaking up.

Bolshevik Advantages. Yet the Bolshevik accession to power was no popular uprising, nor did it result from widespread pressure to put the Bolshevik program into effect. It came rather through withdrawal of loyalties from a Provisional Government which lacked determination to give Russia the purposeful authoritarian government needed in the emergency. The liberals were unready for action or responsibility, and the extraordinary incoherence of the afflicted middle classes virtually invited radicals to assume power.[19]

In a situation inviting charismatic politics—loss of legitimacy of the old authority, inability of the state to keep order, and poorly developed political institutions[20]—the Bolsheviks were well organized and purposeful. Lenin at least was supremely confident in his destiny and ready to shoulder the burdens of power in a difficult situation. With extensive German financial support,[21] the Leninists had an agitational apparatus, party press, and paramilitary troops, means of power the other parties could not match. Lenin was tactically flexible; hence he borrowed the rival Socialist-Revolutionaries' program of land for the peasants instead of socialization of agriculture. Moreover, the democratic pretenses and facade of the Bolshevik party served Lenin in 1917 as they have served the Soviet Union since. The other parties did not seriously believe that Bolshevik power could mean dictatorship and extinction of their freedom. Dictatorship could come from a generals' coup, not a "socialist" party.

The road was consequently paved for the Bolshevik take-over of November 1917. The abortive attempt of General Kornilov in September to drive out the leftist Provisional Government cost it the support of conservatives and armed the Bolsheviks physically and politically. They kept the guns they received to defend the government and played on the fears aroused by the would-be putsch. With no tsar and no traditional loyalties, the officers were not prepared to fight for a semisocialist government, and the non-Bolshevik socialists had no great enthusiasm for a government which seemed incapable of remaking Russian society.

The Capture of Power. Lenin might then have seized power fairly democratically through Bolshevik votes in the councils, or soviets, but he preferred to inaugurate the new era with violence. The Bolshevik-dominated Military Revolutionary Committee organized the seizure of power. Soldiers fearful of being sent to the front, not class-conscious workers, gave Lenin victory; it was a

---

[19] Allan Monkhouse, *Moscow, 1911-1933* (Boston: Little, Brown, 1934), p. 60.
[20] F. LaMond Tullis, *Politics and Social Change in Third World Countries* (New York: John Wiley and Sons, 1973), pp. 81-82.
[21] Documented in Z. A. B. Zeman, *Germany and the Revolution in Russia 1915-1918* (London: Oxford University Press, 1958), passim.

triumph more of anarchism than of Marxism. The Congress of Soviets, which served to legitimize Bolshevik rule through a show of popular support, was immediately dismissed to prevent its interfering in the new state.

Catapulted to the seat of the Romanovs, Lenin shared the general assumption that the Bolsheviks probably could not hold power[22] —he doubted that his government could remain in power as long as the Paris Commune (71 days). He also had very little idea, beyond some characteristically vague Marxist platitudes, what kind of state he was to build. He was, however, as resolved to hold onto power as he had been to achieve it, and the Soviet state took shape largely through Lenin's moves to affirm and protect his position. He proceded rapidly to curb the non-Bolshevik press, first papers of middle-class backing and then competitive socialist organs. He then reinstituted the political police and loosed it against enemies and potential enemies. His order to nationalize industry sought to bring some order to a chaotic economy and to mobilize resources under unified state control. With the commencement of civil war in the summer of 1918, terrorism was added to Lenin's political armory.

The November 1917 seizure of power merely signalled the beginning of the Russian Revolution. The ensuing civil war that lasted until late 1920 eliminated both anti-Bolsheviks and moderates, and also provided the Bolshevik party with cadres hardened to obedience and a population accustomed to their rule. It resulted in stringent controls over the economy and all aspects of life, so-called "War Communism," justified partly by wartime necessity and partly by ideological drives to purge the country of Western capitalism.[23] Conflict, hardships, and terrorism completed the destruction of independent classes and social forces.

The war gave Bolshevism a military cast and washed out what remained of Social Democratic humanitarianism in Lenin's party. Victory gave confidence and conviction of rightness. Local autonomy had been destroyed, and competing parties had been practically outlawed. The mode of maintaining de facto centralized rule over the minorities while allowing them a superficial autonomy had been set. Shortly after the contest had been decided, the party leadership, no longer able to avail itself of wartime drives, moved more systematically to repress dissent. From the time of the Tenth Congress, March 1921, potential opposition was ever more repressed, both within the party and outside. Bolshevism also became self-reliant and basically nationalistic. During the civil war, Lenin and company had persistently scanned the skies for signs of the European revolution which was to save them. The storm clouds never burst, however; and

[22] John Keep, "The Bolshevik Revolution: Prototype or Myth?" in *The Anatomy of Communist Takeovers,* Thomas T. Hammond, ed. (New Haven: Yale University Press, 1975), p. 53.

[23] Moshe Lewin, *Political Undercurrents in Soviet Economic Debates* (Princeton: Princeton University Press, 1974), p. 80.

the Russians always afterwards sought their own salvation, guided not by visions of utopia but by the elite's mandate of self-preservation.

It was thus by no design but quite by circumstance—and the accessibility of an unrealistic but appealing ideology—that the Russians turned away from the prevalent Western tradition and created their own partly modern, partly antique state. Only a large, self-regarding empire could have so set aside the libertarian and rationalistic ideas of the age, and only an empire accustomed to the reality of autocratic government while continually borrowing and adapting from the West could have developed the Leninist answer to dilemmas of modernization. Unlike the February Revolution which overthrew the tsar, Lenin's October Revolution did not represent a real break with Russian political tradition but a reassertion of fundamental values.

China

Grounds of Communism

Thanks to the Red Army, aided in many areas by local converts, Lenin's Revolution in effect saved the Russian empire. Except for the Western marches, its territory was coextensive with that of the Romanov empire. Efforts to institute Communist regimes in such states as Hungary and northern Persia were frustrated. Nonetheless the Soviet Union continued to back the spread of its version of society, especially by means of political parties affiliated directly with Moscow. Ironically, success came after many years of failure had dampened belief in the idealistic mission and it came in ways unforetold by Marxism and not to be surmised from Lenin's road to power.

Fittingly, however, the first great country after Russia to come under Communism was an empire in a basically similar situation, China. This was an ancient state steeped even deeper in the pride of its traditions than Russia, poorer and more backward relative to the industrial West, more injured by the cultural, economic, and political onslaught of the West, and less touched by Western ideas. Such a state was even more suited for restored autocracy than Russia, for which constitutionalism, although unlikely, was conceivable. Perhaps for these reasons Chinese Communism has been more extreme in most respects—the use of blood purges being the principal exception—than the Russian original. It should be remembered, however, that Chinese Communism has been derivative, dependent on the Soviet model for its inception and main forms. China never labored under the secular ambivalence of Russia and presumably for this reason could never have itself invented the Communist form; it was able only to borrow what proved successful elsewhere. European-Asiatic Russia was the indispensable bridge between Marxism and the peasant-nationalist revolution in Asia.

China under the Dynasties. Ancient China was the epitome of the sustained highly developed universal empire. In isolated grandeur-much larger than the

Roman empire at its zenith—the Chinese empire had almost no idea of foreign relations and competing states, there being only tributaries to the Son of Heaven and barbarians beyond its boundaries. The power of the emperor was universal and unlimited, with only philosophic restraints. Competing political organizations were anathema, a blemish on the supreme order, and absolutism was deemed the sine qua non of a united and harmonious realm. Order was to be kept primarily by suasion and moral authority.

The cement of the empire and basis of moral authority was Confucianism, a holistic, universalist moral–political philosophy like Marxism-Leninism, a guide to government and social ethics. It served to sustain the superiority of the elect and to determine a proper hierarchical structure.[24] Like Maoism, it opposed selfish and individualistic impulses as harmful to the social order.[25] The required studies were designed above all to inculcate wholehearted obedience. There was no idea of individualism or freedom in principle—ordinary people were forbidden to use fancy clothing, much as later the Maoists attired all, from peasant to engineer, in boiler suits. Private property was little respected, commercial values were disdained, and status was achieved by official service and mastery of Confucianism. Society was composed, basically, of the peasants and the gentry, those with education and official standing who ruled, like a Communist party, supposedly by merit and moral superiority, forming a group based less on heredity than shared self-interest and philosophy.[26] Yet below the emperor there was no formally hereditary status and theoretically anyone could climb up the official ladder.

The elaborate edifice of Chinese imperial government, based upon the civil service examination system, was strong and effective when fresh, when the literati were capable, loyal, and hardworking; but through Chinese history dynasties did not last more than about 250 years. The ruling bureaucrats would lose their sense of responsibility and turn their positions of public trust into means of private enrichment. Burdens upon the hapless peasants would be increased beyond measure, as parasites fattened and producers starved. Corruption would spread through the entire society, and the rulers would become debauched and incapable until the rotten edifice was ready to collapse.

The last to go through the cycle from vigor to incapacity was the Manchu (Ch'ing) dynasty. Established in 1644, it was senile and obviously decaying from the first part of the nineteenth century, decadence unhappily coinciding with increasing pressure of industrializing Western powers on the ancient realm. Into the proud but impoverished and immobile country came strangers who could only be seen as complete savages in their ignorance of Chinese civilization yet who bore many a remarkable device of which the Chinese were ignorant, including irresistible engines of war. The exalted self-esteem of the Chinese was

---

[24] O. Edmund Clubb, *Twentieth Century China* (New York: Columbia University Press, 1964), p. 3.

[25] Lucien Pye, *China: An Introduction* (Boston: Little, Brown, 1972), p. 344.

[26] Michael Ganter, *China's Struggle to Modernize* (New York: Knopf, 1972), p. 11.

brutally bruised by evidence of their relative incapacity as small numbers of foreigners defeated them in numerous encounters, beginning with the unsavory Opium War (1839–1842).

The Clash with Westernism. China was forcibly opened to Western trade, compelled to receive foreign ambassadors as representatives of equal powers instead of tributaries. More and more concessions were extracted from the helpless Chinese, and the felt injury was much less from abstract comparisons by literati disillusioned in the power of their laborious learning, or from humiliation suffered in diplomatic circles, than from the intrusion and arrogance of countless individuals and businesses. Europeans began making themselves at home in China, protected by special power; often half-educated, they might treat cultivated Chinese as near-beasts, at least as cultural and racial inferiors. They brought disruptions of change with them, like those producing Marxism in Europe. For example, in building a railroad, the foreigners might break the rice bowls of porters, river or canal boatmen, and local traders; cheap imported goods, such as textiles and cutlery, bankrupted native manufacturers. The privileged alienness of foreign enterprises and the haughtiness and seemingly undeserved riches and power of foreign entrepreneurs not only embittered the Chinese against the invaders but redoubled the inherited antipathy to capitalism.

The intrusion was not entirely predatory. Many Westerners tried to help the Chinese build factories or reform the administration. The foreign concession areas in leading Chinese cities were islands of order and good government. But as the dynasty continued to rot at the beginning of this century, the Western presence became ever less restrained and less respectful; and Chinese intellectuals increasingly blamed it for all their troubles.

China was unable to react like Japan, closing ranks, reorganizing the state, and purposefully learning from the West to defend the national integrity. The Chinese had no such effective government, adaptable social order, and national cohesiveness. On the contrary, the Chinese bureaucracy was stiffly conservative and wedded to its institutions. The dynasty, moreover, was foreign in origin, basically insecure, and fearful of change in principle.[27] For the last half century of its existence, the court was dominated by the ignorant and illegitimate ex-concubine Dowager Empress Tz'u-hsi, for whom patriotism came far behind concern for her own status and pleasures—a role faintly like that of tsarina Alexandra in the last years of the Romanovs.

In the 1860s, after two defeats by European powers, the mandarins started a "self-strengthening movement" in order, as they put it, to "learn superior barbarian technique with which to repel the barbarians."[28] But political corruption was rampant; and when the empress appropriated naval funds for her pleasure craft, it came to seem that national restoration presupposed social

---

[27] Immanuel C. Y. Hsü, *The Rise of Modern China* (New York: Oxford University Press, 1970), p. 492.
[28] *Ibid.*, p. 10.

revolution. As in the twilight of any dynasty, there were secret societies, banditry, peasant disorders, and popular uprisings, the more frequent because the dynasty was alien. Of these, the most important was the Tai-p'ing, 1851-1864, the first Chinese insurgency to involve a semi-Western ideology, outwardly adopting Christianity instead of simply claiming the Mantle of Heaven. The Tai-p'ing state in many ways presaged that of Mao: monistic and centralized, it made all classes equal, abolished private land ownership, and set up something of a communal society. The soldiers cultivated state farms. The status of women was raised, foot binding, polygamy, and prostitution being outlawed. Indulgences such as opium, tobacco, and alcohol were forbidden. Symbols of the old order were destroyed, and Chinese sovereignty was reasserted against the West.[29] Westerners responded to these changes by helping the Manchu government to defeat the partly Christian Tai-p'ings. They lived on as heroes for later Communist leaders, and they are cited as precursors of the successful revolution.[30]

Democracy and Nationalism. From the beginning of this century, there evolved a small but dedicated class of intellectuals more or less endowed with Western learning, who spread the opinion that China might be saved by democracy and a Western-style constitution, somewhat like the pro forma Japanese constitution. When the dynasty collapsed (1911-12), a democratic republic was instituted in the approved Western style; but it rapidly degenerated, with coercion and corruption, into dictatorship and warlordism, to the discredit of Western liberal ideas. When the Versailles peace conference determined in 1919 that Japan should retain formerly German-held Shantung, student riots were the result. The May Fourth Movement, a singular upsurge of national feeling which the Communists still hail as a beginning of modern popular revolutionism, tolled the death knell of Western liberalism.

From this point on, the Chinese intelligentsia tended to drift leftwards, as the old order disintegrated with no unifying principle or authority to replace it. The classical written language was abandoned and the vernacular established, thereby severing the bond between the intellectuals and China's past. Avenues of advance were disrupted, and the underemployed educated felt lost between untenable Chinese and unacceptable Western approaches. There was rapid economic change, and the number of factory workers rose to nearly two million at the beginning of the 1920s. The small but growing middle classes were caught up, as Mao noted,[31] between foreign ("imperialist") interests and native society.

---

[29] Eric R. Wolf, *Peasant Wars of the Twentieth Century* (New York: Harper & Row, 1969), pp. 120-124.

[30] Edgar Snow, *Journey to the Beginning* (New York: Random House, 1958), p. 21; see also; *Peking Review*, April 18, 1975, p. 5.

[31] Jerome Ch'en, "Development and Logic of Mao Tse-tung's Thought," in *Ideology and Politics in Contemporary China*, Chalmers Johnson, ed. (Seattle: University of Washington Press, 1973), p. 82.

It was a time of painful breakup of old patterns and felt need for new authority to put the pieces back together.

For a generation, the strongest party attempting to do so was the Kuomingtang or Nationalist party effectively founded by Sun Yat-sen in the upsurge of national feeling in 1919. Sun undertook to free China from the imperialistic intrusions of the Western powers and admired Lenin's success in reaffirming Russian independence. He was also critical of the disorderliness and inequality of Western society, while he saw good organization in the new Soviet state. Then, too, the Western powers were deaf to his appeals, while the Russians offered help. Sun Yat-sen's semisocialist program, bolstered by a party organized on the Bolshevik pattern—with the assistance of Soviet advisors, chiefly Mikhail Borodin—stood for single-party dictatorship during an indefinite period of tutelage. After Sun's death, Chiang Kai-shek turned against Communism and the Soviet Union, but much of his thinking still ran in the old channels. He blamed the Western powers for China's woes and called for social change, an end to the system "under which man is now subordinated to technique."[32] When his party proved incapable of controlling China, it was not remarkable that its successor should be a Communist party.

The Ascension of Maoism

Since the KMT was socialistic and anti-imperialist, at least in its early years, there might seem to have been little need for a strictly Communist party in a country eminently unsuited, according to Marxist theory, for a socialist revolution. Indeed, the road to power was long and tortuous, and many a different turn might well have condemned Communism in China to the futility it has encountered in a large majority of less developed countries. Much of the credit for the success of Communism must go, as indicated earlier, to the Japanese invasion. The weakness and short-sightedness of the Nationalists were also crucial, as were the leadership qualities of Mao Tse-tung.

The Marxist idea of class struggle has never had great appeal in China (the Maoists use the terminology very loosely) because it is largely inapplicable to Chinese society, which has always been much more concerned with political than economic status. There was a minor vogue for anarcho-syndicalism among "progressive" intellectuals before 1920,[33] but Marx remained unnoticed in China until after the Russian Revolution. Then, in 1919–1920, China encountered not Marxism but Marxism-Leninism, a ready-made doctrine of successful revolution, an idea that had no competing rival interpretations. As for the lack of a proletariat, that was easily solved by translating "proletarian" into "propertyless," a large class in China. That the Comintern represented a foreign power

---

[32]Chiang Kai-shek, *China's Destiny* (New York: Roy Publishers, 1947), p. 232.
[33]Robert Scalapino, ed., *Communist Revolution in Asia* (Englewood Cliffs, N. J.: Prentice-Hall, 1965), p. 3.

was also of no matter; Soviet Russia, at odds with the European imperialist powers, became the first great power to recognize China as an equal and had ostentatiously renounced the treaties giving tsarist Russia special rights in Manchuria.[34] Leninist elitism fit perfectly where traditionally a few had been called upon to rule on the basis of their mastery of doctrine. Neither was the Bolshevik conspiratorial approach a novelty for the land of secret societies. In fact, the authoritarian approach of Leninism, coupled with the facade of modern, democratic forms—a "higher democracy" to serve the purposes of national strength[35]—suited perfectly the needs of a society where the despots traditionally proclaimed their devotion to the people.

The creed also appealed to China's need to rationalize its bad experiences with the West. It squarely placed the blame for China's woes on the intruders, and not only promised revenge but gave Asians, too, a role in the remaking of the world—a restoration of dignity especially important for the Chinese. The doctrine promised as a distant goal a society not unlike a perfected and purified empire of tradition. Best of all, it offered a new means of national strength by sweeping away the parasitic classes, compromised by foreign interests and money, and involving the masses in a supreme renewal. Democratic or parliamentary government, so far as the Chinese saw it, was an invitation to factionalism, graft, and special privilege, at best too weak and slow. Something stronger was needed to end feudalism, landlordism, and warlordism and to galvanize the nation, to solve the problems of poverty, disorder, and foreign encroachment.[36]

The Party: First Steps. For such reasons, a few persons began discussing the Soviet example and Marxist-Leninist theory in several cities; and emissaries of the Comintern were able to help organize the founding "congress" of the Chinese Communist Party in July 1921, a convention of a dozen delegates representing somewhat over fifty members, a humble beginning but one of the first Communist parties established outside Russia. Most of the members of the new party had enough education to separate them from the masses and the Chinese mainstream but not enough to qualify them, properly speaking, as intellectuals. They came largely from those parts of China most affected by foreign penetration.[37] Mainly from the upper-peasant or small landholder class, their backgrounds were similar to those of KMT leaders, except that the Nationalists were of a somewhat more bourgeois origin.[38]

Unlike Lenin, who was a revolutionary before he became the founder of a state—indeed became maker of a state only as a last resort—the Chinese

---

[34] This generosity was later partly retracted.

[35] Scalapino, *Communist Revolution in Asia*, p. 4.

[36] James C. Hsiung, *Ideology and Practice: The Evolution of Chinese Communism* (New York: Praeger, 1970), p. 40.

[37] Robert C. North with Ithiel de Sola Poole, "Kuomingtang and Chinese Communist Elites," in *World Revolutionary Elites: Studies in Coercive Ideological Movements*, Harold D. Lasswell and Daniel Lerner, eds. (Cambridge: MIT Press, 1965), p. 376.

[38] Wolf, *Peasant Wars of the Twentieth Century*, p. 151.

Communists were nationalists before they were revolutionaries. In the original Leninist conception, the state was a means to the new society; for the Chinese, revolution was rather a means to national resurrection.[39] They had read little of Marx; Communism was to them an active program, not a theory to be garnered from books but what the Comintern proposed.

This attitude was characteristic of Mao Tse-tung, who with Chou En-lai was one of the founders, though not of the top leaders. Son of a peasant who had prospered, a school teacher by training, Mao never seems to have absorbed much Marxist materialism. In 1918 he was foreshadowing his idea of "contradictions" with such idealistic statements as "the high is the low, the impure is the pure. . ."[40] An active and practical revolutionary, he was never bothered by inconsistencies in thought; one idea, however, remained paramount, and that was China as a nation. He never displayed special attachment to Marx's appointed class, the factory workers, but manifested concern for the dispossessed in general, many of whom Marx would have dismissed as "Lumpenproletariat." His approach to the theory of class struggle was simple. A lesson of a workers' night school he organized ran, "Rich people's tables have the best wine./ Their tables offer the best dishes./ The wine is the blood and sweat of the common people,/ the dishes are their flesh and bones!/ Awake, you who are being eaten by others!"[41]

The Chinese Communist Party, however, did not prosper for several years, perhaps mostly because the Nationalist Party had a long head start and seemed much more promising. The Russians, too, perceived the KMT as more useful to their purpose of attacking the interests of Britain, France, and Japan. Hence the Comintern instructed its Chinese followers to support the KMT, and in 1923 arrangements were made for the Communists to enter that party as individuals. Coexistence proved feasible while the Nationalists were pushing slowly up from their base in Canton and so long as Sun lived; it brought in fact a large increase of membership to the Communist Party. But conflicts of interest surfaced after Sun's death in 1925; each party wanted to use the other and neither had illusions about its rival's ultimate intentions. In 1927, Chiang turned on the Communists and their working-class supporters. Stalin ordered the Communists to retaliate by organizing revolutionary uprisings in the cities; but this tactic failed abysmally, and much of the leadership as well as the basis of the party was wiped out.

Mao, however, determined to engage the long suffering peasantry, in the ancient Chinese tradition of agrarian revolt against bad government, thereby becoming the first Marxist-Leninist of importance to regard the peasants as more than auxiliaries to the urban-oriented revolution.[42] Others, including Stalin and

---

[39] Lucian W. Pye, *The Spirit of Chinese Politics* (Cambridge: MIT Press, 1968), p. 60.

[40] Hsiung, *Ideology and Practice*, p. 29.

[41] *China Reconstructs*, January, 1975, p. 34.

[42] Hsiung, *Ideology and Practice*, p. 61.

Comintern leaders, advocated working with the peasants; but Mao saw them as the vanguard in the fight against feudal forces even before the urban failure. For Mao the class question was simple: a peasant (or anyone else) became a proletarian by joining the revolution; and, obviously, if a revolution by industrial workers was appropriate for an industrial country, an agrarian country should expect to have an agrarian revolution.[43]

The Army Fights for Power. With some difficulties, Mao and Chu Teh, the outstanding Red Army leader, established a guerrilla base south of the Yangtze, and in 1931 proclaimed in Kiangsi a Chinese Soviet Republic. Pushing a stern program of land reform, they were sufficiently successful that Chiang mounted a major series of campaigns to exterminate them. In late 1934 the Communist forces broke out of the siege and undertook what became the legendary Long March south, west, and north, to the northwestern province of Shensi, where they could have direct contact with the Soviet Union. On the way, however, they had no communication with the Comintern for nearly a year;[44] and during this time of isolation, Mao became informal head and factual master of the party and its military forces. This was an epic of tempering hardships and unforgettable deeds, but it was also a nadir of Communist fortunes. In 1934, Mao had some 180,000 men; about 100,000 began the Long March; less than 8,000 came through.[45] Party membership was about 300,000 in 1934; in 1936 only some 30,000 remained.[46]

Communism was lifted from the slough by the war with Japan. The encroachments of the Japanese became serious with the seizure of Manchuria in 1930, and in the following years they pressed into other north Chinese provinces. The Chinese mentality, once nearly indifferent, had so evolved toward nationalism that surrender was inadmissible. The intellectuals moved farther left under pressure, and by 1936 Marxism dominated all sectors.[47] Taking up the nationalist cause as their chief rallying cry, the Communists became, at Yenan in the northwest, more moderate in policies. Class warfare was toned down to expropriation of absentee landholders, restriction of rents and interest rates, village self-government, etc. The Communists refrained, under their "Three Thirds" system, from holding directly more than a third of governing positions. Their success in mobilizing the peasants rested less upon class interest than upon political organization[48] catalyzed by Japanese aggressions. With some reason, the Maoists appeared to Western observers to be agrarian reformers, not

---

[43] Wolf, *Peasant Wars of the Twentieth Century*, pp. 145-146.

[44] James P. Harrison, *The Long March to Power: A History of the Chinese Communist Party 1921-1972*, (New York: Praeger, 1972), p. 243.

[45] Hsü, *The Rise of Modern China*, p. 159.

[46] Cf. Harrison, *The Long March to Power*, Chap. 11, for an account of this episode.

[47] Lucien Bianco, *Origins of the Chinese Revolution 1915-1949* (Stanford: Stanford University Press, 1971), p. 47.

[48] Wolf, *Peasant Wars of the Twentieth Century*, p. 148.

Communists as the world had understood Communism. As nationalists, the Communists also became increasingly independent of the Soviet Union, which had lost interest in the Chinese revolution[49] and was continuing to support the KMT Nationalists as the party capable of resisting Japan.

In 1937 the Japanese launched a large-scale invasion of central China and proceeded to occupy the principal cities and densely populated areas. The Chiang government was driven away from its bases of support into the interior, where it grew more conservative and corrupt. There was a great deal of anarchy, looting, banditry, and irregular fighting, a situation that brought many recruits into the Communist fold and played up Communist talents for bringing order and direction.[50] The Communists became leaders and coordinators of the guerrilla fight behind the lines, and the Japanese counterattack on Communists as guerrilla leaders, along with the general anti-Communist line of Japanese propaganda, helped to make the Communists appear as the only true patriots. Chiang was compelled more or less to collaborate with the Communist forces, which were placed nominally under his command; the war thus legitimized Communism as a contender for authority.

The movement prospered as mobilizer of the people for the common defense. The Communists sought to involve everyone, including women and children, in the cause on a basis of equal dedication, accepting peasant fighters alongside party activists. High and low shared hardships and pride of achievement. When a man entered the Red Army, it is said, he ceased to think of himself as an individual but talked only of battles and victories.[51] In these years of heroic struggle, the Chinese Communists developed that special blend of values and priorities that has since distinguished them—distrust of elites, self-reliance and initiative of ordinary workers and soldiers, and independence of anyone outside. In 1938 Mao made clear that Marxism should be treated not as a literal truth but a "viewpoint and methodology" and called for its Sinification,[52] an achievement made possible by the long struggle for supremacy.

Soviet concentration on the European theater left Mao even freer to go his own way during the years when the Sino-Japanese war merged into World War II. During this period Mao finally cemented his leadership of the Chinese party; in 1943 he became chairman, and Mao Thought was established as party doctrine by the rectification campaign of 1942-1944. The party, too, swelled; by early 1945, the Communist armies boasted nearly a million men, plus two

---

[49] Robert C. North, "The Sino-Soviet Alliance," *China Quarterly*, no. 1 (January-March 1960), p. 53.

[50] Chalmers Johnson, *Peasant Nationalsim and Communist Power* (Stanford: Stanford University Press, 1962), emphasizes the importance of the war emergency for the growth of Communism in China.

[51] Snow, *Journey to the Beginning*, p. 129.

[52] Hsü, *Rise of Modern China*, p. 69.

million in militias. It had become even more thoroughly a peasant party; only two of 44 Central Committee members of 1945 had definitely urban-proletarian background.

By the end of the war Chinese Communism had become a force to be reckoned with, governing areas with a population not far from a hundred million. It was still opposed by the internationally recognized Nationalist government, with forces almost three times as large and much better equipped, thanks to American aid. But the contest was hardly in doubt. In the race to reoccupy the Japanese-held areas, the Nationalists took the cities but the Communists swept across the countryside. The Nationalist regime sank into a morass of inflation, inefficiency, and self-seeking.[53] The Russians, who came to an agreement with Chiang in 1945, probably preferred to see the Communists control only north China and hence remain dependent. Stalin in fact advised Mao to come to an agreement with Chiang.[54] But after Mao's forces completed the occupation of Manchuria, thanks in large measure to Soviet assistance, Nationalist-held cities fell one after another, and a Communist victory over the mainland was assured. On October 1, 1949, the People's Republic was proclaimed not in Nationalist Nanking, but in Peking, the ancient imperial capital. As in Russia, in a time of national upheaval, the best organized, ideologically best cemented, most militant, and most consistently anti-Western party had become heir of the old autocracy.

Imposed Communism

The global conflict that enabled the Communists to mobilize the peasants and gain power in China also raised Communist parties, mostly very small or practically nonexistent previously, to the rulership of eight states of eastern and central Europe: Poland, East Germany, Hungary, Romania, Bulgaria, Czechoslovakia, Yugoslavia, and Albania. For the first five of these, the presence of Soviet armed forces on the national soil was a prime factor in the installation of Communist governments. With a few exceptions, where Soviet troops came as a result of military movements they stayed to guide political evolution. The war also brought Communism to the northern parts of Vietnam and Korea, where again the Soviet army was a major accessory. It was thereby proved that a functional Communist state can be established not only by a Leninist-type coup or a Maoist peasant-backed liberation war but by the fiat of a sufficiently powerful occupational force.

---

[53] On the Nationalist dissolution, cf. A. Doak Barnett, *China on the Eve of Communist Takeover* (New York: Praeger, 1963).

[54] North, "The Sino-Soviet Alliance," p. 53.

The process by which Stalin put Communist regimes in place has been amply described and is of less interest than the rise of independent Communisms. It is not certain that Stalin actually planned the Sovietization of occupied countries, but he did demand obedience, and this was most readily attained when the rulership consisted of trained and dedicated Communists. For the most part these were Moscow-domesticated leaders, formerly affiliated with the Communist International. Stalin outwardly dissolved this body in 1943, but its cadres were held in reserve in the Soviet Union until the time was ripe for their dispatch to Soviet-occupied territories. Native Communist parties had been outlawed before the war in all those countries that later entered the Soviet sphere, with the exception of Czechoslovakia. There were hence few indigenous Communists to greet the Russians, and there was no pretense of immediate revolution but a usually gradual, almost stealthy buildup of absolute Communist control, masked by the language of patriotism, anti-fascism, and democracy.[55]

In the transitional stage, the Soviet army exercised its authority, either unofficially or officially as occupation power in the former enemy states. Infiltrating Soviet police agents, an ever present force to this day, were instrumental in gaining control of the ministry of interior, through which the Communists directed the satellite country's police force. Propaganda was coupled with the repression of independent voices and publications. In Bulgaria and Romania, the Soviets simply imposed governments of their choosing. In most places there was a United Front, or Popular Front, in the name of which the Communists could cover their actions.[56] In Poland and Hungary, there were coalitions or pseudo-coalitions until 1947 when the initiation or intensification of the cold war made the Sovietization of Eastern Europe more urgent. A formally Communist government for the Soviet-held part of Germany was delayed until 1949 because the Soviets wanted to bargain for an all-German state. Under these circumstances Communist parties grew as rapidly as the Russians desired; for example, in August 1944, when the pro-Axis Romanian government was overthrown, there were less than 1000 Communists; a year later, there were 800,000.[57]

Much the same occurred in the Soviet-controlled part of Korea. A few native Communists had survived the Japanese repression; they were joined by returnees from China and the Soviet Union. Kim Il Song, a onetime guerrilla fighter with Chinese Communists in Manchuria who had joined the Soviet army some years before 1945, entered the country in the uniform of a Soviet

---

[55] Thomas T. Hammond, "The History of Communist Takeovers," in *The Anatomy of Communist Takeover,* T. Hammond, ed. (New Haven: Yale University Press, 1975), pp. 22-24.

[56] Malcolm Mackintosh, "Stalin's Policies toward Eastern Europe, 1939–1948," in *The Anatomy of Communist Takeover*, T. Hammond, ed. p. 238.

[57] Julian Hale, *Ceauşescu's Romania* (London: Harrap, 1971), p. 22.

major, along with a few score Koreans also in nominally high military positions.[58] Non-Communists were rather quickly eliminated. Kim, although he had no popular following,[59] was apparently named chairman by the Russians; but he owed his success to his own organizational capacity as well as Soviet favor.[60] In September 1948, as the Soviet forces were about to leave, the Democratic Republic of Korea was proclaimed under Kim's leadership.

Thus by 1948-1949 the Sovietization of the Eastern European satellites, as well as parts of countries occupied by Soviet forces was approximately complete. The several states were not incorporated into the Soviet Union, presumably for foreign policy reasons, although the Soviet state was explicitly set up as the nucleus of a world state, from which, when revolutionary zest was fresh, the movement should spread and override all boundaries. The sovietized lands were not even called "Soviet republics," like the Ukraine, Georgia, etc., presumably from deference to Soviet superiority. Instead, the category of "Democratic Republic" was invented for them. But they were with remarkable speed pressed into the Soviet mould with fully panoply of controls (except for lagging collectivization) to surpass the political achievements made by the Soviet Union over a much longer period.

Contributory Conditions in Eastern Europe. Soviet actions may be seen as an adequate explanation of the triumph of Communism in Eastern Europe and North Korea, much as Soviet military occupation in the aftermath of the Russian civil war suffices to explain the Sovietization of Outer Mongolia. It is not improbable, however, that the Communists would have come to power in many or most of these countries without foreign intervention, as they did in Yugoslavia and Albania and would have done in Greece but for British-American resistance. The presence of Soviet forces was in fact a millstone for local Communists in some ways. They behaved badly, in Korea as in Europe, both in formerly enemy countries such as Hungary and in allied countries such as Yugoslavia, in sharp contrast to the usually more idealistic behavior of the Chinese Communist army. Their looting and maltreatment of civilians reinforced the hatred of most of these occupied countries for the Russians and the view that they were cultural inferiors or (as in Poland, Hungary, and Romania) national enemies.

Regardless of the presence of Soviet forces, conditions were propitious for Communism in Eastern Europe in the wake of the world war. The old regimes had been destroyed in formerly anti-Nazi Poland and Yugoslavia and

---

[58] K. Chung, "The North Korean Peoples Army and the Party" in *North Korea Today*, Robert Scalapino, ed. (New York: Praeger, 1963), p. 106.

[59] Dae-Sook Suh, "A Preconceived Formula for Sovietization: North Korea," in *The Anatomy of Communist Takeover*, T. Hammond, ed. p. 483.

[60] Robert E. Simmons, *The Strained Alliance: Peking, Pyongyang, Moscow, and the Politics of the Korean War* (New York: Free Press, 1975), p. 28.

thoroughly discredited in those nations that had collaborated with the Nazis—Hungary, Romania, and Bulgaria. The earlier political tradition was of elitist empires, Russian, Turkish, or Austro-Hungarian, and there was an irksome sense of inferiority to richer Western Europe and resentment at the scorn to which the "Polacks" and other East Europeans were subjected. Extensive state interference in the economy was the rule, and the commercial classes lacked standing. Democracy had been tried everywhere after 1918 and everywhere (except in Czechoslovakia) had failed. The ensuing dictatorships had usually been corrupt and oppressive; Hungary and Romania, for example, suffered semi-fascist governments during the war. The interwar years were bleak; only in Czechoslovakia did the per capita income at any time in the 1918-1939 period exceed the pre-war level.[61] The old order was also blamed for the chronic bickering among these nations, their destructive and often pointless quarrels, Poland against Czechoslovakia, Hungary and Bulgaria against Romania, etc. There followed the exhaustion of war, impoverishment, and the weakening of the middle classes in the turmoil.[62]

The Communists offered themselves as leaders out of chaos to national revival if not utopia. Because of hierarchic structures, tight organization, and ideological cohesion, Communism is well adapted for underground politics; and Communists were usually the most active fighters against fascist occupiers.[63] When the main preoccupation was to do what the Communists did best, not only did party members qualify for leadership on merits—the moderates were often pushed to one side. Many nationalists who were repelled by Communism tended to slacken their efforts or, as especially in Yugoslavia, to drift into cooperation with the fascists.

People crawling out from the wreckage of the old order were ready to grasp at a vision of total renewal. "Demoralized by so much horror, the population of Central Europe was in a poor position to summon up strength to revive society from within. The Communists alone had a clear goal."[64] The Communists presented themselves as agents of progress, proponents of land reform and rapid economic reconstruction,[65] and they claimed to build not an imitation of the Soviet Union but a "People's Democracy." Soviet power and presence made Communism anti-national, but it answered the difficult circumstances.

---

[61] Cyril E. Black, "Eastern Europe in the Context of Comparative Modernization," in *The Politics of Modernization in Eastern Europe: Testing the Soviet Model*, Charles Gati, ed. (New York: Praeger, 1975), p. 35.

[62] Charles Gati, "Hungary, The Dynamics of Revolutionary Transformation," in *The Politics of Modernization*, C. Gati, ed. pp. 51, 84, sees the stage preset for Communist social revolution in Hungary.

[63] R. Burks, in *Communist Systems in Comparative Perspective*, Leonard J. Cohen and Jane P. Shapiro, eds. (Garden City, N.Y.: Doubleday & Co., 1974), p. 47.

[64] David Pryce-Jones, *The Hungarian Revolution* (London: Benn, 1969), p. 21.

[65] Zbigniew Brzezinski, *The Soviet Bloc, Unity and Conflict* rev. ed., (Cambridge: Harvard University Press, 1967), pp. 6-7, 28-29.

Czechoslovakia

The Communization of Czechoslovakia represents an exception to the process among Eastern European states of a more authoritarian tradition, where the Soviet army was direct master. As the only nation of the region to maintain a democratic tradition through the interwar period, and as the richest and most modern, Czechoslovakia took pride in its Western affiliation. The Western powers were discredited, however, by the Munich agreement compelling the Czechs to yield the Sudetenland to Nazi Germany; the Soviet Union meanwhile presented itself as stalwart champion of Czech freedom.

At the close of the war, the prestige of the Soviet victors was high; the Soviet armies that had liberated Prague did not stay long enough to wither their laurels. There was also a common Slavic feeling and pride in the glories of their victorious Russian fellow-Slavs; the Comintern had long been relatively successful with Slavs of East Europe, especially those on a somewhat more backward level, including the Slovaks.[66] The old Czechoslovak state had been entirely destroyed, and many of the upper classes, including industrialists who had produced for the Nazi war machine, were tainted as collaborationists. The Communists gained leadership in the resistance movement and a head start in the political reorganization of the country. With 38 percent of the vote, the Communist party won a plurality in the elections of 1945. On this basis, the party qualified democratically for the premiership and the key ministries of interior and defense, and it could probably have seized total power if the Soviets had desired.[67]

For a few years, Czechoslovakia was a unique example of a democratic country in which a Communist party held the leading role. With a multiparty parliament and free press, it was proud to be a sort of bridge between East and West, although its slant was eastward. But this compromise would probably have been unstable even without the tensions of the beginning cold war. In any case, the popularity of the Communist Party was visibly declining in 1947, and public opinion polls threatened it with severe losses in the upcoming 1948 elections.[68] To preclude loss of power, the Communists reacted by advocating single-slate elections and trying to undermine other parties. When the Communists tried to tighten their grip on the police, non-Communist ministers resigned to bring a showdown. The Communists then demanded full powers, threatened civil war, and organized demonstrations by workers' militias in imitation of Lenin's seizure of power. Soviet troops on the borders seemed prepared to intervene if needed. Faced with Communist control of the police,

[66] H. Gordon Skilling, *The Governments of Communist East Europe* (New York: Thomas Y. Crowell, 1966), p. 31.

[67] R. V. Burks, "Eastern Europe," in *Communist Systems*, L. J. Cohen and J. P. Shapiro, eds., p. 60.

[68] Pavel Tigrid, "The Prague Coup of 1948: The Elegant Takeover," in *The Anatomy of Communist Takeover*, T. Hammond, ed., pp. 414-415.

army, and means of communication, the non-Communist president, Eduard Beneš, yielded. Czechoslovakia was rapidly Stalinized and became indistinguishable from the Soviet-occupied satellites.

Other Communisms

Yugoslavia and Albania

Stalin was the director of "revolution from above" in the Soviet Union, and the Communization of most of Eastern Europe was as much an exercise of Stalinist Soviet politics as a genuine Communist movement. In Yugoslavia, however, the Communist revolution was the work of Yugoslavs acting essentially on their own—not quite so independent as Mao's party in China but able to contemplate going their own way.

Tito earned a special place in history by making his the first of Marxist-Leninist countries to shed obedience to the Russian center, and that at a time in the lingering euphoria of victory when it was difficult to conceive separatist Communism. The 1948 defiance of Stalin was the more remarkable because Tito, who was chosen by Stalin for his loyalty,[69] had been perhaps the most determinedly Communist, if not fanatic, of East European leaders. More royalist than the king, he was possibly even prepared voluntarily to submerge his nation in an enlarged Soviet Union.

But the roots of independent thinking went far back. In its first years, the Yugoslav Communist Party had a strong attraction not for urban workers but for backward peasants and fringe nationalists in Montenegro and Macedonia.[70] The party, outlawed in July 1921 after the murder of a minister, had to struggle against powerful repressive forces; nevertheless it had a reputation in the 1930s for nonconformity to Comintern directives. Tito, one of the few leaders who survived Stalin's purges, proceeded to make it a definitely Yugoslav party, independent of Comintern financing.[71] In October 1940, he held a party congress without a Comintern presence.

It was Tito's fortune that the Nazi attack on Russia came only a few weeks after the occupation of Yugoslavia and he could join patriotic feelings to socialist devotion in good conscience. His partisans had the advantage that they alone stood for an all-Yugoslav policy; other resistance (and collaborationist) groups

---

[69] Milorad M. Drachkovitch, "The Comintern and the Insurrectional Activity of the Communist Party of Yugoslavia in 1941–1942," in *The Comintern: Historical Highlights*, M. M. Drachkovitch and Branko Lazitch, eds. (New York: Praeger, 1966), p. 188.

[70] Phyllis Auty, *Tito, a Biography* (New York: McGraw-Hill, 1970), p. 46.

[71] *Ibid*, pp. 101, 137–139.

were particularistic, Serbian, Croat, etc.[72] Tito also had the usual Communist advantage of being undeterred by human suffering. Others hesitated to take anti-German actions for fear of massive retaliations, promised and sometimes carried out; the massacre of a village was too high a price for the removal of a German soldier or two. Tito did not hesitate and hence acquired a reputation as a fighter, while refugees streamed into his ranks.

Tito claimed to be fighting for freedom and democracy on behalf of the whole people,[73] but his struggle was difficult and often doubtful, a war not only against German and Italian invaders but against various native factions of more conservative bent. In it, the Titoist Partisans received no material help from the Soviet Union until 1944 and then much less than from the Western powers. They were almost without news of the outside world except for a tenuous radio link with the Comintern until the Italian surrender in 1943.[74]

At the end of the war, Tito, commanding forces of 800,000 men[75] and a functioning administration, had at his feet a destructured society. The war had cost the lives of one in nine of the population, and nearly a quarter had been interned.[76] It was the more devastating to the traditional order as conflicts of nationalities, cultures, and religions swirled through the war against the fascist occupiers. Nationalization of major economic enterprises had already been accomplished incidentally to the war. As a diplomatic gesture, Tito took three "bourgeois" leaders into his government, but they lasted only half a year. There was a purge of officeholders, as those who had merely survived were replaced by men who had earned political stature in the Partisans. Yugoslavia adopted a close copy of the Soviet constitution in 1946, and in the years up to, even after the 1948 split with Stalin, Yugoslavia was ahead of the rest of the Soviet sphere in economic planning, collectivization, and the implementation of Marxism-Leninism.

An echo of the Communization of Yugoslavia was that of Albania. The flight of the repressive King Zog at the time of the Italian invasion, April 1939, left a political vacuum in the poor, backward, and xenophobic country. A nationalist resistance movement arose during the war and was joined by a few scattered groups of Communists. These formed a Communist Party, with the

---

[72] R. V. Burks, "Eastern Europe," in Cyril E. Black and Thomas P. Thornton, eds., *Communism and Revolution: The Strategic Uses of Political Violence* (Princeton: Princeton University Press, 1964), p. 95.

[73] Paul Shoup, "The Yugoslav Revolution: The First of a New Type," in *The Anatomy of Communist Takeover*, T. Hammond, ed., p. 255.

[74] Vladimir Dedijer, *The Battle Stalin Lost* (New York: Viking Press, 1971), pp. 54-55.

[75] Robert F. Byrnes, *East-Central Europe under the Communists* (New York: Praeger, 1957), p. 150.

[76] Johnson, *Peasant Nationalism*, p. 172.

assistance of Yugoslav Partisan emissaries after the Soviet entry into the war; but it operated under the guise of a National Liberation Movement, with an entirely democratic program.[77] As in Yugoslavia, the Communists fought a dual contest against non-Communists as well as Axis occupation forces; they were victorious with a little material assistance from the Western powers and under indirect Comintern guidance via Yugoslav comrades. In November 1944, Enver Hoxha and Koci Xoxe assumed leadership in the formation of a Communist government and proceeded to destroy what remained of their actual and potential enemies.

Vietnam

The coming of Communism to Vietnam was rather like its advent in China and Yugoslavia, with the principal difference that Ho Chi Minh was able to eliminate rival parties and factions by political means.[78] So far as the Communists had to fight fellow-countrymen in the later stages of the thirty-year long war, these appeared clearly as clients if not puppets of an outside power. Hence Communism in Vietnam was exceptionally nationalistic.

Vietnamese Communism has also been especially nationalistic because of the depth of injury by the West. Vietnam had an old, self-satisfied civilization, close to that of China, with an anti-Western mandarinate.[79] Like China, it was decadent in the nineteenth century; like China and unlike Japan it could devise no means of saving itself by borrowing from the West.[80] The conquest, begun in 1859, was completed only in 1883, when Vietnam became a full-fledged French colony, in which settlers and adventurers treated the natives as inferior beings.

Resentment against the foreign masters who took the best land and slapped their coolies never ceased, simmering during the entire period of French rule, occasionally boiling up. It did not help that the French permitted a few Vietnamese youth to receive an education in France; they returned to their homeland without rights or prospects, subject to abuse by uneducated colons. And if there was some glitter of prosperity in the chief cities, the countryside was the more degraded.[81]

[77] Stephen Peters, "Ingredients of the Communist Takeover in Albania," in *The Anatomy of Communist Takeovers,* T. Hammond, ed., pp. 273-292.

[78] For a detailed treatment, see Alexander B. Woodside, *Community and Revolution in Modern Vietnam* (Boston: Houghton Mifflin, 1976).

[79] Joseph Buttinger, *Vietnam: A Dragon Embattled* (New York: Praeger, 1967), Vol. I, p. 113.

[80] Hoang Van Chi, *From Colonialism to Communism* (New Delhi: Allied Publishers, 1964), p. 5.

[81] Cf. Snow, *Journey to the Beginning,* p. 44.

Early Stirrings of National Liberation. Vietnamese hopes were stimulated by the Japanese victory over Russia in 1904, by the 1911-1912 overthrow of the Manchu dynasty, by the Wilsonian vision of self-determination, and by the Russian revolution. The modernization of Japan greatly impressed many, including the outstanding non-Communist nationalist, Phan Boi Chau, a follower of Sun Yat-sen. A Nationalist Party on the model of the KMT was founded in 1927, but after a widespread uprising in 1930, it was practically wiped out.

The way was thereby opened for Communist leadership in the movement of national liberation. Capitalism represented not merely an alien but an oppressing force. Denial of political rights by the colonial rulers precluded any growth of democratic sentiments or institutions and suggested that improvement could come only by violence. The Communists were prepared, by mentality and organization for the conspiratorial, underground revolutionary work called for by these circumstances. Moreover, a big international agency, the Comintern, was prepared to furnish guidance, leadership, and material support.

Ho Chi Minh. Yet the triumph of Communism in Vietnam, as in Russia, China, Yugoslavia, and Cuba was very much the work of one man. Ho Chi Minh (as he came to be called late in his career) was born in a fairly well-to-do family of strongly nationalist sentiments. He left his country in 1912 at age 22, travelled widely as a ship's mess boy, and came to Paris in 1917. There he was attracted to Western ideas of freedom and democracy, the ideas of Wilson as well as those of Lenin.[82] But the socialists were sympathetic, the statesmen at Versailles deaf to the pleas of Vietnamese nationalism. Socialism, or rights for the poor, became nearly synonymous with anticolonialism, rights for oppressed peoples. When the French socialists split over affiliation with Lenin's Comintern, Ho went with those who paid most attention to the colonial question and became, on December 30, 1920, a founding member of the French Communist Party.[83] Thereafter, he became an agent of the Comintern and spent many years in its service, in and out of Moscow and occasionally in jail. Ho also set about destroying rivals; in 1925 he seems to have arranged the arrest by the French of the leading Vietnamese nationalist, Phan Boi Chau.[84]

In 1930, Ho pulled together a number of leftist organizations to found the Indochinese Communist party. In the wake of the 1930 debacle of the Nationalists, his group assumed the leadership of the anti-French movement, and it became the first to seek the support of the masses, in non-Oriental fashion. However, for a decade, success was elusive; the French were able to maintain security throughout their colony with slightly more than ten thousand troops on hand. But in September 1940, Japanese forces entered Indochina and destroyed French prestige.

---

[82] David Halberstam, *Ho* (New York: Random House, 1971), pp. 20, 30-31.

[83] Bernard Fall, *The Two Vietnams: A Political and Military Analysis,* 2nd ed. (New York: Praeger, 1967), p. 90.

[84] Robert F. Turner, *Vietnamese Communism, Its Origins and Development* (Stanford: Hoover Institution Press, 1975), p. 9.

The Vietminh. In March 1941, Ho set up the Vietminh, "Alliance for the Independence of Vietnam," a broad national front, which may have represented a real attempt at a broadly nationalist position.[85] The Vietminh became active following the German invasion of Russia, but it turned pro-American after Pearl Harbor and in effect joined the Allies' war against Japan, which was not at war with the Soviet Union. It was the only broadly nationalist organization, and its objectives were overtly anti-fascist, liberationist, and democratic. The largest number of its recruits were from petty officialdom.[86] It tried to make itself useful both to Chinese Nationalists and American intelligence.[87] It is only to be conjectured what orientation a Vietminh government might have had if it had not been driven to fight against Western power.

As the Allied victory neared, General Giap had infiltrated a large sector of Vietnam adjacent to China with some 5,000 troops. The Communist-dominated Vietminh was the only functioning nationalist organization, and it came to power in Hanoi in August 1945, replacing the puppet administration which the Japanese had installed. In a euphoric wave of popular support, Ho on September 2, 1945, proclaimed the independence of the Democratic Republic of Vietnam, citing the American Declaration of Independence and the French Revolution's Declaration of the Rights of Man. The new government, in which men of Ho's party held the ministries of interior (police), defense, education, and finance, allowed a wide measure of freedom while setting out to reform colonial and oligarchic institutions.[88] In the interest of national unity the Communist party formally dissolved itself, although it continued to function covertly.[89]

When Ho several times requested American assistance, even tutelage, he was unanswered; and the world paid little heed to his plea for independence. The British, assigned by inter-Allied agreement to take the surrender of the Japanese in the southern part of the country, took it for granted that Indochina was again to be a French colony, and facilitated French reoccupation. However, as soon as the French tried to reestablish their government, low-grade warfare began. In the north, Chinese occupiers, while removing such valuables as the Japanese had left behind, tolerated the Vietminh, partly because they were bribed, partly because Ho admitted nationalists to his government; and they delayed French reentry until March 1946. The Vietminh regime was by that time sufficiently firm that the French could with difficulty enter by force. They consequently came to an agreement whereby France recognized the independence of Vietnam in the French union and 15,000 French troops were admitted to specified positions in the country.

---

[85] As believed by Halberstam, *Ho*, p. 63.

[86] Wolf, *Peasant Wars of the Twentieth Century,* p. 185.

[87] Turner, *Vietnamese Communism,* p. 34.

[88] Buttinger, *Vietnam,* pp. 346, 349.

[89] Hoang Van Chi, *From Colonialism to Communism,* pp. 48-49.

In reaching this agreement, Ho alienated many nationalists; but he strongly desired to avoid conflict. Undoctrinaire in outlook, he seems to have desired French economic cooperation and to have regarded France as a potential partner and associate of an independent Vietnam.[90] Moreover, he used the truce with the French to eliminate rivals of all shades; the French were glad to cooperate, in effect, with the Vietminh to destroy independent nationalism. The assembly elected under an overtly democratic constitution was purged of nearly all non-Communists.[91] Many nationalists also went to the South.

The Anti-Imperialist War. But the truce could not last. The French, assuming that Indochina was to be theirs again, tried gradually to move back into positions of overlordship. By July 1946, the forces fixed by agreement at 15,000 had swelled to 67,000.[92] In September Ho made such extensive concessions to French demands as to endanger his popularity, but there could be no real compromise. The French accented their impatience by the bloody bombardment of Haiphong on November 23, 1946; and Ho launched a surprise attack on French garrisons December 19. In the ensuing war, the French took the cities without difficulty, but they never thoroughly reconquered the villages. The poorly armed Vietminh retreated to a guerrilla war of scorched earth, ambushes, and hit-run attacks, wherein any rice paddy was a battlefield and any peasant a potential fighter. For the first several years, the Vietminh received no outside aid—Stalin abstained from lending any support.

But the situation gradually became more difficult for the French. Not only were the human losses more bearable for the Vietnamese than for the French, but the guerrillas showed great ingenuity and energy in supplying their own wants, rice as well as simpler munitions. The French made the same mistake as had the Japanese in China a decade earlier: they branded all their opponents "Communists," driving them to Communism and the Vietminh "National Front," although Ho's men rather freely murdered independent nationalists and attacked all groups, including religious sects, which refused to subordinate themselves to his organization. Like the Japanese in China, the French made peasants into guerillas.

Ho concentrated on mobilizing the masses through propaganda and organization. He also recognized the minority nationalities of Vietnam and provided the only framework for their cooperation, somewhat as Tito brought together the nationalities of Yugoslavia.[93] After Mao's victory in 1949, aid began to flow, not only from China but from the Soviet Union and the East European Communist states. The French tried to turn the war into a civil contest by set-

---

[90] Jean Lacouture, *Ho Chi Minh: A Political Biography* (New York: Random House, 1968), p. 147.

[91] Fall, *The Two Vietnams*, p. 131.

[92] John T. McAlister, Jr., *Vietnam: The Origins of Revolution* (New York: Knopf, 1969), p. 311.

[93] Fall, *The Two Vietnams*, p. 141.

ting up the hereditary emperor, Bao Dai, as a Vietnamese figurehead and organizing an army under his nominal rule. But he was not permitted enough independence to make his regime a moral alternative, and spartan dedication on one
side contrasted with corruption, profiteering, and cynicism on the other. Finally, in 1954 the ragged peasants destroyed or captured the flower of the French
forces at the outlying fortress of Dienbienphu, and the first phase of the war was
over.

Communist domination became total in the anti-French war. After Mao's
victory, Chinese Communist influence and propaganda hardened the movement.[94] In 1951 the party was reorganized as the Vietnam Workers' Party, and
the Vietminh was replaced by a looser organization leaving the Communist Party
more openly dominant. Land reform also signalled a social revolution wherever
the Communists had the power to enforce it.

The Communist Party under Ho Chi Minh thus came to power with the expulsion of the French in 1954. The establishment of the ensuing Communist
regime was facilitated by the departure of nearly 900,000 potential or actual
anti-Communists (with the aid and encouragement of the U.S.) for the southern
part of the country. The tasks of social revolution could proceed unhampered
by opposition, just as the exodus of Whites in the Russian civil war facilitated
the consolidation of Lenin's state and the emigration of anti-Castro Cubans
made easier the Communization of that island. The departure of the French left
much property in state hands, and small craftsmen were gradually brought into
cooperatives and nationalized. A land reform program of 1953-1956 not only
deprived "landlords" and "rich peasants" of plots as small as two- to three-acres
but eliminated many of them physically, as landless peasants were encouraged
to denounce and judge their crimes. Some 10,000 to 15,000 were killed and
another 50,000 to 100,000 imprisoned or deported.[95] This excessive and
capricious campaign, plus onerous requisitions, sparked serious disturbances in
November 1956. The government moved in 1958 from land distribution to collectivization on the Soviet model. Economic planning, Soviet style, with emphasis on industrial plant was also instituted, with Soviet help. Opinion controls
were tightened from 1957 onward. The new war against American and South
Vietnamese forces, intensifying in 1965, strengthened the Communist character of the mobilized state and united it for general safety (and the sacred
purpose of reunification).

The extension of Communism to the remainder of what had been French
Indochina was delayed for over two decades by American intervention. Ho and
his associates never gave up the purpose of extending their revolution to the
South, although they insisted that the fight against the Saigon forces and the

---

[94] Nhu Phong, "Intellectuals, Writers, and Artists," in *North Vietnam Today*, P. J.
Honey, ed. (New York: Praeger, 1962), pp. 74-75.

[95] Buttinger, *Vietnam*, pp. 911-912.

[96] Mary McCarthy, *Hanoi* (New York: Harcourt, Brace and World, 1968), p. 74.

Americans was not Communist.[96] After the Americans withdrew in 1973 under a shaky truce, it required only a determined shove to send the Republic of Vietnam tumbling in April 1975. The inevitable side effect of the Communist triumph in Vietnam was to give victory to allies in Cambodia and Laos, where likewise Communism made itself the most effective exponent of nationalism and anti-Westernism.

Cuba

If Mao, Tito, and Ho showed that a peasant revolt could be turned to Communism, Fidel Castro has proved that Communism can come, under propitious conditions, through charismatic leadership. Castro's was revolution strictly from above with no popular uprising—proletarian, peasant, or otherwise—without even significant popular pressure for socialization. Yet the Cuban revolution became thoroughly Communist, one of the most militant and militarized. Castro has expressed surprise that anyone should differentiate between Communism and Castroism—with some justification, because the Castroite system not only subscribes formally to Marxist-Leninist ideology but follows the Communist model in economic planning, treatment of labor, organization of the ruling party, police controls, education, and so forth.[97]

Pre-Castro Cuba. It has been often pointed out that pre-Castro Cuba was ripe for social change. The difference in standard of living between Cuba and nearby Florida was growing. Although the Cuban economy progressed rapidly in the first quarter of this century, in the last decade before Castro per capita income had actually declined, with population growth outpacing production.[98] A Cuba that had led Latin America in general education in 1925 was by 1958 in one of the last places.[99] Obvious reasons for decline included economic dependence on sugar, a commodity often in oversupply, and pervasive corruption. Instability and frequent unemployment counterbalanced relatively high income levels. The special status of Cuban sugar in the U. S. market, in return for which Cuban duties on U. S. manufactures were kept low, increased dependency upon U. S. markets and capital. Business class involvement with alien interests was complemented by a large amount of foreign landholding and foreign (U. S.) ownership of utilities; in fact, Americans frequently behaved like masters of the house.[100] The U.S. naval base on Cuban territory (Guantanamo) was a minor sore point. Although the Platt Amendment had been repealed and U.S. intervention in Cuban politics halted since 1934, these intrusions were remem-

---

[97] Hugh Thomas, *Cuba: The Pursuit of Freedom* (New York: Harper & Row, 1971), p. 1487.

[98] James O'Connor, *The Origins of Socialism in Cuba* (Ithaca: Cornell University Press, 1970), p. 17.

[99] R. Paulston in *Revolutionary Change in Cuba*, Carmelo Mesa-Lago, ed. (Pittsburgh: University of Pittsburgh Press, 1971), p. 379.

[100] Thomas, *Cuba: The Pursuit of Freedom*, p. 502.

bered.[101] Then, too, Cuban culture was often derogated by not entirely attractive importations from the mainland. In short, Cuba was a prime example of a semi-colony, with little real political, economic, or cultural autonomy.

Yet the economy Castro inherited at the beginning of 1959 was still relatively prosperous by Third World standards. There was a large middle class, literacy was high, and in most indicators of development Cuba ranked near the top among Latin American countries and well ahead of Mexico.[102] Indeed, a decade of mismanagement and political agitation was required to bring Cuba to the point where a Communist revolution might be expected to start.[103] Many potential forces of foment were noticeably absent; for instance, there was a fairly large class of factory workers, but they were quiet and played virtually no part in bringing Castro to power. A Cuban Communist Party, founded in 1925, exercised little influence. It had a long-term modus vivendi with the Batista dictatorship,[104] having sacrificed its former militancy to expediency.

Anti-imperialism, anti-Americanism since 1898, was an old theme of Cuban politics; and the U. S. was naturally blamed for most of Cuba's troubles. But anti-Yankeeism was more potential than actual, and the major Cuban grievance in the last years before Castro was less economic than political. Fulgencio Batista was a thoroughly illegitimate ruler, having seized power (for the second time) in 1952 and ruling by force and terrorism, with a government made up of "time-servers, opportunists, and thieves."[105]

The Bases of Castro. Castro came to power as a rebel against the Batista dictatorship without the benefit of Communist theory, an exemplar of the tendency of Communism away from Marxist philosophy and toward pure action. "Castroism is a leader in search of a movement, a movement in search of power, and power in search of an ideology."[106] "Communism was not a cause of the Cuban revolution; it was a result."[107] The revolution was made simply by Castro and his followers.

Fidel Castro Ruz was the son of a Spanish immigrant who became a wealthy landowner by individual enterprise. He turned to radicalism during his law student years at the University of Havana, a crowded institution with low academic standards and part-time instructors, where students had plenty of time to talk, ruminate, and agitate and from which they emerged with a feeling

---

[101]Theodore Draper, *Castroism: Theory and Practice* (New York: Praeger, 1965), pp. 107-108.

[102]Draper, *Castroism*, p. 100.

[103]Maurice Halperin, *The Rise and Decline of Fidel Castro* (Berkeley: University of California Press, 1972), p. 39.

[104]Hans Enzensberger, "Portrait of a Party," in *The New Cuba: Paradoxes and Potentials*, Ronald Radosh, ed (New York: William Morrow, 1976), pp. 109-110.

[105]O'Connor, *Origins of Socialism*, p. 280.

[106]Draper, *Castroism*, pp. 48-49.

[107]Herbert L. Matthews, *Fidel Castro* (New York: Simon and Schuster, 1969), p. 165.

of superiority but not much useful education. Castro gravitated toward politics. In 1953, at age 27, he tried to overthrow Batista by an attack on an army barracks at Santiago; he and his followers were killed or captured. Imprisonment from 1953 to 1955 gave him an opportunity to ripen his philosophy. After release, he went to Mexico where he formed his own party, continued working against the Batista government, and prepared a new assault. On December 2, 1956, he landed from the yacht "Granma," with 81 followers, on the coast of eastern Cuba.

Thus far the movement was wholly middle class, and Castro was entirely in the Cuban tradition of José Martí and Antonio Guiteras—a romantic endeavor to overthrow a tyrant. But after the Cuban army had killed many of the group and scattered the remainder, he took a new and unplanned turn. Instead of withdrawing abroad again, about fifteen who reassembled[108] went into the mountains and began a guerrilla movement to bring down the Batista government or to await its collapse.[109]

Contact with and dependence on the peasantry radicalized the movement, and in the Sierra Maestra Castro took up agrarian reform and promised betterment for the backward farmers. Moreover, some of the guerrilla leaders, including Fidel's brother Raúl and his lieutenant, the Argentine Ernesto "Che" Guevara, were fairly close to Communism. The latter even seems to have read Marxist texts.[110] Yet in later years Castro reminisced that he had no idea that his was going to turn out to be a Communist revolution.[111] Castro gave no sign of being a Marxist intellectual; he took pride in having read only a few pages of Capital,[112] although he did claim to have read the *Communist Manifesto*.[113] His 1953 program was indistinguishable from that of other liberal Cubans,[114] and the programmatic statement he drew up while imprisoned, "History Will Absolve Me," contained only one reference to "capitalism," no other Marxist language, and less anti-U. S. rhetoric than used by most other Cuban nationalists.[115] In Mexican exile he emphasized leadership and party discipline more than social aims.

During the guerrilla period, Castro repeatedly called for democratic rights and the restoration of the 1940 constitution, as though his chief concern were for free elections.[116] In February, 1958, he spoke of the need for foreign investment to advance industrialization.[117] On the other hand, he blamed the

---

[108] Thomas, *Cuba: The Pursuit of Freedom*, pp. 898-901.

[109] Draper, *Castroism*, p. 23.

[110] Andrés Suárez, *Cuba: Castro and Communism* (Cambridge: MIT Press, 1967), p. 39.

[111] Lee Lockwood, *Castro's Cuba, Cuba's Fidel* (New York: Macmillan, 1967), 1967), p. 251.

[112] Matthews, *Fidel Castro*, p. 187.

[113] Lockwood, *Castro's Cuba*, p. 138.

[114] Draper, *Castroism*, p. 6.

[115] Thomas, *Cuba: The Pursuit of Freedom*, pp. 850-851.

U. S. for supporting Batista, proposed nationalization of U. S.-owned utilities, and spoke sometimes of agrarian reform, even agricultural cooperatives, objectives revolutionary in implications.

The democratic manifestos with which Castro wooed popular support may have been opportunistic. In December 1961, he wrote that, if in the mountains they had said, "We are Marxist-Leninists," then "possibly we would not have been able to get down to the plain."[118] Meanwhile the Cuban Communist Party was rather unsympathetic, regarding Castro as a "bourgeois adventurer." In April 1958 the Communists torpedoed Castro's bid for a revolutionary general strike.[119] Not until June were there serious dealings between Castroites and Communists. Then a sort of secret alliance was formed, but very few Communists took part in the guerrilla fight.[120]

The guerrilla onslaught was at first not visibly successful. Castro had only about 300 men to face the offensive Batista organized to liquidate the *foco* in August 1958. But the government forces, demoralized and unprepared for this type of conflict, disintegrated during the following months. Moreover, the U. S., unaware of Castro's potential radicalism, helped him morally and militarily by an arms embargo against Batista beginning in March 1958. In the general repugnance for the violence and corruption of Batista's regime, support for the old dictator collapsed. Fidel Castro, age 32, surrounded by followers in their twenties, rode to power to general hurrahs on January 1, 1959.

Castroism becomes Communism. In his first months, Castro was or seemed to be a practical, non-ideological reformer who wanted to lead all Cubans to a better future. He installed a government of moderate liberals, Manuel Urrutia as president and José Miró Cardona as prime minister, while himself retaining the command of the armed forces; only in February did he assume the prime ministry. In April, he went to the U. S. on an unofficial visit, taking with him the ministers of economy and finance and the president of the national bank, as though he expected to negotiate for economic assistance from the U. S.[121] In his first months of power he made numerous anti-Communist statements, even comparing Communism to fascism and capitalism, and promising "humanistic freedoms" for Cuba.[122]

But Castro, critical virtually from the first of the U. S., soon began gravitating toward Communist positions. He rejected collaboration with other anti-Batista forces, asserting his own leadership to carry through his social objec-

---

[116] Draper, *Castroism*, pp. 14-15.

[117] A. James Gregor, *The Fascist Persuasion in Radical Politics* (Princeton: Princeton University Press, 1974).

[118] Draper, *Castroism*, p. 17.

[119] Lockwood, *Castro's Cuba*, p. 276.

[120] Halperin, *Rise and Decline*, pp. 28-29.

[121] Suárez, *Cuba: Castro and Communism*, p. 48.

[122] Draper, *Castroism*, p. 37.

tives; he at once needed power to make a social revolution and social revolution to justify arbitrary power. The initial decision not to call elections and permit himself to be duly elected president was probably decisive. Democracy meant limiting and dividing his authority,[123] and the middle-class moderates would certainly restrict his freedom of action. Castro and the Castroites, a set of eager and confident young men, impressed by their victory in the face of overwhelming odds,[124] badly wanted to change things, although they had at first only vague ideas of how. They were, moreover, in a much better position to do so than many another victor in a Latin American struggle for power because they had their own, albeit modest, force of personally loyal guerrilla veterans, and the old regime had collapsed completely.

Castro began immediately confiscating holdings of Batista supporters, freely interpreted. This meant socializing large amounts of property.[125] He also executed much more liberally than customary in the aftermath of Latin American revolutions (some 600 going "to the wall"). A stream of refugees began to flow away, especially to Florida, where many of them started to scheme the downfall of their persecutor. Castro also began to expropriate big holdings of persons in no way associated with the former regime, because he saw great fortunes and big landholdings as a source of political corruption, and a cause of unemployment and peasant misery. The initially warm reception of the American press rapidly chilled because Americans suffered the largest economic losses and because the trials and executions of Batista henchmen neglected judicial formalities. Criticism and snubbing by the Eisenhower administration during his trip to the U. S. did not chasten but infuriated Castro and his compañeros; and when he was accused of Communism he became an anti-anti-Communist. As early as February he was charging the American ambassador with interfering in Cuban affairs.[126]

He also began moving toward Communism. Fidel's near-Communist brother Raúl Castro was named second-in-command. In July 1959, President Manuel Urrutia was removed for attacking Communism no more violently than Fidel had done a few weeks earlier. He was replaced by Osvaldo Dorticós, a former Communist youth league member; and anti-Communists were purged from Castro's movement. The Communist Party was the only political organization, aside from Castro's 26th July Movement, permitted to operate. Castro turned to the peasants and workers for support against the middle classes who acted as a brake on his actions. Credit for the success of the revolution was transferred to the "proletariat," although the victory was due to the defection of all classes from the Batista regime.[127] Communists and Communist doctrine were instru-

---

[123] Matthews, *Fidel Castro*, p. 183.

[124] Halperin, *Rise and Decline*, p. 38.

[125] Boris Goldenberg, "The Establishment of Communism in Cuba," in *The Anatomy of Communist Takeover*, T. Hammond, ed., p. 590.

[126] O'Connor, *Origins of Socialism*, p. 296.

mental in the drive for change. Having won power with one ideology, Castro now substituted a different one more suitable for its exercise.

The quarrel with the U.S. also escalated rapidly. Castro expropriated more and more American holdings. In February 1960, there was a Cuban-Soviet trade agreement, probably including arms. The following month Eisenhower authorized the training and arming by the CIA of anti-Castro Cubans. In June 1960, American oil companies in Cuba refused to refine Soviet crude oil; and they were seized in retaliation. The U.S. reduced and then ended the Cuban sugar quota. Castro took over remaining U.S. properties; the U.S. embargoed trade with Cuba and severed diplomatic relations. In this situation, the Soviet Union and Third World radicals seemed to be the chief hope of support abroad; Castro turned to close relations with the former, and to encouragement and assistance for the latter—all to the increasing fury of the American administration, which took the cold war and anti-Communism very seriously. The time seemed opportune for Castro: Latin America was showing a leftist trend, much of the Third World was becoming vocally anti-imperialist, and Khrushchev was feeling somewhat exuberantly expansionist.

In October 1960, Castro nationalized remaining important enterprises. With an essentially socialized economy on his hands, he needed an organization like the Communist party to help manage it.[128] He had considerable distrust for the Communist Party as a bureaucratic contradiction to his charismatic style,[129] but there was no better instrument at hand. By the end of 1960 he had probably decided to fuse his movement with the party—remaking the latter, of course, to his taste.

Cuba did not become a genuine Communist state, however, until the confrontation with the U.S. became violent. Castro first spoke of his revolution as "socialist" at the funeral of victims of an air bombardment preliminary to the Bay of Pigs invasion, April 16, 1961.[130] The landing created a national emergency and the occasion to wipe out resistance and potential resistance, and the victory gave the government prestige and confidence to pursue its revolutionary policies.[131] The emergency was made permanent by the plausible assumption that the capitalist-supported attempt to overthrow the revolutionary state would be repeated on a large scale. Meanwhile, large numbers of anti-Communist and potentially anti-Communist Cubans, a large fraction of the educated and persons of independent mentality, had wisely emigrated; and the

---

[127] Draper, *Castroism*, p. 63.

[128] René Dumont, *Cuba: Socialism and Development* (New York: Grove Press, 1970), p. 31.

[129] I. Horowitz, "Cuban Communism," in *The Anatomy of Communist Takeover*, T. Hammond, ed., p. 7.

[130] Dumont, *Cuba: Socialism and Development*, p. 59.

[131] Matthews, *Fidel Castro*, p. 199.

end of trade with the U.S. and most other nations of this hemisphere negated the economic interests still opposed to Communism.

Resistance was thus dissolved, and Castro had reasons enough for turning Cuba into a full-fledged Communist state. Communism provided an ideology, the only practical one, for the total power which he had acquired; it gave an orientation for policy making; it provided an organizational framework for rule; and it promised the alliance of a superpower, which he probably believed would guarantee Cuban security against the U.S. It also promised glory, the inauguration of the first Spanish-language, New World Marxist-Leninist state and the leadership in what Castro believed would turn into a glorious revolutionary movement in the Americas.

In December 1961, Castro claimed to be and (somewhat ambiguously) always to have been a Marxist-Leninist. He had earlier amalgamated his movement with the Communist (called "Socialist") Party as the United Revolutionary Organizations, which was after other name changes finally (1965) to be designated plainly as the Communist Party of Cuba. Many old-line Communists were placed in high positions, and Castro pledged allegiance to the party, but he made it strictly his tool and filled its top ranks with his own followers.

The Communist movement had come a long road from Marx's idea of an elementary upsurge of the workers taking over an economy which had outgrown the fetters of capitalism, through Lenin's semi-military coup in a defeated pre-industrial state and Mao's mobilization of the peasantry for a war of national liberation, to an energetic and ambitious leader's adoption of the Communist party and ideology for domestic and foreign political purposes. If more states are to become Communist, Lenin's way appears unlikely unless there is a major war. The way of Mao and Ho is unlikely because no "bourgeois" state seems disposed to fight for control of a less developed state. Castro's way, however, may well be followed if a dictator resolves to change society and decides to lean on Soviet power.

Chapter three

The Giants of Communism

The Soviet Socialist Fatherland

Leninist Creation

Most revolutions have decayed rapidly; the extraordinary peculiarity of the Communist revolution has been its stability and the degree to which the ideas and political organization of the revolution-making party went into the making of the permanent state. With a few shifts of emphasis, the ideology of revolutionary drive became the ideology of statist discipline, and the close-knit radical party made itself the close-knit governing party.

From Revolution to Dictatorship of the Proletariat. The making of the Communist state in Soviet Russia, where everything was new and had to be tried, was slow. But it was purposeful and unidirectional. Lenin, in contrast to nearly all Western Marxists, made much of the "dictatorship of the proletariat" despite the fact that he could speak for only a handful of agitators; and he moved forthwith to establish the dictatorship as soon as he got the reins of government in hand in November 1917. The grip of the state grew steadily tighter, with hardly an ebb, from the shaky rule of the first weeks of Soviet power down to the solidification of Stalinist despotism in the latter 1930s, when all Russia quaked before the semi-deified ruler, peasants sowed and reaped at his decree, workers built his projects, painters glorified his image, and poets hymned his genius.

The steps toward totality of rulership in a country where most people confidently expected liberation as the result of the downfall of the tsar, were so numerous that their direction would seem to have been predestined by the conditions of Russia. The first and one of the most crucial was Lenin's insistence that the party carry out the coup on its own and thus assert a claim to power for itself alone. Then came Lenin's determination to keep the government wholly in Bolshevik hands despite the widespread assumption, even among Lenin's followers, that cooperation with other parties was indispensable in order to govern. For a few months there was a sort of coalition with the radical left wing of the Socialist-Revolutionary party; but they never were allowed any real power and this minor concession to pluralism broke down early in 1918 in disputes over peace with Germany and the requisitioning of grain from the peasants. It was also settled at the outset that the elected soviets, in the name of which Lenin ousted the Provisional Government, should have a mere pro forma role in the new state. The Congress of Soviets, which accepted Lenin's revolution, was not asked to debate anything but sent home next day.

From his first days in power Lenin began to reimpose in the name of the party, the proletariat, and the socialist revolution controls which had lapsed under the Provisional Government. Censorship was gradually reinstituted, competing political parties were curbed, then outlawed—except so far as they cooperated with the Bolsheviks in the civil war—after it abolished entirely. Any opposition became class treason, betrayal of the revolution. Independent trade unions and other organizations were infiltrated or destroyed. Controls over the economy were gradually extended until they reached totality in the War Communism of 1919-1920.

Lenin freely applied arbitrary force, and this rapidly degenerated into terrorism. By December 1917, well before the beginning of the civil war, Lenin was calling on his followers "to purge the land of Russia of all vermin," the rich and "the lackeys of the bourgeoisie."[1] The instrument of "class struggle" was a revived political police, which began to grip the land within a few weeks of Lenin's coup.[2]

It was also accepted that workers and Communists should sacrifice for the cause. Rations shrank, the peasants had to surrender much or most of their crops virtually without compensation, and party leaders were to receive no more pay than the average skilled worker. Lenin told the representatives of foreign parties in 1920, at the second congress of the Comintern, that they should expect their workers to sacrifice, as the Russian workers had done.[3]

It was necessary to organize a systematically functioning state structure. To this, the Leninists had given little thought, partly because they were too preoccupied with winning power to plan what they would do with it, partly because their ideology precluded the existence of a separate Russian socialist state. For a few years after the seizure of power the leaders still saw their

---

[1] *Selected Works,* Vol. II (Moscow: Progress Publishers, 1970), p. 524.

[2] On the Cheka, see G. H. Leggett, "Lenin, Terror, and Political Police," *Survey,* 21 (Autumn 1975), 157-187.

[3] Adam B. Ulam, *Expansion and Coexistence* (New York: Praeger, 1974), p. 118.

movement as truly international, bound up with a world movement, only accidentally restricted to Russia.[4] In a letter of August 19, 1919, Lenin wrote to an Italian comrade: "The material and final victory, regardless of all difficulties, regardless of rivers of blood, the white terror of the bourgeoisie, etc., will inevitably come in all countries of the world. . . . Long live the republic of Soviets of the whole world."[5] That the craved-for spread of revolution would relegate Russia once again to relatively backwardness seemed to be of no consequence.[6]

The Bolsheviks Turn Nationalistic. Yet step by step the vision of worldwide Communism gave way to nationalistic policies. A major break was the peace with Germany (March 1918), whereby revolutionary Russia was compelled to recognize and to enter diplomatic relations with a capitalist state. Thereafter the Bolsheviks purposefully undertook to build a functional administration for an indefinite tenure of power in Russia. The civil war, viewed as a contest with world capitalism, renewed the internationalist temper, but the end of the war and subsequent defeat of the Red Army before Warsaw largely put an end to dreams of widespread revolution to save Russia and solve its problems.[7] It was only a recognition of reality for Stalin in 1924 to espouse "Socialism in One Country."

To govern, the Bolsheviks needed the cooperation of skilled persons, and Lenin, in his flexible practicality, encouraged the hiring of "bourgeois experts," appropriately paid for their service to the revolutionary state. In fact, most of the old apparatus continued in place; as Lenin saw it, there were at the top "at most a few tens of thousands, of our own people. But at the base of the hierarchy, hundreds of thousands of former fuctionaries that we have inherited from the Tsar and bourgeois society . . ."[8] The servants of the old regime were, contrary to Marxist-shaped Bolshevik fears, fairly loyal and effective servants of the new.[9] They did not emigrate in numbers because they were too much tied to Russia and had no skills useful abroad; with some hesitations and exceptions, they went to work to administer the Soviet state in ways not greatly different from those of the old regime.

There was, however, a major change of approach. Autocracy was no longer frank and open but concealed and qualified, outwardly if not in spirit, by

---

[4] Bertrand Russell, *The Practice and Theory of Bolshevism* (London: Allen and Unwin, 1920), p. 31.

[5] Lenin, *Polnoe sobranie sochinenii* (Moscow: Gosizdat, 1965), Vol. 39, p. 150.

[6] As Lenin states in "'Left-Wing' Communism—An Infantile Disorder," *Selected Works in Three Volumes* (Moscow: Progress Publishers, 1973), Vol. 3, p. 349.

[7] Norman Davis, "The Missing Revolutionary War," *Soviet Studies*, 27, no. 2 (April 1975), 190.

[8] Speech at Fourth Congress of Comintern, November 19, 1922. *Polnoe Sobranie Sochinenii*, 5th ed. (Moscow: Gosizdat, 1958-1965), Vol. 45, p. 290.

[9] Moshe Lewin, *Lenin's Last Struggle* (New York: Vintage Books, 1970).

radical Marxist forms and a democratic facade. Busts and portraits of Marx were far more abundant across Russia than those of the emperor had been,[10] although they were few compared to the proliferation of the image of Stalin in later years. Ministers became people's commissars, who bowed formally to the representatives of the masses. As Solzhenitsyn put it, "The Revolution had hastened to rename everything so that everything would be new."[11] The delegation sent to negotiate peace with Germany in December 1917 included, purely for ornament, a worker, a peasant, a sailor, and an ordinary soldier.[12] Although de facto privilege, including special ration cards and access to closed stores began within a year or so of the revolution, leaders were expected to conduct themselves like true members of the proletariat, living and dressing simply, and joining volunteer labor on occasion.

A written constitution was adopted, under which political power was based on the system of elected soviets. But elections to the soviets had always been at best haphazard and subject to manipulation, and the Bolsheviks used their skills to influence results even before the coup of November 1917. Afterwards, they held all the tools of coercion and pressure, and by the end of the civil war even local elections were little more than a show of support for the ruling party.

The Leninists introduced a basic change in the state structure, the placing of decision-making power in the ruling party instead of the official government. There were several causes for this extraordinary innovation. The Bolsheviks were clannish and accustomed to discussing and deciding among themselves, a habit that was retained even after the revolution. It was the more necessary since the administration was staffed by holdovers; thus, to assure party control, it was better to formulate policy in the Central Committee or the Politburo rather than in the Council of Commissars surrounded by ex-tsarist bureaucrats. Keeping real power in the party also made it easier to preserve the essence of autocracy while dressing up the state in legal and quasi-democratic forms. Moreover, the party was the principal bond of unity between the Russian center and the minority regimes organized as nominally independent soviet republics. Leninist nationality policy permitted nominal freedom to the minority peoples while keeping them under the close rule of branches of the centralized Bolshevik party.

This concession to democratic-libertarian sentiments and political necessity gave the Bolsheviks a major advantage in the civil war, since it was easy to believe that those who promised freedom would at worst allow more autonomy than the Russian-imperialist conservative forces who talked of a united Russia.

---

[10] H. G. Wells, *Russia in the Shadows* (New York: George Duran, 1921), p. 83.

[11] Alexander Solzhenitsyn, *The Gulag Archipelago, 1918-1956* (New York: Harper & Row, 1974), p. 436.

[12] Ulam, *Expansion and Coexistence*, p. 57.

But the freedom of nationalities was subject to Marxist class logic and the determination of the party that opposition to the policies of Moscow was "bourgeois" and inadmissible. This policy was the basis for the effective restoration of the empire, ruled the more strongly because its rule was not simply based on force and contempt for the conquered (in the way of most historic empires) but on claims of equality and justice. The claim was not entirely hollow as long as Lenin (himself of mixed non-Russian ancestry) held the helm. Various non-Russians had been overrepresented in the Bolshevik party and had contributed greatly to the making of the revolution; at one time, Lenin's chief defenders in Petrograd were a Latvian rifle corps and Estonian and Finnish sailors. Russian nationalism was condemned, and minorities were encouraged to use their own languages. It became briefly disadvantageous to be a Russian in the Ukraine. There, as in other minority areas, natives were recruited and preferred in the party and government apparatus.

Yet the long-range goal of Leninism was centralization in the name of the ideological cause incarnated in the party elite, the controlled and engineered state. Lenin liked order. Thus, at the beginning of his New Economic Policy he saw small capitalists as the enemy, while he regarded big capitalist enterprises as useful examples of organization and discipline for the socialist state;[13] socialism consisted more of control than of equality. The peasants were for Lenin "petty bourgeois" elements, inherently inimical to the managed order. In the same spirit, he had little use for science as independent thinking, but he eagerly subsidized the work of Ivan Pavlov, when the state was virtually bankrupt, in hopes that conditioned reflexes would make possible behavior modification.[14]

Centralization and discipline were more than a response to danger, however. After the civil war emergency, the freedom of discussion that had formerly prevailed within higher party circles gradually diminished, until even the Central Committee became largely a rubber stamp for decisions of the inner circle—the Politburo with Lenin and his confidants. The proletariat having been much reduced by the degradation of the economy and war losses, the party ruled all the more arbitrarily. Terror became a frequent method of administration.[15] The rulership became the more resolved to suppress other parties and opinions because of the narrowness of its base. As Lenin expressed it in a speech of March 31, 1920, "Soviet socialist democracy is not in the least incompatible with individual rule and dictatorship. The will of a class may sometimes be carried out by a dictator who can sometimes do more all by himself and who is frequently more essential."[16]

---

[13] Lewin, *Lenin's Last Struggle*, p. 27.
[14] Albert Parry, *The Russian Scientist* (New York: Macmillan, 1973), p. 88.
[15] G. H. Leggett, "Lenin, Terror, and Political Police," p. 173.
[16] *Polnoe sobranie sochinenii*, 5th ed., Vol. 40, p. 272.

As a result of its victory over the Russian Whites and the Allied interventionists, the party had great self-confidence and a firm grip on power, the opposition having been eliminated. Yet the original vision was gone, the country was impoverished and starving, and the ideological basis for the building of socialism had been destroyed. Trotsky and others tried to carry on the revolution by turning the huge forces built up during the civil war into labor armies. They were to use the organization which had won the war to rebuild the economy, raise the cultural level, and bring the triumph of communist spirit.[17] This failed; men could not be made to fight against backwardness in the same way they had been led to fight against the Whites. In the general breakdown, Lenin had to retreat and permit considerable economic freedom in order to stimulate reconstruction, had in fact to administer a dose of capitalism with his New Economic Policy. However, there was no idea of political relaxation or of sharing power; the party reaffirmed its doctrinal superiority, banned organized differences of opinion within the party ("factions"), and outlawed political competition.

The Stalinist Completion

The Soviet Communist state was to a large extent the work of Lenin. His was the guiding hand at critical junctures, and his was the propelling will. Yet the machine kept rolling, as of itself, after his hand was removed. It was left to Stalin—in part perhaps because Lenin could exercise leadership little more than a year after the end of the civil war before his disabling stroke of May 1922— fully to utilize the totalitarian potentialities. Stalin essentially completed the formation of the Communist state which has continued with little change in Russia up to this day and has served as the progenitor-model for other Communist states. Lenin's Communism for all its harshness was still tinged with the spirit of Western social democracy that had characterized the debating-society atmosphere of the early Russian Marxist party. In Lenin's Russia, there was still that effervescence of freedom that welled up with the liquidation of the old autocracy and its repressive rule, as witnessed by a high degree of vivacity and creativity in the arts and literature. But Stalin's stern despotism levelled, harnessed, and compressed all innovation. Until Stalin's Second Revolution, most people in Russia lived much as they had before 1917. Stalin made all, so far as humanly possible, servants of the state.

Character of Stalin. Lenin was an internationalist by background and temper; Stalin nationalized the revolution and became, despite his Georgian origin, the single greatest force toward centralization and Russification. Lenin thought in terms of class change and based his legitimacy on the rights of the

---

[17] Isaac Deutscher, *The Prophet Unarmed* (New York: Oxford University Press, 1959), p. 25.

oppressed; for Stalin, revolution was not social change but reorganization of society under central rulership, industrialization, and the magnification of power. Lenin was a revolutionary modernizer, equalitarian in spirit; Stalin was an antiequalitarian managerial modernizer.[18] Lenin's Russia was more inspiring, Stalin's more imitable by aspiring autocrats. If Lenin went back to the young Marx, Stalin reverted beyond Marx to Hegelian Prussianism and the apotheosis of the state.

How much of this may be due to accidents of Stalin's personality is questionable. That he had a withered arm must have caused a sense of frustration; that he was pockmarked may have sharpened an inferiority complex.[19] As a half-educated young man, with incomplete seminary training, unequipped for any regular profession, Stalin had hardly anywhere to go except into the revolutionary movement; apparently almost incapable of warm human relations, he became cynical not only about the established order but about people in general.

Yet Stalin was a quite reasonable man, generally speaking, before his personality became distorted by power.[20] In many party debates, his was the voice of moderation and unity. According to Khrushchev, Stalin impressed party delegates by his democratic manners, in contrast with the haughtiness of many.[21] Stalin was given many a party assignment with little fear that he would misuse authority, and he willingly took on jobs others did not desire. In Lenin's illness, the oligarchs, tasting independence, made him a front man in dealing with the sick boss (who reacted with the bitter comments of his "Testament"). His colleagues did not perceive him as a potential autocrat but as a useful operator. His fellow triumvirs after Lenin's death, Kamenev and Zinoviev, wanted to keep Stalin in the Secretariat, partly from fears of Trotsky as a more dangerous man, partly because Stalin became increasingly the man who held the party together in its still somewhat doubtful rulership.[22]

Stalinism Triumphant. Stalin made himself dictator through his supposed indispensability to party unity and so to the party dictatorship, plus his skillful use of the levers of power in the apparatus. But again, objective conditions favored despotism. Not only had the liberal classes of tsarist times been removed by terrorism, starvation, and emigration, but a new generation had grown up with very little schooling because education had nearly come to a halt in the civil war and its aftermath. The exiles, the pamphleteers and theoreticians

---

[18] In the sense of John H. Kautsky, *Political Consequences of Modernization* (New York: John Wiley and Sons, 1972), p. 67.

[19] For speculations on such psychological determinants, see Robert C. Tucker, *Stalin as a Revolutionary, 1879-1929: A Study in History and Personality* (New York: Norton, 1973).

[20] Ulam, *Stalin*, pp. 105-106.

[21] *Khrushchev Remembers* (Boston: Little, Brown, 1970), pp. 27-28.

[22] Ulam, *Stalin*, pp. 216, 239.

who had largely made the revolutionary movement and whose authoritarianism had been infiltrated by a touch of Western liberalism, yielded place in the new state to hard-bitten bosses and pragmatists. The old-style Bolsheviks were further discredited by the failure of the world revolution with which they were identified, while "Socialism in One Country" fit the needs and mood of the hardening Soviet state. Moreover, the Stalinists were in a position to impose greater controls because the party cadres and organization had been built up to the point that they could effectively manage the country. Lenin's ability to carry through a radical program in 1920 was limited by shortage of personnel and weakness of organization. A decade later, by virtue of recruitment, replacement of holdovers, and the growing habit of obedience to party orders, Stalin had an apparatus capable of executing a second revolutionary upheaval.

If the political instrument had become potent, the idealism of the revolution had been frustrated. The revolution had brought very little of the expected benefits; but it was impossible, especially for party members but also to a degree for ordinary Russians, to tell themselves that the great experiment had been a failure and a mistake. Rather, it had to be incomplete. Stalin thus offered to fulfill the political revolution by an economic one, and many were ready to follow his leadership to a renewed promise of socialism.

The sacred ideals of Marxist ideology and of the revolution formed the alleged basis for Stalin's driving the peasants into collective farms, where they could be forced to farm under the management of the party and their harvests could be appropriated for whatever return Stalin deemed necessary. Collectivization was also in the interests of modernization and mechanization, at least in theory, and hence beyond criticism. Again, in the name of socialism and the revolutionary class struggle, the more prosperous peasants, dubbed "kulaks," were destroyed as a class, millions of them literally annihilated. Through collectivization, Stalin eliminated the last large unsovietized sector of the population and potential support for an opposition, while thousands of party men moved into positions of new authority over the peasants as a new class of village lords.

Similar considerations lay behind the rapid industrialization program of the Five-Year Plans. According to the Marxist scheme socialism was preconditioned by highly developed industry, so in Russia industrial development should fulfill the socialistic vision and set the country on the way to the higher social order and utopia. It was modernization in the true Russian tradition of government pushing the economy to catch up with the West, basically for purposes of prestige and power, economic independence, and military security. Already at the beginning of the drive, in 1928, Stalin saw himself as successor to Peter the Great.[23] Like collectivization, industrialization under state planning greatly increased the power of the central authorities and did away with

---

[23] *Ibid.*, p. 312.

most small-scale and artisan producers, while making the populace totally dependent on the state. This development also brought an army of apparatusmen into new positions of authority. Lenin had shown the way with his passion for electrification, but it was Stalin's contribution to make industrial growth for many Five-Year Plans the fetish and preoccupation of the Soviet state.

The Purges. Ideology and self-interest somewhat similarly combined to make possible the purges. Stalin moved, as usual, outwardly in defense of the revolution and the unity of the party; and these sacred twin concepts persuaded many to support his actions and others to submit with little or no resistance. How could a revolutionary oppose the will of the party or set his personal convictions against its decrees? Confession was felt ordinarily necessary; but jailers were ruthless in their use of psychological and physical torture to secure it. Peasants might be shot for gleaning a handful of grain or soldiers (in the war) for having lost identity papers, or anyone for a careless word or a suspicion in Stalin's mind.

Moral conviction was necessary to make the terror effective; the police seem to have felt they were doing their true duty. Revolutionary idealism also prevented potential victims from combining and acting in their own defense. Not even the military leaders, in possession of the chief means of force, made a gesture toward halting the madness.

So many were killed in the purges—about thirteen million—either by execution or imprisonment in unbearable labor camps,[24] that the Soviet people were beaten and cowed for decades to come. The dimensions of the disaster may be roughly judged by comparison with the total of about 35,000 victims of the famed Terror of the French Revolution.[25] Besides the total elimination of opposition, the purges also raised up a new layer of bosses and managers at once beholden to Stalin for their advancement and much aware that their security depended upon unimpeachable loyalty to the powers above. Best of all, fawning became internalized. To survive it was necessary to demonstrate love for Stalin; like beaten dogs that cringe and lick the hand that whips them, men convinced themselves that they truly loved the threatening boss, somewhat as hijack hostages frequently love their abductors.

The great purges were madness; they weakened the Soviet Union and probably for a time gravely endangered the unbalanced dictator. The Soviet interpretation, since Khrushchev undertook de-Stalinization in 1956, is that they were the result not of the Soviet system but of a quirk of personality. It may at least be said that no other Communist leader has executed on a comparable scale or similarly annihilated a host of faithful followers.

As was to be expected of such a paranoiac personality, Stalin mixed rewards with punishment, lavishing political and material privileges on his servants.

---

[24] For an account of the purges, see Robert Conquest, *The Great Terror* (New York: Macmillan, 1968).

[25] Peter Gay and R. K. Webb, *Modern Europe* (New York: Harper & Row, 1973), p. 494.

By the mid-1930s, engineers may have earned 80 or 100 times as much as un-skilled members of the proletariat,[26] and political elite came into princely privilege. The vast enlargement of the governing apparatus put in place a new ruling elite unlike any the world had known before. In 1936, Stalin proclaimed that classes had ceased to exist in Russia; but his meaning was the opposite, that by Marxist definition proletarianism no longer shadowed the status of the new governing class.

Stalinism. Fundamentally indifferent to Marxism, a power-bent administrator of the revolution to which he was heir,[27] Stalin was a consistently strong centralizer. He deprived the minorities of the small degree of autonomy Lenin had permitted them, indirectly as a by-product of the extension of controls through collectivization, industrialization, and purges, directly as official policy. Stalin oversaw the gradual Russification of a party that had once espoused internationalism, as old Bolsheviks dropped out or were purged and the party was staffed with new, home-bred recruits. It was typical, too, that Stalin quietly went back to the old Russian attitude of anti-Semitism. It may be assumed that Stalin did not Russify from any personal predilection for Russian people or culture—he was a Georgian nationalist in his youth—but because the retreat of revolutionism implied Russian dominance. Effective rule from the Kremlin meant rule by Russians, whose self-interest lay in the maintenance of the supreme authority of Moscow.

By corollary, Stalin built up, in the name of proletarian internationalism, an essentially nationalistic dictatorship. From the early 1930s he reversed much of the logic of the revolution by restoring tsarist Russia, with its hero-warriors and expansionist wars, to respectability and glory; the tsarist empire was found to have been "progressive." The army was built up and privileges and distinctions of officers, reduced or abolished in the fever of the revolution, were restored or magnified. The press indulged in raptures over the "defense of the fatherland." Women were urged to have many children for the fatherland, and divorce was made difficult to strengthen the family Bolsheviks once wanted to abolish. Experimental art forms were replaced by traditional, and artists and writers were mobilized to glorify the state, the party, and the leader.

As a nationalist Communist, Stalin was shielded and upheld by a simplistic Marxism-Leninism of clear goals and simple solutions. His semi-deified person became in practice the chief article of faith. If the party was the vanguard of the workers, Stalin was the vanguard of the vanguard; all organizations, including the party, were ultimately to serve only his will. He was to be venerated and obeyed without question because he incorporated the destiny at once of Russia and of the proletarian socialist revolution, destined to lead humanity to new

---

[26] Max Eastman, *Stalin's Russia and the Crisis in Socialism* (New York: Norton, 1940), p. 39.

[27] Lucio Colletti, "The Question of Stalin," *New Left Review*, 61 (May-June 1970), 75.

glories. He lived in seclusion and enveloped his state in a degree of secrecy novel for the age. In the 1920s, Soviet Russia, desirous of telling the world about its experiment in social engineering, had released a flood of statistical and other data; Stalin cut this down to a stream of propaganda, disclosure of any factual information being punishable as communication of state secrets. He isolated Russia from the outside world, allowing only the most trusted to depart and few to enter. At the same time, he gave his subjects a new and more democratic constitution (during his lifetime, the so-called "Stalin Constitution") with a most impressive set of rights and freedoms and democratic procedures, the unreality of which was perhaps the most impressive testimony to the power of the master. Ordinary Russians supposed that they were free,[28] and many an educated foreigner, from Sidney and Beatrice Webb to György Lukács, agreed.

Settled Sovietism

At the Eighteenth Congress of the party, in March 1939, Stalin blamed subordinates for the excesses and declared the great purges at an end. The transformations ensuing from the revolution were complete, and the Soviet state settled down to bureacratic management and the enjoyment of rulership.

Having achieved the utmost in internal power, Stalin was turning his attention to power abroad, to the newly interesting and promising international stage stirred up by the fascist wave. By the Nazi-Soviet agreement of August 1939, he gave the signal for a conflict which he doubtless hoped would gravely weaken the Western powers while leaving him to pick up the spoils. His reward for this service was a large swath of territory from the Black Sea to the Gulf of Finland.

Effects of War and Conquest. Stalin's calculations were not unrealistic, except for the fact that the fresh and purposeful German dictatorship was stronger than Stalin (or the British or French) had reckoned. Thus from June 22, 1941, the Soviet Union found itself battling for its life. During the struggle, after the shock of the early defeats had been absorbed and translated into national determination to survive, the Soviet system changed in tone and character. Marxist ideology became only a secondary adjunct of the battle against the cruel invader. Secrecy and cruelty remained; a wartime statute, for example, provided imprisonment for relatives of soldiers taken prisoner. But there was a freedom of sorts. Self-sacrifice was taken for granted, but initiative was welcome; writers, for instance, could write freely and truthfully so long as their theme remained the national one of beating the Germans under Stalin's leadership. The Orthodox Church was also released to support the war, and Russian tradition came strongly to the fore. Lenin's Comintern was formally dissolved, although its staff was kept intact to aid in the appropriation of Eastern Europe.

---

[28] Michel Gordey, *Visa to Moscow* (New York: Knopf, 1952), p. 410.

The Soviet state became most Russian-nationalist when it was reduced by German conquest of the Western borderlands, the Ukraine, and parts of the Caucasus. As it recovered the minority areas, still more as it moved into domination of large parts of Eastern Europe, it brought back Marxist-Leninist indoctrination, the ideological world picture, and strict party-mediated dictatorship. Reinvigorated by the fight, buoyed by victory, the Soviet state settled down, after probes in Iran, toward Turkey, etc., had been turned back, to xenophobic enjoyment of rulership by the new apparatus elite and its godlike leader. There was no more will to change. Stalin had in him enough of the revolutionary idealist (or the jealous boss) to resent the privileges of the governing caste he had created but not enough to undertake to abolish them.[29] He maintained terrorism at a level sufficient to keep his aides filled with fear but not enough to risk shaking the structure of the state. Intellectual creativity was more stifled than ever. Minimizing foreign contacts and denigrating Western culture, he tried practically to de-Europeanize Russia.[30] Stalin's bent for secrecy and his distrust of everyone grew as his capacities declined, his absolutism unameliorated by his senility.[31] The top bodies of the party, the Congress, Central Committee, even the Politburo, fell into disuse, as the despot governed through his court.

The Khrushchev Style. After Stalin's death, the oligarchs, led by Georgi Malenkov, who had stood next to Stalin, and Lavrenti Beria, former police boss, took charge and reorganized the top level of party and government. They had antithetical fears—on the one hand, of a purge, such as Stalin had evidently been preparing at his death, and on the other, of relaxation leading to the loss of power. As Khrushchev put it in his memoirs, "We were afraid the thaw might unleash a flood which we wouldn't be able to control and which might drown us."[32]

Stalin had sufficiently downplayed the party that Malenkov, as leading individual in the new government, seems to have preferred the position of Chairman of the Council of Ministers to that of Secretary of the party. He undertook a limited rationalization and loosening, with emphasis shifted slightly from military strength to the satisfaction of consumer wants. In the maneuvering for power, however, the leading party secretary, Nikita Khrushchev, was able, in February 1955, to force Malenkov from leadership as too soft. But Khrushchev, once on top, carried on something of the Malenkov policy of limited easing of tensions and softening the impact of the state.

---

[29] Svetlana Alliluyeva, *Twenty Letters to a Friend* (New York: Harper & Row, 1967), p. 166.

[30] Ivar Spector, *An Introduction to Russian History and Culture*, 5th ed. (Princeton: Van Nostrand, 1969), p. 461.

[31] Khrushchev stressed over and over in his memoirs how little he, as a member of the Politburo, knew of official policies.

[32] Nikita S. Khrushchev, *Khrushchev Remembers: The Last Testament* (Boston: Little, Brown, 1974), p. 79.

Khrushchev, a thorough Stalinist as long as the boss lived, seems to have been imbued with a certain realistic idealism from his wartime experiences.[33] He wanted to release the Soviet Union from the extreme strictures of Stalinism, to return to what he viewed as the purer revolutionary ethos of Leninism, and to reinvigorate the party as an institution. Although his de-Stalinization, begun in a secret speech at the Twentieth Congress of the Communist Party, February 1956, and promoted publicly in 1961, was no doubt a political attack on rivals, it seems to have come from the heart.

Unlike Stalin, Khrushchev ventured out of the Kremlin, mixed with his underlings, and engaged in mundane discussions of all manner of policies. He permitted more foreign trade and slightly opened the borders. Recognizing that war must no longer be considered inevitable in the nuclear age, he viewed "Peaceful Coexistence" as a drive for the supremacy of socialism by nonviolent means. He continued the curbing of the powers of the secret police, begun by deposing Beria not long after Stalin's death. He did not try to shoot defeated rivals but eased them from power—a precedent which may have been involuntary, because of inability to muster support for harsher reprisals, but which in any case made it possible for his own aides to conspire against him in 1964. To release the economy from overcentralization, Khrushchev undertook in 1957 to transfer a large part of supervision to over a hundred regional councils. He acknowledged that writers knew what to write better than the party and somewhat eased controls over literature and art, even though he occasionally shouted at writers and artists. The high point of post-Stalinist liberalization was surely the publication, by Khrushchev's dispensation, in 1962, of Solzhenitsyn's labor camp sketch, *One Day in the Life of Ivan Denisovich.*

Khrushchev was both a liberalizer and an authoritarian, and while loosening in some ways he tightened in others. Thus, he closed most of the churches which Stalin had allowed to remain open and revived atheism as Soviet doctrine. He also reapplied the death penalty for a variety of economic crimes. In both directions, however, he was a Leninist and a populist, putting into effect the ideological disapproval of religion and expressing the popular anger at those who fattened by taking advantage of the weaknesses of the Soviet state. Other Khrushchevian policies were in the same general mode: revival of equalitarianism by reducing income differentials and requiring youths to have work experience before entering higher education; "comrade courts," wherein the assembled people should exercise mostly moral suasion on minor miscreants; exile of "parasites" from major centers; some effort to turn over minor governmental and regulatory functions to the citizens' organizations (under party guidance). Hesitantly and inconsistently, Khrushchev wanted to turn from mobilization to participation, from the strictly party state to a popular state. As he put it at the 1961 (22nd) Party Congress, "For the first time there has arisen in our country a state which is not a dictatorship of any one class but

---

[33] Edward Crankshaw, foreword to *Khrushchev Remembers*, p. xvi.

the instrument of society as a whole, of all the people."[34]   But he proposed no relaxation of the party's grip on power, and he permitted an impressive cult of his own personality.

The New Conservatism. Fear that Khrushchev's policies might lead to a weakening of the party's authority, plus a distaste for his sometimes rather frenetic schemes for betterment—and the consequent reorganizations and shifts of personnel—seem to have turned his colleagues against him. Khrushchev was removed (and converted into a non-person) by a coup in October 1964, singular in the history of Communism, and of Russia, as the semilegal and bloodless removal of a sovereign ruler.

The new oligarchs, led by First Secretary Leonid Brezhnev, seemed determined to avoid adventures, internally and externally. They moved only gradually and rather methodically on the diplomatic stage to strengthen not the world revolutionary movement or the socialist cause but Soviet strategic positions. They reversed Khrushchev's efforts to cut down the armed forces and military expenditures.

Internally, the gray leadership attempted to rationalize the economy to revive industrial and agricultural growth but backed away from liberalization of economic controls. The few reforms they undertook were moves either toward restoration of Stalinist practices or toward further centralization of controls. There was practically no evidence of controversy over policies among the oligarchs. They reemphasized ideology, especially after the invasion of Czechoslovakia in August 1968, but in tones rather of Soviet socialist pride than social change. De-Stalinization was ended, although Stalin's name and photograph only very slowly reappeared in the Soviet press. The cult of Lenin was inflated as never before, but he was made a symbol not of revolution but of order and authority. Khrushchev's equalitarian changes were largely undone. His slight tendencies to populism were replaced by renewed emphasis on "dictatorship of the proletariat," that is, strict party rule.[35]   In 1971, the Twenty-Fourth Congress of the party adopted a new conservative rule permitting longer periods between congresses and giving secretaries more security of office.

Leonid Brezhnev, who had been next to Khrushchev, presided over this conservative, bureaucratic regime. Initially only first among equals, he gradually succeeded in replacing rivals and potential rivals with friends and supporters on the Politburo. In 1966 he took Stalin's old title of General Secretary. By 1970 he was negotiating on behalf of the Soviet Union, and the 1971 Congress was virtually his show. By 1976, his cult of personality was so advanced that quotations from his mundane works largely replaced Lenin's in the papers, books were written about him, his recorded speeches were on sale, and documentary films glorified his deeds.

---

[34] "On the Party Program," at the Twenty-Second Congress of the CPSU. N.S. Khrushchev, *Kommunizm—Mir i Schastie Narodov* (Moscow: Gosizdat, 1962), pp. 216-217.

[35] Peter H. Juviler, in *Contemporary Soviet Law*, Donald D. Barry et al., eds. (The Hague: Nijhoff, 1974), p. 42.

The Soviet System

The Soviet political structure, now in its seventh decade, is a successful and well-engineered social construction, remarkably cohesive and stable. It has guided the destiny of a great society and maintained the rule of a single organization, the Communist Party, from the war-torn, backward Russia of 1917–1920 to the industrialized society of today. Kept on course through three successions, it has functioned effectively under single leaders and collective leaderships alike. It has educated, modernized, promoted economic growth, and shaped the lives of its citizens to a degree hitherto inconceivable.

The Military and the Use of Force. All this has been possible because the Soviet state is a tightly articulated framework of mutually reinforcing elements. One of these is the use of force. In the disorderly days of 1917, the Bolsheviks were prepared to employ violence when most other parties shrank from it, and they effectively wielded the sword of terror in the civil war. The purges were probably counterproductive even for Stalin's dictatorship, but they left a docile if not monolithic society.

Mass purge seems no longer possible, barring an emergency, revolutionary conviction no longer being strong enough to justify murder; and the party leadership's number one priority seems to be security. Yet the party-state will not hesitate to use coercion whenever it feels useful, and people know it. The political police, the KGB with its half-million army, is a major organ of the state—its chief, Yury Andropov, sits on the Politburo—and it is restrained in actions against persons considered dangerous by little more than dislike for adverse publicity. Dissenters are not shot, as in Stalin's day, but are subjected to persuasion, chicanery, and low and medium grade molestations, from questioning, searches, threats, discharge from employment, eviction from housing, to beatings and imprisonment. Such measures usually suffice to ensure prudent compliance, although the limits of free talk have expanded considerably as fear of authority has diminished. Those who stubbornly transgress the limits may be treated as insane, which they are by the norms of the system, and confined in psychiatric institutions. Those who are found most perverse may be sentenced to labor camps. These have only a tiny fraction of the inmates of Stalin's time, but they reportedly hold some ten thousand prisoners, mostly religious or ethnic dissidents, with a sprinkling of recalcitrant intellectuals.

Looming behind the political police is the army, the guarantor of order. It is especially vital as the bulwark of Soviet domination of Eastern Europe. Within the Soviet Union, its chief utility is perhaps in the socialization and indoctrination of youth and the inculcation of discipline. "Ours is an army," said Marshal Grechko, "in which the officer as well as every soldier is called upon to be a political warrior, an active propagandist and agitator."[36]

---

[36] *Krasnaia Zvezda*, November 27, 1969.

There is an immense program of military–patriotic indoctrination, ranging from the collection of trophies to lessons in nuclear defense for schoolchildren. The inspirational side of combat has been idealized more than in any other state of modern times (except some other Communist states and Nazi Germany and fascist Italy). Indoctrination and military and paramilitary training of youth have been carried to extremes.[37] This has hardly abated during the international relaxation of tension in the 1970s. In 1973-74, for example, a sample of Soviet shows comprised one about the navy, one about the airforce, a gripping war-spy series, an anti-crime film, and one comedy.[38]

The military emphasis contributes to the maintenance of a degree of tension with the outside world which the Soviet state seems to find necessary for its morale. In 1956, Khrushchev realistically discarded the old Leninist proposition of the inevitability of war and espoused the idea of Peaceful Coexistence, but he had still to maintain ideological warfare and contend that the rival social systems were engaged in life-and-death competition, symbolic war. In the 1970s trade with Western powers and technological borrowing have seemed more important to the Russians than the promotion of Communism. Yet the old themes of militancy have been persistent, although the danger is no longer seen in specific countries but in "imperialism" (the military side of capitalism). *Pravda* warned of relaxation: "It is well known that the forces of imperialism, despite the failure of their aggressive adventures, by no means renounce their goals."[39] Brezhnev underlined: "The CPSU stood and stands on the principle that the struggle of two systems—capitalist and socialist—in the realm of economics, politics, and of course ideology, will continue. It cannot be otherwise, for the philosophy and class goals of socialism and capitalism are opposite and irreconcilable."[40]

The Economic Sphere. The economy also continues to revolve around military production. Not only is the proportion of national income spent on defense double that of the United States; but industrial development since the first Five-Year Plan (1928) has been structured around heavy industry and military needs. This priority has always been maintained, and at present it is difficult to suggest whether it is the purpose of the military to defend the civilian economy or of the latter to support the military.[41] Centralization of the economy is virtually complete, ownership being vested not in any subunits or the Soviet

---

[37] Cf. Leon Goure, *The Militarization of Soviet Youth* (New York: National Strategy Information Center, 1973).

[38] Klaus Mehnert, "Moskauer Fernsehen und Film 1973–74," *Osteuropa*, 24, no. 5 (May 1974), 319–331.

[39] Editorial, March 16, 1973.

[40] Speech for the Soviet Union's fiftieth birthday, quoted by *Pravda*, March 31, 1973, p. 4.

[41] William E. Odom, "Who Controls Whom in Moscow," *Foreign Policy*, 19 (Summer 1975), 113.

national divisions but in the people as a whole, that is, the government in Moscow. Managers of enterprises are only agents of the state. They may be permitted to retain a share of profits for incentive purposes, but their primary duty is to fulfill the quotas and objectives of the economic plan, and the central authorities allocate the basic commodities in the production process.

State control of the economy makes it possible to allocate resources and investments for political and social as well as strictly economic purposes, and it has in the past assured a high rate of growth of industrial output. It also helps to hold the system together. Everyone must work, in effect, for the state, that is, for the party; outside its sphere there are only illegal or semilegal activities, which constitute "parasitism." Advancement in any career means working within the party-dominated framework, and those who have climbed the ladder have acquired a vested interest in the system.

Difficulties of central management have always been most evident in agriculture, the least successful sector of the Soviet economy, with periodic harvest failures only partly attributable to weather. The productivity of labor in Soviet agriculture is only ten to twenty percent of the American, and it seems incongruous in a modern state that offices are emptied for weeks in the fall as white-collar workers are marshalled to pick potatoes or cotton. Despite the far greater productivity of the small private plots permitted peasants and some workers—the 3% of land cultivated privately yields as much as ten times per hectare as the collectives—perhaps in reality *because* of their relative productivity, they are under continual pressure,[42] and inducements are offered for possessors to give up entirely this vestige of individual farming.[43] Workers who had been allowed to cultivate patches of .1 hectare were ordered to plant only .01 hectare so they could not possibly raise enough to supplement incomes.[44]

Many distortions result from the attempt to direct the entire economy from Moscow and from the substitution of political for economic levers—difficulties similar to but much greater than those resulting from relatively modest efforts to control production by governmental fiat in the West. There are multiple confusions, waste, profiteering, and difficulty in securing technical innovation—reasons for the dependence on technological imports sixty years after the revolution. Productivity of labor remains far below that of leading Western countries despite decades of heavy capital investment.

The planners know well that production could be greatly enhanced by permitting more latitude to factory managers on the spot or by breaking up the huge collective farms into smaller units that would allow the farmers to see more direct benefit from their endeavors. Many such proposals have been made, and experiments have shown the practicality of such relaxations; yet no fundamental

---

[42] Karl-Eugen Wädekin, "Income Distribution in Soviet Agriculture," *Soviet Studies*, 27, no. 1 (January, 1975), 6.

[43] *New York Times*, October 24, 1974, p. 18.

[44] *Izvestia*, December 4, 1974.

changes are made because they are seemingly perceived as too dangerous for party authority. Similarly, individual, even cooperative but non-state handicraft production is more or less illegal, despite the large and obvious gains for the public from permitting small-scale entrepreneurs to fill the gaps left by the state's failure to satisfy needs for various commodities and particularly services.

The role of money is kept as low as feasible, because money means independence. Much effort is made to motivate by "moral incentives," both general idealism and patriotic dedication and special recognition, honors and status, for outstanding performance. Outstanding workers receive ceremonial recognition, certificates, medals and lifelong privileges. Many things are to be had primarily as perquisites, not for cash, such as preferred housing, vacations, and travel; usually even such a material possession as an automobile is a reward of service instead of an outright purchase (at an exorbitant price), and loyalty is the price of continued enjoyment.

Total control of the economy is thus an essential pillar of the political structure, hence infinitely precious.[45] For the controllers, the reformers who would allow more autonomy or more reliance on market mechanisms are anti-state, so anti-socialist. And happily for the Soviet system, economic statism with its apparatus of controls has pleasing aspects. It gives security; there are jobs for all, security in employment, and few economic uncertainties. It is popular in principle; workers can feel that the factory somehow belongs to them, as they are often told. Nationalization of industry seems to be popular even with persons antagonistic to the party.

Propaganda. An equally indispensable pillar of the Soviet edifice is the manifold management of minds, intended to be as total as the control of production. The means of information—press, broadcasting, all organized meetings, art, and literature—are at the disposal of the authorities and are to be used for purposes of edification and enlightenment, with whatever concessions to entertainment are necessary. It is even prohibited (since 1972) to use the telephone for "purposes contradicting state interests." Artists and writers, so far as they are cooperative, are generously subsidized by the party. If uncooperative, they are excluded from the Writers' or Artists' Union, that is, from the profession. Censorship is enforced mainly through the caution exercised by writers and editors, but all publications must have a specific imprimatur. In addition to the usual means of propaganda, there is a vast apparatus of strictly party indoctrination, including party schools, with 20 million students in 1976.[46]

As in economic matters, overcontrol in the intellectual sphere must needs be counterproductive and deadly to initiative and creativity. Artists and writers must not only refrain from opposing state and party but must also conform to

---

[45] A theme of Moshe Lewin, *Political Undercurrents in Soviet Economic Debates* (Princeton: Princeton University Press, 1974).

[46] *Pravda*, June 12, 1976, p. 1; cf. Ellen Mickiewicz, "The Modernization of Party Propaganda in the USSR," *Slavic Review*, 30 (June 1971), 257-276.

canons of "Socialist Realism"—simple, even simpleminded presentation with the proper accent on socialist values and without real conflicts except between accepted values of good and evil, wherein the good inevitably emerges as victorious. So little that is merely interesting or amusing can appear in the newspapers that their value as propaganda is seriously diminished. Yet canons are not to be bent, because permitting individualistic deviations would mean opening cracks to subversive Western influences and offering a nucleus on which anti-Soviet sentiments might crystallize, a handle for attack on party rule.

Opinion control requires a faith in which minds are to be molded, just as the use of coercion and the monopolization of the economy need an ideal legitimation. A mixture of idealism and rationalization for the use, perhaps abuse, of power, Marxist-Leninist ideology fills in the Soviet system the multiple functions suggested earlier. It is at once a formalized language of politics and a standard of virtue by which to decry individualism and consumption-mindedness. It does not significantly guide policy but serves as a means of denouncing what is disliked and defining duties. It is a means of setting workers against intellectuals. It serves to redefine words; "freedom" or "democracy" signify the opposite of the originals when prefixed by "class" or "proletarian." It is the criterion of the interpretation of reality, any alternative to which is anti-Soviet, hence by definition false. As a Russian put it, "The truth may also be a class enemy."[47]

The critical element in Soviet ideology is faith in the party and its leadership, the loyalty which holds the system together. As representative of the workers, the party cannot err; even victims of the purges felt they had to agree that their suffering was ordained.[48] Anything done against the will of the party is class-hostile and counterrevolutionary. Ideology also makes loyalty easily definable. The profession of belief and, even more, its internalization—a necessary condition to advancement within the party—is a prophylactic against mental independence. Ideology as loyalty is as critical within the party as between people and party, perhaps more so; so long as the party, holder of all key positions, remains united, it is secure.

Marxism-Leninism is regarded as a science, the ramifications of which can be studied forever. As stated by a Soviet philosopher, "The entire practice of building a new communist society is based on an unshakable foundation of science, above all social science. Such a science, taking in all sides of social life, is Marxist-Leninist theory."[49] For this reason, higher education, a mixture of indoctrination and useful training, is the primary path to elite status in the Soviet Union.

---

[47] George Feifer, *Russia Close-Up* (London: Jonathan Cape, 1973), p. 34.

[48] Cf. Solzhenitsyn, *The Gulag Archipelago*, Vol. 1, pp. 104 ff.

[49] A. M. Rumiantsev, "Lenin's Ideas on the Relation of Politics and Culture," *Voprosy Filosofii*, no. 1 (January 1975), p. 20.

Ideological interpretations coincide with the self-interest of the rulership, and it may be assumed that the leaders, while cynical about many pieces of information and misinformation they permit the public, basically believe in the creed in which they have been educated and which serves their status. Khrushchev, for example, in his memoirs repeatedly speaks in terms of kitchen Marxism, of class conflict and dangers of war from the capitalist-imperialists; he laments the sufferings of the workers under the yoke of capitalism,[50] untroubled by the earlier admission[51] that he was better off as a metalworker under the tsarist regime than Soviet workers in his day. Conformity comes more easily because ideology is intrinsically elitist, setting up its warranted possessors as superior beings. As Stalin said, "Comrades, we Communists are a people of a unique mould. We are made of a special stuff. We are those who form the army of the great proletarian strategist, the army of Comrade Lenin. There is nothing higher than the honour of belonging to this army."[52]

Ideology in the Service of the Party. Marxism-Leninism is in any case indispensable as the basis of the very existence of the Soviet Union as a state.[53] "Soviet" delimits not a national group but a collection of many nationalities; it can logically be integrated only on an ideological-universalist basis. The Soviet peoples, half of them non-Russian, are not joined by community of language and culture, like the French or the Swedes, and are as much divided as united by historical experience. They find, however, a common ground in the community of the working class in Marxism-Leninism, the socialist family of Soviet nationalities standing together (with allies in Eastern Europe) against the capitalist-imperialist evil. The minorities are congratulated on their freedom while they are told that it would be unthinkable to use it. The anniversary of a Soviet republic's annexation is celebrated as a gala national holiday. The interests of the proletariat or workers of the Ukraine, Transcaucasus, etc., are by definition identical with those of the Russian proletariat and are perfectly expressed by the Communist Party. Any suspicions that Russians may derive special advantages from the union imply a nationalistic and narrow, anti-proletarian attachment to "bourgeois" interests. There is no such thing as proletarian nationalism.

Marxism-Leninism thus represents a powerful combination of broad ideals with Russian self-interest. For patriotic Russians, Marxism-Leninism may be the only obvious way to sustain Russian greatness in the modern world. This may also be the reason that ideology in formal detail, Marxist-Leninist scholasticism, seems to be much more important for the Soviet Union than for other Communist states, none of which has a nationality problem of comparable magnitude.

---

[50] *Khrushchev Remembers: The Last Testament*, p. 149.

[51] *Ibid.*, p. 87.

[52] Joseph Stalin, "On the Death of Lenin," *Works* (Moscow: Foreign Languages Publishing House, 1953), Vol. VI, p. 47.

[53] Cf. R. Wesson, "Soviet Ideology: The Necessity of Marxism," *Soviet Studies*, 21, no. 1 (July 1969), 64-70.

Like the collectivization of the economy, mind control also has psychological benefits. The picture of the world presented to Soviet citizens is simple, and since Stalin's times comforting and usually placid, a mosaic of the great and small triumphs of Soviet socialism and those of its friends, made brighter by the evil forces remaining in the world without. Soviet citizens are not alarmed by natural calamities or portents of disaster, by sensational crime news, by the horrors of transportation crashes or industrial accidents in the land of socialism. Their envy is not aroused by reports of prosperity outside the socialist sphere or by information regarding the earnings or indulgences of their betters in party or state, nor by the troubles or personal affairs of the latter. Even if there should be a drought the media informs them of it only long afterwards if at all. Least of all is one bothered by controversies over policies or accounts of political contest. There are no scandals, except so far as the party attacks abuses from time to time. There have been some mild debates in the press, most frequently on economic subjects, but (at least since the slightly greater openness of the Khrushchev era was closed down) they have not been such as to engage the passions of onlookers, who should limit their shouting to sports matches. The limitation on information is effective, even when facts are widely known; the new Soviet generation, for instance, has only the faintest idea of the excesses of the Stalinist era. With reason, Ambassador Kohler remarked that the Kremlin was not a mystery, just a secret.[54]

The Soviet people enjoy "the happiness of simplification,"[55] along with the conviction that their society, whatever its temporary or superficial shortcomings, is—because of the wisdom and heroism of Lenin, the current leaders, the party, and the noble people—the most just and progressive on earth. As a Moscow taxi driver averred, private property "means jealousy and hate and greed."[56] The contradictory politics of the pluralistic society and competing parties are incomprehensible and undesirable. The Soviet citizen sees a clear-cut universe in which he is burdened by no problems of values—indeed, by few autonomous choices—and no critical voices jar the harmony decreed by the supreme powers.

The Party Hierarchy. But ideology serves the party, not the reverse. The party is the mesh that holds together the various elements of the Soviet system—police, military, governmental bureaucracy, economic administration, trade unions, and the intellectual community—and prevents their inevitable conflicts of interest from tearing apart the tight-knit system. The party has long been especially afraid of the potential independence of the armed forces, and has developed an elaborate control apparatus infiltrating the services with police agents and political officers responsible not to the military command but to the Central Committee. Furthermore, officers nearly all belong to the party and are hence subject to party discipline.

---

[54] *New York Times*, January 23, 1975, p. 3.
[55] Solzhenitsyn, *Gulag*, p. 162.
[56] Observer, *Message from Moscow* (London: Jonathan Cape, 1969), p. 178.

Party control of other organizations and agencies is exercised primarily through the control of staffing. At each territorial level, party secretaries are responsible for filling all important positions in a list called the "nomenklatura," not only government posts but leadership positions in all organizations. At each level also, departments of the respective party committee—for village, city, district, and so on—are responsible for determining that persons under their jurisdiction act in accordance with party policies. At the lowest level, party members within any organization, no matter how humble, are obligated to form a "party fraction" to guide the organization according to party dictates. The party aims to govern everything from inside. In this way, all organizations in the Soviet Union can be considered specialized affiliates of the party. (With the exception of the churches, only a partial exception because the favored churches are party-dominated.) The trade unions may be viewed as the labor branch of the party, the Writers' Union as the literary branch, the 34-million member (1974) Komsomol as the youth sector, etc.

Much as the party directs the country, the professional apparatus and the central nucleus direct the party. The 16 million members theoretically elect both the officers of their primary organizations and delegates to local conferences, who in turn elect delegates to higher conferences or congresses; these high-level representatives theoretically choose members of the Central Committee, and they in turn elect its Secretariat and Politburo. But in fact party officers at each level suggest who should be elected at levels below them, elections are generally not by secret ballot, and results may be set aside if necessary, so there are few surprises. The secretaries are the line officers of the party, the backbone of the structure, and they select, from the top down, the secretaries and other professionals, to the number of about 300,000 (excluding secretaries of primary organizations).[57] About a third of these comprise the Soviet political elite. Members of this ruling group are practically above criticism or chastisement as long as they abide by the party's code of behavior; they comprise a closely bound group which rallies to protect its membership from any outside encroachment.

A narrower, more privileged group, those who may be considered candidates for top positions, are the approximately 6,000 persons forming the buros of provincial central committees plus their superiors. The next top aristocrats are the members of the Central Committee, slightly over 400 in number. They are provincial first secretaries or regional bosses, leaders of organizations, ministers, Politburo members and the like—the power elite. As a committee they seldom exercise much power, since they meet only about twice yearly. The Central Committee,

---

[57] T. H. Rigby, "Soviet Communist Party Membership under Brezhnev," *Soviet Studies*, 28 (July 1976), 317; Mervyn Matthews, "Top Incomes in the USSR: Towards a Definition of the Soviet Elite," *Survey*, 21 (Summer 1975), 24.

however, is the focus of the central apparatus, including 23 departments which are chief overseers of the party's management of society and the party itself. The Central Committee also has a Secretariat of 11 (in 1977), most of whom are in command of a department, such as heavy industry, agriculture, relations with foreign parties, education and propaganda, etc.

At times under Khrushchev it seemed that the Secretariat might be the dominant party organ, or at least that Khrushchev wished to make it so. The fact that the Secretariat is, according to the rules, authorized to nominate to party positions might indicate its superiority. But since Khrushchev's downfall in October 1964, the Politburo has clearly been supreme. With 15 voting members in 1977, it regularly brings together (reportedly every Thursday) the outstanding personages of the Soviet system: the General Secretary and four other Secretaries of the Central Committee, the Chairman of the Council of Ministers, his deputy, the ceremonial head of state, Ministers of Defense and Foreign Affairs, the chief of the political police, the Chairman of the Party Control Commission, and the most important provincial chiefs, those of Moscow, Kazakhstan, Leningrad, and the Ukraine. The name "Politburo" suggests that it decides governmental policy in general, but it is also the governing arm of the party itself. It apparently determines its own membership.

Within the Politburo one man has clearly stood out as the leader except for brief intervals in the aftermath of the disappearances of Lenin, Stalin, and Khrushchev, sometimes first among near equals, sometimes rather firmly in command, in Stalin's case so superior that he could ignore the Politburo as he saw fit. Since Lenin, the top individual has always been the ranking Secretary, and there has been a general tendency for his authority to grow through the years until he is overtaken by senility. This may be partly custom; an oligarchy generally seeks leadership from a single individual, primus inter pares, from whom it can accept a verdict. However, it may also be because the General Secretary, although he is not free to remove persons at the top (even Stalin seems to have been restrained; he felt the need, near the end of his life, to blow up a security scandal to purge the Politburo) can place his friends and followers in high places.

There is no formal provision for replacing the top leader, but he must be acceptable to his colleagues on the Politburo. This probably means, among other things, that he must not seem dangerous. That neither Stalin nor Khrushchev seemed leading candidates for dictatorship was a major advantage for both in their climb to supreme power. Brezhnev apparently made a commitment, when Khrushchev was overthrown, to respect the Politburo. There has never been a designated successor, and under Brezhnev it has usually been unclear who—Kosygin, Podgorny, or Suslov—might be second in authority. Yet succession crises have been easily overcome because of the spirit of party unity.

How important decisions are reached is shrouded in a veil of secrecy which was only slightly lifted during the Khrushchev era (1953-1964) and since then has remained opaque and tight. Khrushchev's memoirs reveal a highly irregular and rather haphazard type of decision making, with little or no reference to general principles;[58] there seems also to be some jostling among various ministries and committees, with unclear lines of authority. Various actual or potential pressure groups have been cited as probably influencing decisions, chiefly the military or sections within the military, the police, the administrative bureaucrats, and the economic managers; but these are probably more potent in vetoing what they dislike than in pushing positive programs. The party leadership consults expert opinion on various matters, from foreign affairs specialists to economists and jurists; but there is no technocracy. The experts are used or disregarded as the political rulers prefer.

The principle of the party is unity, which must be maintained by the concentration of power. This implies the law of oligarchy, that it is impermissible to appeal to inferiors or outsiders. No faction in the party since 1918 has ever tried to strengthen its case by joining forces with any non-party group or by mustering support among workers or peasants. Any attempt to do so would be held treasonous to the party. It is likewise illicit to garner support among lower levels of the party, as Trotsky and Zinoviev tried to do in 1926-27. This means going outside and hence against the brotherhood. Since the party is structured for control strictly from the top down, it is even rather difficult for the man at the top of the apparatus to use his control of the base to remove his colleagues. Thus Stalin, although effectively boss of the party apparatus from 1924, did not get rid of Trotsky until the end of 1927. Khrushchev, despite his ability to name secretaries at lower levels, was unable to rid himself of persons he found inconvenient. Only in the beginning of 1964 could he secure expulsion from the party of Molotov and others who tried to remove him in 1957. On that occasion, Khrushchev transgressed the law of oligarchy by appealing to the Central Committee the decision of the Presidium (Politburo) majority to oust him—an action which seems to have taken them by surprise. It is thus dangerous to try to build up a power base outside the system—a sin which contributed to the downfall of many, such as Shelest, former Ukrainian boss.

The long indoctrination which party leaders have necessarily undergone is an essential factor in their willingness to follow the rules. Moreover, all persons in positions of authority owe everything to the party. For all who climb, the party must be virtually a purpose in itself, because the great qualification is dedication and loyalty. Status in the party means everything for those who would be insignificant without it, and the web of belonging is the more gripping because each layer of authority has its superiority over those below.

Even outside the web of Soviet controls, the sense of belonging is powerful; real Communists never broke away from the Comintern because of facts or the

---

[58] See Khrushchev, *Khrushchev Remembers* and *Khrushchev Remembers: The Last Testament.*

misery and terror rampant among the Soviet peoples, only because of doctrinal quarrels.[59] The rulership of the party-state is held together not only by shared ideology but by the sense of self-fulfillment of the self-chosen elite, this fraternity of the elect, whose commitment combines the features of a religious order and a secret society. Ordinary folk, too, are tied into the system. Many forms of participation help people identify with party and government, give a sense of belonging, and provide an outlet for energies and idealism.[60] Fear of disorder is widespread and people are grateful to authorities who establish order; some even seem to long for a return of Stalinist firmness to set the country aright.[61]

In sum, the Soviet party-centered system is extremely effective and for this reason has been copied by other Communist countries. Its principles of concentration of authority and leverage throughout society enable it to organize the energies of the people with remarkable efficiency so far as the elite is clear in its purposes. It is upon this basis that the Soviet party could, under Stalin, carry on virtual warfare against a large majority of the population and force through an industrialization program which for some years lowered real wages by nearly half. It is also for this reason that the Communist party is outstandingly powerful in the conduct of war.

Chinese Communism

Divergence

The two great autocratic empires of China and Russia were in many ways alike and consequently reacted similarly to intrusion of Western power and in their attempts to save the authoritarian society by reshaping it. But inherent differences eventually led the Chinese Communists to diverge from the Soviet model they had once uncritically accepted.

When the imperial regimes were falling apart, China was far poorer than Russia, the masses ignorant and near starvation. In China, there was practically no industrial proletariat, and the intelligentsia was both much smaller and less westernized than in tsarist Russia. Culture and mentality were (and remain) much more alien to the West. Europeans in the nineteenth century suspected the Russians of being Orientals beneath the surface, but they found the Chinese impenetrable. The Chinese mind has been frequently characterized as prone to

---

[59] Branko Lazitch, *Biographical Dictionary of the Comintern* (Stanford: Hoover Institution Press, 1973), pp. xiv–xv.

[60] Jerry Hough, "Political Participation in the Soviet Union," *Soviet Studies*, 28 (January 1976), p. 15.

[61] Hedrick Smith, *The Russians* (New York: Quadrangle/New York Times, 1976), pp. 245-246.

mystic reasoning, lacking a sense of individualism, basically indifferent to technology, and without feeling for long-range progress.[62] The Westerner who travels from Peking to Moscow finds himself halfway back home when he reaches Russia. The Chinese continue to have less respect for Western culture. An attack on Western classical music as "bourgeois" poison, such as the Chinese conducted in 1974 (chiefly but not entirely against Beethoven and Schubert),[63] would hardly be thinkable in the Soviet Union. The Chinese are apparently immune to the Russian passion for Western clothes, modish tunes, detective novels, etc.

A decisive factor of Chinese imperial civilization was its relative isolation by ocean, deserts, and mountains. Chinese culture remained almost completely indigenous, in marked contrast to constant and close Russian contact with the European state system and the Russian tradition of eager and often indiscriminate appropriation of Western culture. Just as nineteenth-century Chinese were half-hearted in their efforts to learn from the West, so has present-day Chinese Communism much less consistently striven to catch up materially, emphasizing instead self-reliance and typically Chinese answers.

The impact of the West on China was more humiliating than it ever was on Russia, and the breakdown of order in the decades following the fall of the dynasty was deeper. In this situation, leadership of the radical movement fell to men who (except Chou En-lai) had no direct experience of the West and limited knowledge of it—less than most Chinese intellectuals of their generation.[64] To make a radical revolution, rejecting both the injurious Western and the bankrupt native tradition, they needed a doctrine and a model, and they found what suited them in Soviet Russia. For this reason, and no other, they remained outwardly loyal to the Comintern which had proved its incapacity to guide them and to the Soviet state which, for its own purposes, helped the anti-Communist Nationalists.

The doctrine and the model also proved decisive when Mao achieved victory much sooner than Stalin (and probably than Mao) had expected; he and his fellows adopted the Soviet Union's "socialist" society as China's guide to Communism. Mao claimed to have felt his revolution to be an integral and subordinate part of the Soviet-led movement. In his version of a discussion with Stalin a few months after the proclamation of the People's Republic, he told Stalin, 'If I disagree with your proposal, I shall struggle against it. But if you really insist on it, then I shall accept it.' This was because I took into account the interests of socialism as a whole."[65]

---

[62] Cf. Lily Abegg, *The Mind of East Asia* (London: Thames and Hudson, 1952), *passim.*

[63] Cf. *New York Times*, January 15, 1975.

[64] Robert A. Scalapino, *Elites in the People's Republic of China* (Seattle: University of Washington Press, 1972), p. 74.

[65] Cited by John Gittings, "New Light on Mao: His View of the World," *China Quarterly*, no. 60 (October-December 1974), p. 759.

Adoption of the Russian Model. The entire structure of the new Chinese state was closely constructed after the Soviet pattern. Chinese pragmatism as well as lack of a true proletarian class led, however, to the state's being organized not as "Dictatorship of the Proletariat" but as a "People's Democratic Dictatorship," with the participation of a half-dozen subservient "parties" to represent various "classes" acceptable on the basis of their adherence to the revolution.[66] Perhaps in imitation of Soviet policies of the mid-1920s, commercial and industrial owners were treated relatively leniently; this was easier because the Chinese party from the first enjoyed popular support such as the Soviet did not obtain until World War II. But the Soviet organizational scheme of governing party, secretaries, committees, Politburo, etc. was adopted bodily. There were "parliamentary" bodies corresponding to soviets, a written constitution on the Soviet pattern, and pretensions to "socialist legality." In 1953–1954 Soviet-style general elections were held.[67] The former guerrilla army was reshaped in the Soviet image, professionalized with emphasis on technical proficiency, separated from the party and subordinated to it. The chief thrust of ideology was to follow the ways of the Soviet big brother, with loyal adherence to the Soviet line in world affairs and gratitude for Soviet assistance at home. Soviet engineers planned Chinese projects, and Chinese schoolchildren learned Russian and studied translated Soviet texts.

The Chinese took the Soviet economic model for granted and adopted it without discussion.[68] Land reform already underway in previously Communist-held areas was carried to completion throughout China by 1952, accompanied by the execution of a million or so landowners. Collectivization began immediately after land reform. It was more judiciously managed than Stalin's, with graduated steps, mutual aid teams, small and partial collectives weaning the peasants gradually from independent ways; but the goal was the same. By 1957, the Chinese masses had been brought into collective farms much like Soviet kolkhozes. The Soviet educational system was also copied as closely as feasible, with emphasis on the training of engineers and other experts. Rudimentary economic planning was begun immediately, and a five-year plan officially implemented in 1953, with heavy stress, in the Soviet fashion, on urban industry; only eight percent of investment was budgeted for agriculture, which occupied close to nine-tenths of the population.[69] The idea of economic incentives was also taken over, with salary differentials (excluding top ranks) of twenty to one.[70] Such policies were successful in that recovery and industrial

---

[66] Lucian W. Pye, *China: An Introduction* (Boston: Little, Brown, 1972), p. 186.
[67] L. La Dany, "Shrinking Political Life," *Problems of Communism*, 23, no. 5 (September-October 1974), 25-26.
[68] Alexander Eckstein, *China's Economic Development: The Interplay of Scarcity and Ideology* (Ann Arbor: University of Michigan Press, 1975), p. 14.
[69] Edgar Snow, *The Other Side of the River* (New York: Random House, 1971), p. 179.
[70] Klaus Mehnert, *China Returns* (New York: Dutton, 1972), p. 194.

growth were very rapid, at a yearly rate of 14 to 19 percent according to different figures.[71]

Chinese Communism Goes its Own Way. But imitation of the Soviet model was an aberration which could hardly outlast the period of China's weakness and uncertainty. A restored China would feel the confidence to go its own way; the completion of liberation of China from foreign domination meant independence of Russia also. The disappearance of Stalin also broke a link. Although he had been no benefactor of the Chinese—in fact he treated Mao very neglectfully during Mao's lengthy stay in Moscow shortly after coming to power—Stalin was the Comintern leader, comrade of Lenin, respected for three decades. Mao would defer to him but not to the secondary figures who followed. As the senior revolutionary and leader of a much larger party and people, he doubtless expected Khrushchev's deference; but Khrushchev regarded Mao as a simpleminded bumpkin.[72]

A turning point was the Twentieth Congress of the Soviet Party, February 1956, during which Khrushchev enunciated officially his line of Peaceful Coexistence and also made his famous secret denunciation of Stalin as a criminal paranoiac and bungler. Peaceful Coexistence was unacceptable because the Chinese saw their revolution still incomplete, with Taiwan requiring liberation; and the denunciation of Stalin both removed his name as a bond and implied condemnation of the Maoist cult of personality. Soviet prestige was further shaken by troubles in Hungary and Poland. Then Soviet economic aid to China dwindled, even as increasing amounts were being sent to non-Communist countries, including India. Worst was the termination of the Soviet nuclear assistance program, clearly showing that the Russians did not trust the Chinese brothers.

In striking out on its own road, however, Chinese Communism became unstable. The first independent experiment came in 1956-1957, when Mao opened up the "Hundred Flowers" period of "blooming and contending," a period of freedom of criticism quite contrary to Soviet style. Mao seems to have believed that the intellectuals would support him and his policies out of conviction while criticizing the party apparatus, but criticisms soon became deep and bitter.[73] The flowers were branded poisonous weeds and cut down in an Anti-Rightist Campaign, but there remained bad feelings on both sides. Mao was disillusioned with the ungrateful and conceited intellectuals (as he saw them) and resolved to turn to the masses; the intellectuals felt they had been deceived and continued sniping covertly so far as they were able during subsequent years.[74]

---

[71] Eckstein, *China's Economic Development*, p. 33.

[72] *Khrushchev Remembers: The Last Testament*, pp. 240, 257, 260.

[73] For the variety and depth of criticism, see René Goldman, "The Rectification Campaign at Peking University, May–June 1957," in MacFarquhar, ed., pp. 255-270.

[74] Lowell Dittmer, *Liu Shao-chi and the Chinese Cultural Revolution* (Berkeley: University of California Press, 1974), pp. 34, 64.

This failure hurt the influence of Mao, who always wished to be an ideological guide but had little taste for the administrative detail that assured Stalin his position in the Soviet party. In 1957, Mao's name was seldom mentioned in connection with current policies, and his opponents within the hierarchy sought to check him without attacking the symbol of the revolution. He in turn sought Soviet backing to regain power, but it was not forthcoming.[75] Mao countered the bureaucratic apparatus, which he could not manage, and also the Soviet style of Communism, by "placing politics in command" and leading China into the turmoil of a new "revolution from above," the People's Communes and the Great Leap Forward. The parallel to Stalin's launching of collectivization and the First Five-Year Plan as soon as Russia had recovered its pre-war economic level is striking.

Maoism and the Great Leap Forward. The People's Communes were announced as the social unit of the future in August 1958; by the end of that year, 740,000 collective farms had been joined into 26,000 giant communal organizations. These were both production units and local governments; they also represented a leap into the utopian society without private property, as it was proposed (and to some extent realized) that the tens of thousands of members should enjoy socialized meals, clothing, housing, entertainment, and haircuts; children would be raised in communal nurseries—a society organized as a giant military barracks. Members were to work together in the fields, on irrigation projects, and small-scale manufacturing. There were also experiments with urban communes, usually centered on factories.[76] They were designed rather for supplemental than for basic production, to make use of housewives and other persons not fully employed. They also tried to produce as much as possible of the cities' food on adjacent farmlands.[77]

Taking a leaf from the book of the nineteenth-century reformer Kang Yu-wei,[78] Mao thereby gave a slap to the Soviet Union. By revolutionary will and Maoist inspiration, China would leap forward to the higher level of social development while the Russians were lingering at the socialist stage of personal property and monetary incentives.

Mao also sought to demonstrate Chinese superiority by a Great Leap Forward in production. Thanks to leadership and indoctrination, the Chinese should work hard for no specific material reward[79] and do wonders far beyond Soviet laggards. Production of basic commodities was to rise at unheard of

---

[75] Franz Michael, "China after the Cultural Revolution," *Orbis*, 17, no. 2 (Summer 1973), 315.

[76] Cf. D. E. T. Luard, "The Urban Communes," *China Quarterly*, no. 3 (July-Stepember 1960), pp. 74-79.

[77] Ezra F. Vogel, *Canton under Communism* (New York: Harper & Row, 1974), p. 267.

[78] Immanuel C. Y. Hsü, *The Rise of Modern China* (New York: Oxford University Press, 1970), p. 753.

[79] Vogel, *Canton under Communism*, p. 246.

rates. Most famous were the small steel furnaces (in imitation of the Stalinist passion for steel) to be built by peasants in nearly every commune, which were to double, then to triple steel production in a single year. While the peasants were frantically making steel (and adjusting to life in the commune) they were also to produce two or three times as much grain by plowing deeper or planting closer, or mostly by trying harder. In part, it was a declaration of independence; when "politics take command," the party joining hands with the masses, China must be able to go forward without foreign—including Soviet—models. It was "walking on two legs," with rural industry, based on mass mobilization, supplementing modern industry, based on capital investment.

The Maoists also attempted to enroll all able-bodied adults in militias, partly for military but more for political and economic purposes. Ideology in these circumstances became dedication to the communal task, "work experience created in the cause of indigenous production."[80] A new equalitarianism gripped the land; cadres were supposed to go to and work with the peasants, and army officers were required, at least theoretically, to serve one month per year as ordinary soldiers. Colonels were to sweep the floors, and generals took orders from corporals.[81] Art, too, was made equalitarian; the peasants, including the illiterate, composed poems by thousands to exalt the revolution.[82]

By this turn to radicalism, China virtually completed its emancipation. For some years yet the Chinese (and the Russians) would pretend that their alliance was intact; the Chinese hesitated to separate themselves from the Communist movement and the Russians were reluctant to concede the loss of the biggest part of the Sino-Soviet bloc. But after 1958, the Soviet Union for the Chinese was rather a countermodel. In the summer of 1959, when Marshal P'eng tried to criticize Mao, it was a serious handicap for him that he had discussed his ideas with Soviet leaders.[83]

The Cultural Revolution and Recession of Maoism

Statistics purporting incredible advances poured out of China, and the leaders seem to have believed at first—as they led many abroad to believe—that the People's Communes and the Great Leap Forward were an enormous success. But the capacity for mobilization had much outstripped the capacity for rational

---

[80] W. L. Rensselaer, in *Ideology and Politics in Contemporary China*, Chalmers A. Johnson, ed. (Seattle: University of Washington Press, 1973), p. 313.

[81] Ellis Joffe, "The Conflict between the Old and New in the Chinese Army," in *China under Mao*, MacFarquhar, ed., p. 52.

[82] S. H. Chen, "Multiplicity in Uniformity: Poetry and the Great Leap Forward," *China Quarterly*, no. 3 (July-September 1960), p. 4.

[83] David A. Charles, "The Dismissal of Marshal P'eng Teh-huai," in *China under Mao*, MacFarquhar, ed., pp. 28-33.

direction.[84] The statistics reflected wishes, and production sank in confusion and disorder. The communes were loosened, returning the management of production to "brigades," practically equivalent to the previous collectives. Communal consumption was largely replaced by pay, and peasants were allowed garden plots, the produce of which they could sell. Urban communes faded away. To feed the country, priority was given to agriculture, and industrial development languished. Ideological mobilization was largely replaced by banal economic incentives.

Mao and the Bureaucrats. Although it was never admitted that the campaign was less than successful, the debacle was a severe blow to its chief architect, Mao. Liu Shao-chi, who took Mao's former post as head of state (Mao remaining party chairman) in April 1959, and Teng Hsiao-ping, leader of the party secretariat, seemed to be in charge in an era of pragmatic retreat. There was no desire to remove Mao, the symbolic leader and ideologist of the revolution; but he was divorced from active policy making and was subjected to criticism as a poor administrator. Mao spent much time away from the capital in semi-retirement, making pronouncements from time to time which the bureaucracy was likely to ignore as soon as he withdrew.[85]

In August 1959, at a party gathering, the minister of defense, Marshal P'eng Te-huai, ventured a serious and far-reaching criticism of Mao's leadership, perhaps intending his removal from active politics. In this, Marshal P'eng had probably been encouraged by the precedent of the Hundred Flowers; he had also conferred widely before mustering the courage to attack the Chairman. But Mao was still the center of the system. He demanded that the party support him, and it felt compelled to do so. P'eng was ousted as military chief and replaced by the most fervent of Maoists, Lin Piao.[86] Lin proceeded to politicize and indoctrinate the army, raising Mao above the party.

P'eng, however, received widespread sympathy as symbol of rational discontent. The result was a deeper division between the increasingly settled bureaucratic party and state apparatus on one side and Mao supported by the military on the other. The burgeoning and solidifying bureaucracy was increasingly unsympathetic to Mao's populist revolutionary romanticism, while Mao saw "revisionist" and "bourgeois" tendencies as the apparatus reverted toward traditional Chinese ways and a new educated elite grew up to rule the masses. Hence there were covert criticisms of Mao over several years,[87] while Mao in semi-retirement, surrounded by relatives and acolytes, became increasingly impatient with the party majority. He was especially disappointed in the lack of revolutionary fervor of the Communist Youth League, the prospective leaders of the future.

---

[84] Vogel, *Canton under Communism*, p. 353.

[85] Dittmer, *Liu Shao-chi*, pp. 49-50.

[86] A. Doak Barnett, *Uncertain Passage: China's Transition to the Post-Mao Era* (Washington, D.C.: Brookings Institution, 1974), p. 197.

[87] Hsü, *Rise of Modern China*, p. 771.

For several years there was a covert running battle between Mao, who could not manage the bureaucracy, and the bureaucrats who wanted freedom to run the country but who could not well do without Mao. A showdown came in 1966, perhaps basically because of tensions rising out of the escalation of the Vietnam war after February 1965. The Chinese thought they were the real targets and were divided on how to respond. Some, including Liu Shao-chi, wanted to restore the Soviet alliance and on this basis to come to the assistance of North Vietnam; others, including Mao, feared that a joint war with the Soviet Union would be as dangerous as fighting alone and wanted rather to mobilize the people and prepare for guerrilla war if necessary.[88]

The Cultural Revolution. The underlying cause of Mao's wrath and the years of turmoil, however, was his sensitivity to criticism. A play entitled "The Dismissal of Hai Jui from Office" dealt with the unjust discharge of a faithful minister by a capricious emperor; any knowing Chinese, in view of the custom of pointing morals by historical examples and the obvious allusions in the drama[89] would understand that it referred to Mao's ouster of Marshal P'eng. Mao saw a conspiracy of propaganda against him aided and abetted by the high circles.[90] His aim consequently became to attack the "bourgeois superstructure" in the party, reform it as Lin had reformed the army,[91] turn back the process of degenerative institutionalization, and reinvigorate the revolution.

Therewith began one of the most amazing episodes of history, wherein an autocrat called in the popular masses to put down, to discipline if not destroy, the apparatus of government over which he presided—a dangerous plan that might well cost him his rulership. Unable to publish his damnation of the offending author in Peking, Mao launched his campaign in Shanghai. In the spring of 1966, assured of army support, the Maoist-army forces gained control of the *People's Daily* and other important papers. In a propagandistic overkill, a three-week period saw 4,000 articles attacking the hapless playwright.[92] In July, the 72-year-old Mao was reported to have swum nine miles in the Yangtze at a speed worthy of Superman. Simultaneously, attacks on party leaders multiplied and became both harsher and more direct as the instigators behind the offending intellectuals were ferreted out—ultimately the top managers in the party, Liu Shao-chi and Teng Hsiao-ping.

What Mao may have proposed at this juncture is unclear, since there is no evidence that the Great Proletarian Cultural Revolution was planned in advance. But Mao called upon forces as he found convenient. Like Marcuse and the New

---

[88] William F. Dorrill, "Power, Policy, and Ideology in the Making of the Chinese Cultural Revolution," in *The Cultural Revolution in China*, Thomas W. Robinson, ed. (Berkeley: University of California Press, 1971), p. 73.

[89] James P. Harrison, *The Long March to Power: A History of the Chinese Communist Party 1921-72* (New York: Praeger, 1972) p. 484.

[90] Edgar Snow, *The Long Revolution* (New York: Vintage Books, 1971), p. 86.

[91] A. Doak Barnett, *Uncertain Passage*, p. 77.

[92] Dittmer, *Liu Shao-chi*, p. 75.

Left, and presumably aware of the student revolts flaring up in the U. S., Japan, and Western Europe, Mao saw the students as a revolutionary force.[93] "It is right to rebel," Mao pronounced; and he urged, "Bombard the headquarters." They responded enthusiastically.[94] In August 1966, Mao put on a red armband and publicly joined the Red Guards that were springing up among students and other youth everywhere.

Schools were closed (even elementary schools for some months) and millions of young people were set to parading, shouting, marauding, and making pseudo-revolution. Railroads were largely devoted to transporting them; about 10 million travelled to Peking in the months after August to catch a distant glimpse of the godlike figure.[95] They were the principal instrument of Mao's power in those first years of the Cultural Revolution, since they could be sent to humiliate or drive anyone from office and the apparatus found it very difficult to resist them because they were acting in the name of the sacred and irreplaceable leader, for a time with the support of the army.

Liu Shao-chi and his principal aides were accused of treason or favoring the restoration of capitalism; and Mao invoked popular hostility to the Soviet Union to assail his opponents, who mostly favored cooperation with that country. Eventually about half the top elite was forced from office,[96] and the Politburo ceased to function. In the provinces, the party and most of the state structures were wiped out in the disorders. It was speculated that the party might be abolished altogether.[97] Trade unions and other party-led mass organizations also became inoperative, and economic planning ceased. Many latent conflicts, such as between local organizations and the center or between workers and students, surfaced in the turmoil.[98] Extremism and xenophobia reaching a fever pitch during the war in Vietnam, China virtually cut itself off from the outside world; foreign embassies were assaulted and Chinese ambassadors recalled.

The Cultural Revolution seemed to be a confession of failure in that Maoists found so many "representatives of the bourgeoisie" and "capitalist-roaders" in the party, government, and army, which Mao had set up and presided over for many years, and so many "bourgeois intellectuals" after endless rectifications. Yet it had the underlying purpose, like the Great Leap Forward and the

---

[93] David Milton, Nancy Milton, and Frank Schurmann, eds. *People's China: Social Experimentation, Politics, Entry onto the World Scene, 1966-1971* (New York: Random House, 1974), p. 16.

[94] William Hinton, *Hundred Day War: The Cultural Revolution at Tsinghua University* (New York: Monthly Review Press, 1972), p. 20. For a discussion of the Cultural Revolution, see also, C. L. Chiou, *Maoism in Action: The Cultural Revolution* (New York: Crane, Russak, 1974).

[95] Hinton, *Hundred Day War*, p. 63.

[96] James R. Townsend, *Politics in China* (Boston: Little, Brown, 1974), p. 135.

[97] Harrison, *The Long March*, p. 489.

[98] Alan P. L. Liu, *Political Culture and Group Conflict in Communist China* (Santa Barbara: Clio Press, 1976), *passim*.

People's Communes, of raising China to a higher level of social perfection. It was "cultural" not only in the sense of attacking writers and intellectuals but also in seeking to make the New Man without greed or pride. The people were immersed in Mao Thought as no country had ever been submerged in the image and doctrines of a single man. He was venerated like a deity; it was ritual to open meetings with a Mao saying and wishes of long life to the Chairman.[99] Nonpolitical journals were closed, no books but Mao's works were printed, and for a time no others were to be had except for a few textbooks.[100]

In another sense, the Cultural Revolution was an attempt to revive the past, the heroic and inspiring times of pure Communist spirit when young Mao and his comrades were conducting a holy war from the caves of Yenan.[101] China should use its ingenuity to achieve self-sufficiency as the Red Army did in those glorious days; everyone should be wholly dedicated to the cause as those brave soldiers had been. Even Mao's model for education reverted to the university set up there thirty years before.[102] Mao, who had come to greatness in revolution, saw revolution as the means to attack those who opposed him; and he sought remission from the inexorable decrepitude of his revolution by leadership in something which could be called a new "revolution."

Mao apparently thought that by direct contact with the people, incorporated in the Red Guards, he could rule better than through the "revisionist" party apparatus. Naively enough, it was proposed to make cities into giant communes in imitation of the Paris Commune celebrated by Marx and Engels. But efforts to do this failed quickly.[103]

The results must have been the greatest disappointment of the Great Helmsman's long career. He and what there was of a Maoist government, with the Central Cultural Revolution Committee headed by Mao's secretary, Ch'en Po-ta and Mao's wife, former actress Chiang Ch'ing, had little control over the multitudes who waved Little Red Books and fought one another; at one time, the Maoist center controlled only about a third of China.[104] In the loosening of authority, much anti-Communist feeling showed itself. And the Cultural Revolution accomplished very little. It was finally necessary to bring in the People's Liberation Army to restore order, and to establish Revolutionary Committees under military auspices to govern the country.

In the fall of 1968, after the Soviet Union had occupied another dissident Communist country, Czechoslovakia, the Red Guards were finally suppressed

---

[99] Edward E. Rice, *Mao's Way* (Berkeley: University of California Press, 1972), p. 497.

[100] Snow, *Long Revolution*, p. 25.

[101] *Ibid.*, p. 19.

[102] Hinton, *Hundred Day War*, p. 21.

[103] Stanley Kamow, *Mao and China: From Revolution to Revolution* (New York: Viking Press, 1972), p. 286; Franz Michael, "China after the Cultural Revolution: The Unresolved Succession Crisis," *Orbis*, 17, no. 2 (Summer 1973), 319–320.

[104] Hsü, *Rise of Modern China*, p. 776.

as a political force—Mao seemingly having decided they too were in reality "bourgeois."[105] Thereafter the Mao cult was gradually eased. From late 1970, universities began to reopen with simplified work-and-learning courses for youths with work or military experience. Rebuilding of the party commenced and nearly all the victims of the Cultural Revolution—95 to 98 percent—were reinstated.[106] The party was again recognized as a "vanguard, " necessary to run the country.

As the rule of the military diminished after 1970, Marshal Lin Piao, consecrated in 1966 as Mao's second in command and successor, lost stature. As the result of an obscure intrigue, he was killed, apparently in September 1971; and a number of his associates were purged. Thereafter, governing institutions increasingly reverted to old forms. It was said that there must be more and more "revolution" on the way to communism, but this echo of the turbulence also slowly receded.

The practical end of the Mao era came with the Tenth Party Congress, August 1973. Chou En-lai, who had been at Mao's side since 1933, ran the show; Mao was not reported to have spoken. In 1974, there was an extended anti-Confucius, anti-Lin Piao campaign, possibly to vacate the sage's throne for the benefit of Mao; but the affair petered out with a puzzling lack of results.[107] In January 1975, a new People's Congress convened in secret, under a giant portrait of Mao but without his participation, to adopt a new constitution reaffirming the supremacy of the party and consecrating such non-Maoist principles as payment according to work.[108] Teng Hsiao-ping, second highest target of the Cultural Revolution, who had resurfaced in 1973, was given status immediately behind Chou. His famous un-Maoist aphorism was, "It doesn't matter whether a cat is black or white as long as it catches mice."

Thereafter the living Mao (81 and senile at the beginning of 1975) became a godlike figure with limited influence on current political happenings. His instructions or supposed instructions were cited from time to time by the radicals, led or supported by his wife, Chiang Ch'ing; but they did little more than maintain a degree of uncertainty. As long as Chou lived, he and his protege Teng were able to manage the state in non-Maoist fashion while praising Mao. But the old conflicts of ideology versus expertise in education[109] and in the economy, economic versus moral incentives, modernization versus thought reform, etc., remained unresolved. It was a strange situation resulting from the senile leader's obsession with revolutionary romanticism when the revolution had long since been laid to rest.

---

[105] Hinton, *Hundred Day War*, p. 68.

[106] Snow, *Long Revolution*, p. 13; Frederick C. Teiwes, "Before and After the Cultural Revolution," *China Quarterly*, no. 58 (April-June 1974), p. 33.

[107] Chiou, *Maoism in Action*, p. 122.

[108] Chün-tu Hsieh, "The New Constitution," *Problems of Communism*, 24, no. 3 (May-June 1975), 11.

[109] Parris Chang, "Mao's Last Stand," *Problems of Communism*, 25 (July–August 1976), 7-9.

Chou, however, died in January 1976; and without the backing of his prestige Teng was attacked by the radicals as a "capitalist roader in the party" and replaced by a virtual unknown entirely without revolutionary glory, chief of the security forces Hua Kuo-feng. On September 9, the Chinese fifth of humanity was grief-stricken by the announcement of the departure of the great helmsman. The moderates, headed by Hua, emerged in control. It seemed that the office of Chairman might be left vacant, at least for a decent period of mourning—many a high office had gone unfilled for months or years—but Hua was elevated to the post in less than a month. Immediately thereafter, the Shanghai radicals Chiang Ch'ing, Wang Hung-wen, recently named second-ranking member of the Politburo, Yao-Wen-yuan, national propaganda chief, and Chang Ch'un Ch'iao, vice premier, reportedly schemed a coup.[110] But they were arrested and vilified as the "gang of four." Madame Mao was accused of nagging her husband, then of having hastened his death; the equalitarian radicals were portrayed as hypocrites wallowing in private luxury. In the following months, the sins of the radicals and the damage they had allegedly done to the Chinese economy were the principal theme of the Chinese press, even of kindergarten songs. Quotations of Mao were used chiefly to legitimate the new leadership, while the country moved away from Maoist revolutionary romanticism. Production was given priority over ideology, plays banned by Chiang Ch'ing were put on the stage, contacts with the outside world were slightly liberalized, and the government settled down to the difficult task of ruling China.

The Chinese Deviation

The outcome of the Cultural Revolution demonstrated that Chinese Communism could not be reformulated in a mode so very different from the despised Soviet model as Mao desired. It seemed necessary, in order to govern, to revert to institutions basically rather similar to those of the Soviet party-state. It seems clear that the general resemblance of Chinese Communism to the Soviet pattern is due to the imperatives of total rulership. The Chinese system, like the Soviet, is characterized by party direction, military influence, pseudo-democratic institutions, popular participation in execution of party policies, overt equalitarianism, controlled economy, ideology, and mind control.

Role of the Military. Differing personalities, history, and background, however, have brought about different emphases. One is the larger role of the military in Chinese politics. Mao built up his movement as a fighting party or ideological army while Lenin spent the years prior to 1917 as an exile politician in European cafes. It was the army, not the party, that made the Chinese revolution. If prior to 1949 army and party were almost indistinguishable, in

---

[110] *New York Times*, November 9, 1976, p. 9.

the first years after the take-over army and state were indissoluble. *The People's Daily*, July 1, 1950, pointed out that about a million party members had lived on rations without pay. "In other words, they have led a life of strictly military communism," making them "the most outstanding members of the working class."[111] Civilian rule was fairly effective by 1954, but after 1960 the People's Liberation Army was apparently more effective in propaganda than civilian agencies.[112]

In 1964-1965, Lin reversed the conventional Communist Party infiltration of the military by placing military men into regional bureaus of the party.[113] In the Cultural Revolution, the army was Mao's only reliable support. It again became practically synonymous with the government, and military leaders came to head many or most local party bodies and to occupy a majority of places on the Central Committee. The army participated in many construction projects, state farms, schools, and so forth. Army companies were assigned to work regularly with commune production brigades. As Chou En-lai remarked, "We are all connected with the army."[114]

The end of the Cultural Revolution signalled a reduction in the role of the military. At the Tenth Party Congress, in August 1973, the military contingent of the Central Committee was pared from 56% to 41%, and in the Politburo from 44% to 32%. Generals advanced during the Cultural Revolution were shifted around. The military budget, after reaching a peak in 1970-71, declined according to American estimates about 25% during the next few years.[115]

The army continued, however, to play a significant role. In one instance, more than 10,000 troops were sent into the factories of Hangchow to aid the workers and quell unrest.[116] The party and military bureaucracies seem to merge both at top and bottom, and control is exercised through the party-military hierarchy as well as through the party chain of command.[117] The generals seem to have been largely responsible for the defeat of the radicals after the death of Mao, and they have had a very large role in the government headed by Chairman Hua.

Propaganda has been strikingly military in tone. "Chairman Mao's military writings ... are our Party's treasured theoretical wealth ..."[118] The people are called upon, typically, to "concentrate superior force to destroy the enemy

---

[111] Robert Conquest, *Where Marx Went Wrong* (London: Tom Stacey, 1970), pp. 55-56.

[112] Parris H. Chang, "The Changing Patterns of Military Participation in Chinese Politics," *Orbis*, 24, no. 3 (Fall 1972), 780-802.

[113] Hsü, *Rise of Modern China*, p. 774.

[114] Snow, *Long Revolution*, p. 99.

[115] *New York Times*, July 16, 1975, p. 3.

[116] *New York Times*, July 29, 1975, p. 6.

[117] Harry W. Nelson, "Military Bureaucracy in the Cultural Revolution," *Asian Survey*, 14, no. 4 (April 1974), 373.

[118] *Peking Review*, September 20, 1974, p. 9.

one by one";[119] they should "obey orders in all our actions, march in step to win victory."[120] The virtues stressed are Spartan loyalty, determination, dedication, abstinence, and self-sacrifice. "Nothing is hard if you dare scale the heights."[121]

The Party. As the role of the army is proportionately greater, so that of the party is less. The Soviets make a great deal of the history of the party to teach its younger members; the Chinese, on the other hand, have a history of twenty years of heroic fighting. Unlike the Soviet party, the Chinese have no formal program, only whatever may be understood by Mao Tse-tung Thought. The party structure has been much less fixed in China. Party congresses have followed at long intervals: 1945, 1956, 1969, and in Mao's senescence, in 1973. There is little pretense of election from the bottom up in the Chinese party; the rules (as also the constitution) speak rather of election through "democratic consultation."[122] Mao has been able to act against or outside the party as even Stalin could or did not, and in the Cultural Revolution the party was quite set aside. The Chinese have been less impressed than the Soviets with the logic of party control over and separate from government administration, and the hierarchies have been fused at lower levels.[123]

The party could not function so effectively in China as in the Soviet Union because its symbolic and ideological head was unprepared to manage its administration—in sharp contrast to Stalin's willingness, which contributed greatly to his mastery—but rather opposed the high party oligarchs. The Chinese, moreover, do not seem to have been so obsessed with the necessity for unity as the Russians, perhaps because of the absence of important minority divisions. Consequently, there has been a certain un-Soviet and un-Communist looseness and factionalism, and China has for decades seen public expressions of political differences like those that occurred in the Soviet party after Lenin's death in the period from 1924 to 1927. Divisions have centered on Kao Kang, Marshal P'eng, President Liu, Marshal Lin, and others, and Mao's call to revolution against the party was itself the greatest expression of the freedom of faction. In 1976, Teng Hsiao-ping, who had been the acting head of the administration and remained vice-premier, was accused publicly of trying to reverse the cultural revolution and of mocking the proletarian dramas patronized by Mrs. Mao.

The fact that the Chinese party, with its war-forged unity, has never had major blood purges has doubtless made discipline less thorough. From time to time personages have been ousted, but only a few have been executed. In the Soviet Union, moreover, those who are disgraced never return to power. 1975,

---

[119] *Peking Review*, December 27, 1974, p. 5.

[120] *Renmin Ribao*, editorial, *Peking Review*, July 5, 1974, p. 8.

[121] *Peking Review* headline, January 2, 1976, p. 8.

[122] Harold C. Hinton, *An Introduction to Chinese Politics* (New York: Praeger, 1973), p. 158.

[123] Barnett, *Uncertain Passage*, p. 54.

however, saw T'eng working closely with Chang Chun-chiao, who had denounced him in violent terms eight years earlier, and Lo Jui-ching, first prominent victim of the Cultural Revolution, was back in a key position.

In the governmental sphere China has tended to swing between centralization and decentralization, the latter prevailing since 1959. The communes
are permitted much more control over their resources than are Soviet local administrations, and Chinese economic planning has been relatively loose. In 1971
it was reported that each of the 2,000 hsien of China was given the task of self-
sufficiency in food and light industry.[124]

Chinese practice seems in general to be more irregular than Soviet. Thus,
there hardly exist codes to guide criminal courts, there are no set sentences, no
lawyers in court, and only the most informal trials, at which the judge hears the
voice of the "masses." Though the Chinese wrote a requirement for general
elections into their constitution, they have held them only once; the Soviets
perform the ritual regularly at the prescribed intervals. The Supreme Soviet
dutifully meets to rubberstamp policies twice a year; the Chinese People's
Congress of January 1975 (chosen by means entirely undivulged) was the first
in ten years. Many positions have been left vacant for many years, including the
headship of state from 1966 to 1975. The whole machine has thus been less
strictly orchestrated than is the Soviet style. Quite aside from the anarchy of
the Cultural Revolution, the campaign against Confucius and Lin Piao came
across differently in different provinces, and posters at times appeared berating
bureaucrats, who would then proceed to tear them down. From time to time
there are campaigns, such as the criticism of the old novel *Water Margins*, the
thrust of which is unclear to outsiders.

The security forces are invisible, perhaps because the neighborhood committees make them superfluous. People frequently ignore the law in minor
ways—peasants sell private produce openly and traffic is much less disciplined
than in the Soviet Union. Infractions may be leniently treated; a party document took up the problem of absentee managers as follows: "The leading cadres
who left their posts without permission must return to work within two weeks
after this notice is reported to them. If they don't do so, their salary will be
suspended. If after that they still don't return, they may be severely disciplined
by the masses or dismissed."[125]

Equalitarianism. The relative slackness of administrative controls obviously
reflects a greater faith in the people and less emphasis on the party as an elite.
This implies a good deal more involvement of ordinary people in the work of
government than in Russia. The average citizens are not consulted on higher
matters, and workers' councils have no substantial authority, but the party is

---

[124] Rice, *Mao's Way*, p. 481.
[125] *New York Times*, May 15, 1974.

supposed to listen. Brigades and factory groups seem to elect their own leaders, although they are not likely to promote anyone unacceptable to higher-ups.

The ordinary workers are also credited with great qualities—perhaps a virtue of necessity since China has so many. In Maoism, technology should not be a matter for the experts, much less a foreign import, but of and by the masses. In the language of revolutionary reversal, "The lowly are most intelligent; the elite are most ignorant."[126]

The workers are wise, and manual labor is educational and uplifting. There have been many rules that managers, cadres, and officers share the life of their underlings for a certain fraction of the time, perhaps one day per week or one month per year. Whether effective or not, this is quite out of the vision of Soviet Communism. It is likewise equalitarian, distressfully so to many, that urban young people, millions yearly, have been sent to live in peasant communes, for the most part permanently.[127] This is in line with the Marxist desire to bring city and countryside closer together. Both are supposed to profit; urbanites get peasant values and peasants learn from educated youths. They are sent away with festivities and applause,[128] but many try to slip back to the cities and form a disaffected and possibly lawless sector.

Equalitarianism, it may be noted, does not mean freedom; as usual in communal societies, duties are imperative. The Chinese rely mostly on group pressure. Everyone belongs to a party-controlled organization, and what anyone does is everyone's business, in the most neighborly fashion. Controls thus depend to a great extent on the general populace, under the guidance of the authorities—a goal toward which Khrushchev was heading but from which his successors have retreated.

Duty correspondingly is to the people, first of all to the largest collective, the whole of China, last of all to one's personal welfare. To serve the people is a better destiny than to get a higher education.[129] Mao, who once prepared to be a teacher and regarded himself as such,[130] wished to rule by moral suasion, in the manner traditionally deemed virtuous for Chinese emperors. No country has been more propagandized everywhere and at all times; the large loudspeaker has dominated the village, the political meeting occupying countless afterwork hours.

The Importance of "Correct Thinking." A merciful implication of the emphasis on persuasion is that deviants are not to be punished (except as a last

---

[126] Quotation from Mao, *Peking Review*, June 21, 1974, p. 11.

[127] Parris H. Chang, "China's Rustication Movement," *Current History*, 69 (September 1975), 85-89.

[128] *New York Times*, November 7, 1973, p. 5.

[129] Moral of a reportage, "The Countryside is a University, Too," *Chinese Literature* (April 1974), pp. 69-80.

[130] Snow, *Long Revolution*, p. 71.

resort) but remoulded; "thought reform" or "brainwashing" is a Chinese Communist specialty.[131] This may be regarded either as a sophisticated method of depersonalization or as political psychotherapy; the Chinese speak positively of cleansing the mind of filth. The method, originally developed in the guerrilla war to convert captured soldiers to the cause of the people, relies on isolation of the individual, endless repetition, and pressure, preferably from friends and associates. The errant individual must be brought to see the errors of past thinking until he is overwhelmed by feelings of guilt and shame, and so is led to thorough, presumably enthusiastic acceptance of the correct views and reintegration into the group on a new ideological basis. The process has been considered especially necessary for intellectuals.

Faith in such remoulding has made it possible in China, as not in the Soviet Union, for persons found guilty of grave errors to return after a time to high positions. Communist China has never known the hecatombs of Soviet Russia, and the percentage of the population in forced labor, probably never over two million,[132] has been trivial by Soviet standards. There was murderous cruelty only in the early anti-landlord campaigns, presumably a reflection of the peasant prejudices of the party; but even these executions took only a tiny proportion of the population in comparison with Stalin's liquidation of "kulaks." It was not deemed necessary to destroy the other old propertied classes, only to complete their reeducation.

The Chinese Reinterpretation of Marxism. But if correct thinking is all-important, Marxist class analysis has certainly been drained of content. De facto, Marx and Lenin saw attitudes as much more crucial than the economic class origins which theoretically should determine outlooks. Both readily accepted adherents of capitalist background (such as Engels) and damned workers who rejected their politics. But the Chinese Communists have gone further. In the first place, "bourgeois" and "proletarian" were made equivalent simply to "rich" and "poor," and divested entirely of their relationship to the means of production as in classical Marxism.[133] More significantly, "class" standing was made dependent on mentality; in practice, a "proletarian" was one of "proletarian" or popular consciousness, loyal and unselfish; a "capitalist" was a selfish person attached to past or elitist ways.

In this view, the victory of socialism did not mean the end of conflict since backward, "bourgeois" tendencies persist indefinitely. Despite emphasis on ideas and ideology, Maoism has remained inchoate as a creed, inconstant and poorly integrated. It lacks the coherent scholasticism of Marxism-Leninism;

---

[131] Cf. Robert J. Lifton, "Peking's 'Thought Reform'—Group Psychotherapy to Save Your Soul," in *Communist China: Revolutionary Reconstruction and Internal Confrontation*, Franz Schurmann and Orville Schell, eds. (New York: Random House, 1969), pp. 137–147. Also Bao Ruo-wong (Jean Pasqualini), *Prisoner of Mao* (New York: Coward, McCann and Geohegan, 1973).

[132] Hinton, *Introduction to Chinese Politics*, p. 212.

[133] Hsiung, *Ideology and Practice*, p. 58.

Chinese "reeducation" is character training, improvement of attitudes, by talk or by labor with the peasants, based on nothing so sophisticated as Soviet "dialectical materialism." It is more like Confucianist exhortation mixed with folk wisdom and maxims derived from party and guerrilla experience than a Marxist analysis.

Marxism has also been sinicized by the infusion of a great deal of nationalism, anti-Westernism, and Chinese pride. Offended pride was prominent, if not dominant, in the psychology which led to acceptance of Communism, and the revolutionaries exalted haughtiness toward Western powers. The Soviet Union took the place of the U. S. as chief enemy, presumably because there is much more apparent danger of attack from Russia, perhaps also because the Russians were so much in evidence in China during the first decade of Communist power. But Chinese propaganda has continued to lash both superpowers. This reaction is more Chinese than Communist. Overseas Chinese, who are mostly merchants and totally at odds with Peking on economic class grounds, are expected to sympathize and in fact to a large extent do so, finding satisfaction in Communist achievements. According to *Peking Review*, Chinese in ports where a new Chinese-built ship touched were moved to tears; its success allegedly conformed to "not only the common will of the working class and other revolutionaries but the common aspiration of tens of millions of Chinese living abroad."[134] A corollary is self-reliance, a doctrine central to the Yenan tradition. It is reflected in unwillingness, until recently, to accept commercial credits from Western countries.

Marxism in Mao's thinking became part of the moral drama of Chinese history. Mao was the sage philosopher-king of Chinese legend, the lofty figure who would come down from time to time to set his servants right and give them new instructions. In his works, Mao made ample use of historical examples and precedents.[135] He linked his revolution to previous Chinese revolutions, and he seemed to see himself as successor on a higher plane to the great unifier of China in the third century B.C., the First Emperor, of whom he was an admirer as a boy.[136] As he said in 1969, "If you denounce us for being Ch'in Shih Huang, for being autocrats, we admit everything."[137] It did not matter if Ch'in Shih Huang employed harsh methods in remaking China; " 'Burning books and burying Confucian scholars alive' was, in nature, a progressive measure ..."[138]

There emerged a confused ideological picture. Making the peasants the basic revolutionary force was in accord with the traditional Chinese, not the Marxist scheme of history. Thus Chinese history had to be mangled to squeeze

---

[134] *Peking Review*, November 29, 1974, p. 24.

[135] Stuart R. Schram, "Mao Tse-tung: A Self-Portrait," *China Quarterly*, no. 57 (January-March 1974), p. 164.

[136] Rice, *Mao's Way*, p. 5.

[137] Cited by Schram, "Mao Tse-tung," p. 162.

[138] *Peking Review*, May 10, 1974, p. 27.

it into the Marxist framework; the Chinese had to see their own country as archetypical of the Marxist historical sequence.[139]

The key ideological focus was clearly the people, but this was in itself ambiguous. At one time they were all those who opposed the Japanese; subsequently, those who cooperated in the building of socialism; in the Cultural Revolution they were hardly more than those who loyally supported Chairman Mao. Two such disparate characters as Liu Shao-chi and Lin Piao were lumped together as "restorers of capitalism." Before coming to power, Mao spoke of the factory proletariat as the leading class, when it comprised only one-half of one percent of the population,[140] but he looked to the "lumpenproletariat" (ricksha men, street cleaners, etc.) as likely allies,[141] in contravention to Marx's scorn for this "scum". He listed no less than thirteen "classes" comprising Chinese society.[142] All this does not imply that Mao was alien to the spirit of Marx. He was perhaps not far wrong when he said, "Marxism consists of thousands of truths, but they all boil down to one sentence, 'It is right to rebel.'"[143]

Chinese Communism on Balance. While Communism is exalted as a new and higher stage of Chinese history, its overall result has been an extraordinary narrowing and compression of the Chinese mind. If Western music has been held imperialist (although sometimes heard), Soviet is revisionist, and traditional Chinese feudal. In Mao's words, there were "only two kinds of knowledge, knowledge of the struggle for production and knowledge of the class struggle,"[144] and the latter is preferred. "Red" is better than "expert," or more necessary, and "expert" has a connotation of foreignness. Virtue should of itself beget influence and power, in the Confucian way. Education has hence not fared very well, particularly in and after the Cultural Revolution. Seven or eight university graduating classes were lost, a luxury for a nation that would share the benefits of modern technology.

The Chinese mind has been cut off very largely from the present as well as past, from Chinese as well as foreign information. The authorities are much warier than even the Soviets of casual contacts between unofficial or unprepared Chinese and foreigners. Sympathetic students from abroad find themselves isolated in the Chinese university. News from the outside world is skimpy and selective; if Chinese citizens know that astronauts ever walked on the moon, it is not by official design. Of domestic affairs, practically no statistics have been published since 1960, only occasional claims of increases of production or local

---

[139] Harold Kahn and Albert Feuerwerker, "The Ideology of Scholarship: China's New Historiography," *The China Quarterly*, 22 (April-June 1965), 2-10.

[140] Mao Tse-tung, *Selected Readings*, p. 17.

[141] *Ibid.*, p. 18.

[142] *Ibid.*, p. 45.

[143] From 1959 speech on Stalin's birthday, in *People's China*, D. Milton, N. Milton, and F. Schurmann, eds., p. 239.

[144] Mao Tse-tung, *Selected Readings*, p. 124.

triumphs.[145] Even successes may be shrouded; in 1974 the Chinese made known the completion in 1962 of a major hydro project on the Yellow River.[146] Population figures are uncertain by a hundred million or more. Not only are the workings of politics kept under cover; the organizational structures of the party and government and the occupants of leading positions are largely secret from the Chinese people.

Under these circumstances, the balance sheet can only be regarded as mixed. Chinese Communism has achieved its twin goals of organizing and inspiring the masses, but it has fallen far short of the technological advances it overtly despised. Where there had been near chaos, it established order and unity. It restored the self-respect of the nation, making China respected militarily and politically. With the same controls which enabled them to put some 800 million people in near-uniform, it has done much for basic welfare, eliminating or much reducing the extreme poverty that formerly beset a large part of the population. It provided some kind of health care for the masses who formerly had none. It made heroes of common peasants and gave this formerly degraded class cause for pride in its achievements. It has made at least a modicum of education available to the formerly illiterate masses.

The Chinese Communists impressed visitors by their handling of the population problem. Chinese cities, unlike those of most poorer countries, had no huge shantytowns filled with peasants streaming in to urban life. There was no unemployment problem. Nor did Chinese education create a stratum of unemployable semi-intellectuals.[147] Small factories in communes, "intermediate technology," and industrial decentralization were doubtless sound for China's relatively undeveloped economy. There is much to be said for the humanity of the basic Maoist approach to economic development, which is to raise from below.

Yet the negative side weighs heavily. The intellectual level of the state was lowered, modernization of the economy was not achieved, and China failed to train even the specialists needed to replace the older generation. Anti-bureaucratism weakened economic planning without permitting a healthy market economy.[148] Even the army was allowed to stagnate in 1950s technology during the 1970s.[149] Only for a brief period could it be imagined that the Chinese version of Communism was lighting the way to the future.

---

[145] Eckstein, *China's Economic Development*, p. 22.

[146] *New York Times*, October 25, 1974, p. 2

[147] Jan S. Prybyla, "The Chinese Economic Model," *Current History*, 69 (September 1975), 80-84.

[148] Lucian W. Pye, "Mass Participation in China," in *China: Management of a Revolutionary Society*, John M. H. Lindbeck, ed. (Seattle: University of Washington Press, 1971), p. 27.

[149] Edward N. Luttwak, "Seeing China Plain," *Commentary*, 62 (December 1976), 32-33.

Chapter four

Lesser Communist States

Eastern Europe

The Soviet Sphere

The eight Communist states of East-Central Europe, all maintain basically the same apparatus of party over state hierarchies, pseudo-democracy, economic planning, censorship and the like. Albania is independent and anti-Soviet, Yugoslavia independent and more or less pro-Soviet, and Romania independent so long as it does not seriously offend the Russians. Five states may be called Soviet vassals; four (Czechoslovakia, East Germany, Poland, and Hungary) have Soviet military forces inside the homeland. The Soviets have long regarded these countries as virtually theirs. A Soviet editor remarked in 1968 that "we" would not have elected Dubcek if it had been known what a "reactionary" he was. Asked if it was not the Czechs who elected him, the editor said, "You know we run these countries. It is our duty, we are responsible for them . . . ."[1]

In Stalin's time, no one questioned that the Soviet Union had complete control of its Eastern European domain; and no one ventured to rebel. The prestige of Stalin, the servility of the satellite parties, each with its little Stalin (Gottwald, Ulbricht, Rakosi, etc.) sufficed without direct military intervention. The purges that were carried through in most countries between 1949 and 1953 also dampened dissent. But Stalinism was even more stifling in Eastern Europe than in the Soviet Union, where the people were inured to it; and after Stalin, it seemed necessary to find better methods. In 1953 Malenkov introduced a "New Course" for the satellites, paralleling relaxation at home. This was largely

---

[1] John Scott, *Detente through Soviet Eyes* (New York: Radio Liberty Committee, 1974), p. 85.

undone after his fall, but Khrushchev, and after him his successors, have lacked strength to rule as Stalin did and have had to depend much more on institutional, less on personal bonds.

Means of Rule. The means of Soviet domination are various. Most obvious and perhaps most decisive are the Soviet military and the police. Soviet forces are usually not conspicuous nor very numerous in relation to the populations of respective countries (except East Germany), but it is known that they are prepared to shoot and they are backed by the full might of the U.S.S.R. Also instrumental is the coordination of forces through the Warsaw Treaty Organization (WTO), the Soviet-sponsored counterpart of NATO. A Soviet general commands the WTO, and it acts as a Soviet agency, with little more than gestures of general consultation. Equipment is standardized and a great effort is made to indoctrinate officers and men to loyalty to the "socialist camp." In satellite armies, key positions are usually given to Soviet-trained, often Soviet-born officers.

The Soviet political police operates both on its own and as infiltrators of local organizations. Coordination seems to be close.[2] The police were among the few Czechs to welcome the Soviet invasion in 1968. In December 1976, KGB men trooped into East Germany to help repress a wave of discontent.[3] It is said that Iuri Andropov, Soviet Politburo member, is director of operations in Eastern Europe.

Economic levers also hold the Soviet sphere together. Under the Council for Mutual Economic Assistance (Comecon), trade and to some extent production and planning are coordinated and interdependence is created, so that any break with the bloc would require extensive and costly readjustments. By such means, an artificially large proportion of the trade of the satellite countries is with the Soviet Union and one another, from about half to four-fifths in the case of East Germany and Bulgaria, the most loyal. This arrangement has not necessarily been disadvantageous to the East Europeans since the end of the Stalinist era. They receive Soviet raw materials, perhaps more cheaply than available on world markets, and have an assured market for industrial goods, perhaps of less than standard quality. However, they are under pressure to finance the production of more Soviet materials, which ensures increased dependence.

There is likewise a manifold and unending psychological–cultural campaign to convince the East European peoples of the virtues of socialism and the Soviet Union and the necessity of joining their destinies to it. Propaganda, education, and many coordinated activities all supposedly shape attitudes, at least serving to reduce ideas of separatism, individualism, or Western democracy, if they do not generate much enthusiasm. The traffic is one-way, from the Soviet center, representing orthodoxy, to the satellites, potentially a source of subversive ideas for the Russians. For example, the East Europeans are not allowed to broadcast

---

[2] Cf. John Barron, *KGB: The Secret Work of Soviet Secret Agents* (New York: Reader's Digest Press, 1974), pp. 141-146.

[3] *Time*, December 20, 1976, p. 35.

to the Soviet Union even in their own languages; Poland and East Germany are to have no cultural relations with Poles and Germans in the U.S.S.R.

A more basic means of the Soviet state in securing conformity in its sphere of influence is the classic strategy of empire, of support for an elite which depends upon the hegemonic power and so shares its interest in maintaining the relations of vassalhood. The Soviet Union has assisted to power in Eastern Europe many persons representative of minority views who would otherwise be insignificant. Nowhere except in Czechoslovakia were the Communists a mass party at the time of formation of a Communist government; indeed, many of the leaders, such as Novotny in Czechoslovakia and Rakosi in Hungary, have impressed rather by the mediocrity of their political talents. They held power and glory by grace of the Soviet presence, and they had every reason to repay the favor by following Soviet wishes and sovietizing their countries so far as possible in order to stabilize their own power. It is a circular process: the less popular the regime, the more necessary to lean on foreign support, and the greater the identification with Russia, the less popular support. The situation is somewhat ameliorated, however, by Marxism-Leninism. Instead of conceding political dependency on the Soviets, the otherwise insecure regimes profess adherence to the internationalist creed to cover their essentially anti-national position. East European leaders can tell themselves that they are not servants of a foreign power but adherents to the progressive creed of Marxism-Leninism—champions of the international proletarian movement. The reward is all the satisfaction of political power within the limits fixed by the Soviet overlordship, the perquisites of office at home and international recognition abroad, with security of tenure so far as the regime is reasonably competent.

The entire system is well organized and rather successful, as evidenced by the absence of visible protest against occupation armies of a disliked power. Media and schools dutifully teach Marxism-Leninism, the glories of socialism and of the Soviet Union, and the virtues of the local leaders. The economies function at least moderately well. Unemployment and inflation are minimized. Old national frictions and traditional enmities have been extenuated by the peace-keeping Soviet presence. The East Europeans, traditionally poor relations of Western Europe, have also been given some pride in standing by themselves, building on their own, and taking a path which may be seen as "progressive."

The "socialist" form seems to have become fairly well ingrained and accepted, although Soviet Russian domination may be silently resented. In 1953 and 1956, in East Germany, Czechoslovakia, and Hungary there were movements that might well be interpreted as anti-Communist as well as anti-Russian, uprisings that had to be suppressed by force. But many years have passed, a new generation has grown up unacquainted with political pluralism, and ever larger numbers of people have tied their lives to the existent system. Even the Czech deviation of 1968, which the Russians found so threatening, seemed aimed not at overthrowing the Communist structure but at humanizing and democratizing within the "socialist" framework. The Czechs seem to have seen the Communist Party as the best basis for political and economic improvement.[4]

The apparent conclusion is that Communism is a fairly workable system even when imposed from without. Russian domination, after all, is not inherently more alien for Poles and Hungarians than it is for Georgians and Uzbeks. Perhaps the satellite countries have a greater sense of national pride, independence, and modern cultural development, but these are subject to erosion; and the same general policies which hold the Soviet minorities in line with little visible friction serve to keep the nations of the Soviet bloc in harness. Beyond this, there is only a difference of degree from the condition of the Russians or other states whose Communism is native-imposed. In any case, Communism represents a system imposed by a minority under special circumstances, whereby the minority perpetuates the emergency regime indefinitely. That Russian Communists rule Russians or Czechs implies no great difference in principle.

There are, however, differences of emphasis and degree, so that Communism in Eastern Europe can by no means be equated with variants in Russia, Central Asia, or China; the expectations and attitudes of the peoples involved have made modifications unavoidable. The Soviet empire could never again present so monolithic a front after the death of Stalin and especially after de-Stalinization had discredited the cult of personality. Recovery from the devastation and shock of war also contributed to some loosening and the revival of nationalism in Eastern Europe. Controls over art and literature, never so firm as in the Soviet Union, slackened in most countries. As the Soviet Union began to find the management of the economy more complicated than appeared in the early five-year plans and began to experiment, East Europeans did so also; and experimentation means diversification. Hungary, for example, has gone well beyond the Soviet pattern in making room for local initiative and market forces. There is more latitude for private enterprise, and peasant household plots are much more generous than in the Soviet Union. Most East Europeans have never been so wedded to atheism as the Soviets, and they have not been so ideologically dogmatic. In Poland there has been much discussion of "humanistic Marxism," Socialist Realism has been less oppressive, and censorship not so rigorous.

The party elite throughout Eastern Europe has usually been less autonomous and less self-assured than in the Soviet system. The contrast of good socialism and bad capitalism has been less convincing; leaders have felt the need not merely to make a "socialist" revolution but to adapt policies to a complex and changing reality. Western influences and desires for contact with the pluralistic West have been more pervasive. In short, Communism in Eastern Europe has been, with endless variations, less Communistic.

---

[4] Walter C. Clemens, Jr., "The Impact of Detente on Chinese and Soviet Communism," *Journal of International Affairs,* 28, 2, 1974, p. 141.

Bulgaria

Least divergent and least self-willed has been the most backward of the satellites, Bulgaria, the only one which has no visible opposition and which seems gladly to accept Soviet overlordship. This exemplary adherence probably originates with the Russo-Turkish war of 1878 and the liberation of Bulgaria from Turkish rule by the tsarist army. Subsequently the Russians gave Bulgaria relative freedom with a liberal constitution and supported Bulgarian territorial ambitions. Bulgarian intellectuals of the 1890s shared their Russian counterparts' passion for Marxism, and only because of Balkan antagonisms did Bulgaria enter on the anti-Russian side in World War I. Defeat shifted considerable support to radicals, many of whom became Communists.[5] The Communist Party of the interwar period had been virtually destroyed by repression when the Russians entered in late 1944. However, they required the immediate establishment of a Communist government. Within a few months, thousands had been imprisoned or shot;[6] and Bulgaria became in short order a model satellite.

Historical gratitude has combined with the advantages of cooperation with the Soviet Union. The Bulgarians have received more generous Soviet assistance in industrialization than any other country,[7] and a high growth rate has greatly improved the standing of the formerly poor agricultural country. There has been no threat from the U.S.S.R. to the formal independence of Bulgaria, with which it shares no boundaries. On the contrary, the Russians have supported Bulgarian national aspirations in neighboring territories, especially Macedonia; and Russians and Bulgars have shared attitudes toward Turkey.

There was an incipient anti-Soviet move in 1965 but it was quietly purged; since then, Bulgarian leaders seem to have felt that their interests are best served by total adherence to the bloc leader. General Secretary Todor Zhivkov has accepted complete dependence on Soviet backing and has surrounded himself with men entirely dedicated to the Soviet connection.[8] The Soviet ambassador seems to be proconsul; Soviet police and other authorities operate almost as though on home grounds. The maxim of Soviet superiority in everything takes precedence over all national values, and Bulgarians know that they are great but Russians are greater.[9] In 1958 there was a short-lived move to emulate the Chinese Great Leap Forward as the quick way to convert surplus labor into useful capital; once Soviet opposition was expressed, however, the

---

[5] Nissan Oren, *Bulgarian Communism* (New York: Columbia University Press, 1971), pp. 260-261.

[6] Zbigniew Brzezinski, *The Soviet Bloc: Unity and Conflict*, rev. ed. (Cambridge: Harvard University Press, 1967), p. 15.

[7] Nissan Oren, *Revolution Administered: Agrarianism and Communism in Bulgaria* (Baltimore: Johns Hopkins University Press, 1973), p. 182.

[8] M. Pundeff, "Bulgaria under Zhivkov," in *The Changing Face of Communism in Eastern Europe*, Peter A. Toma, ed. (Tucson: University of Arizona Press, 1970), pp. 118-119.

[9] Oren, *Revolution Administered*, pp. 171, 172.

plan was summarily dropped. Otherwise, Bulgaria has unremittingly followed Soviet patterns. It is the only country of Eastern Europe to have farms comparable in size to those of the Soviets, many of them over 10,000 acres, despite resultant low productivity.[10] Bulgarians are the only East Europeans to show a liking for Soviet films,[11] and the only satellite to celebrate Victory Day just as the Russians do, as a great Soviet victory. It has been among the most reluctant of Eastern European states to seek broader contacts with the West.

German Democratic Republic

Second honors for obedience go to the East German government, whose situation may be characterized as antipodal to that of Bulgaria. For the German Democratic Republic, nationalistic feelings do not merge with pro-Soviet Communism as in the case of Bulgaria but directly conflict with it. It would seem that the Bulgarians follow a strict party line because they have little to lose and something to gain, at least from the viewpoint of the rulership; the East German elite conforms, however, because of insecurity and dependence. The German Democratic Republic rules less than a fourth of the German nation, and many or most of its people would like to be reunited with West Germany. Less than any other Communist state can it exclude subversive influences; West German television, for instance, permeates the land.

Defender of the Soviet Model. Striving to justify its existence, which has at times seemed precarious, the East German (Socialist Unity) party has felt driven to emphasize Marxism, internationalism, and Soviet virtues, even becoming more papal than the pope and sometimes mildly criticizing Moscow for unorthodoxy.[12] Nowhere is Lenin a greater hero. At the same time, Marx is made the true exponent of German greatness. This is mixed with quiet emphasis on the German authoritarian-bureaucratic tradition; goose-stepping jackboots are the style of East, not West Germany. Anti-Westernism and anti-Americanism also vindicate the state; Communist Germany sternly fights against the invasion of the language by Americanisms,[13] referring, incidentally, to the purity not of "German," but of "the national language." This semantic device presumably has as its objective the differentiation of East Germany from the common German experience (Abgrenzungspolitik). Of greater consequence, the U.S. has been used as a general bogey, villain of Vietnam and exploitation and oppression around the world; the American government was even cited in the constitution as a menace to the world.[14]

---

[10] Bogoslav Dobrin, *Bulgarian Economic Development since World War II* (New York: Praeger, 1973), p. 174.

[11] Ivan Volgyes, "Political Socialization in Eastern Europe" in *Political Socialization in Eastern Europe: A Comparative Framework*, I. Volgyes, ed. (New York: Praeger, 1975), p. 25.

[12] Bill T. Jones, "East German Cultural Scene," *Survey*, 21 (Autumn 1975), 60.

[13] *Die Zeit*, February 21, 1975.

[14] John J. Putnam and Gordon W. Gohan, "East Germany, the Struggle to Survive," *National Geographic*, 146, no. 3 (September 1974), 302-303.

Every effort is made to contrast East Germany with the Western state as the land of socialism, modern rationality, and equality. The nonrecognition of East Germany by most states outside the Soviet bloc until about 1969, with consequent minimization of contacts, helped to promote the feeling of specialness. The East Germans have been particularly insistent on limiting higher education to those qualified by "class" background, in order to raise up a loyal future elite. While this approach has mostly been abandoned with the passing of the years in other bloc countries, Erich Honecker, the successor of Ulbricht, reemphasized the weight of "political qualification" for admission.[15]

The East German elite has been constrained not merely to talk ideology to bolster their synthetic status but to act like and thereby become true believers in something vaguely called "socialism" and to strive for legitimation by performance.[16]   After the building of the Berlin Wall, in August 1961, people came increasingly to accept the necessity or inevitability of getting along with the inescapable system, some with resignation, some with enthusiasm. Managers have been reported to work seventy hours per week or more,[17] in the style of hard-driving American executives. Many East Germans set out to show what systematic work and organization could achieve; typical of the results is the eminence achieved in international sports competitions, far ahead of West Germany with over three times the population. Thanks to hard work and restriction of consumption,[18] the East German economy has grown rapidly, making East Germany the most productive country of the Soviet bloc, with per capita income in the same range as that of Italy.

Legitimacy came to rest to a large extent on this economic success; East Germans, although still much poorer than their Western cousins, could be proud—and were indeed encouraged to be so—of what they had achieved under difficult conditions. The technical elite reaped a higher status and was even admitted to the higher ranks, comprising a third of the Central Committee, although it remained excluded from the core bodies, the Secretariat and Politburo.[19]   But the experts have not seemed necessarily anti-authoritarian or opposed to party domination; to the contrary, the young elite has been more

---

[15] Peter C. Ludz, "Continuity and Change since Ulbricht," *Problems of Communism* (January-February 1972), p. 64.

[16] Heinz Lippman, *Honecker and the New Politics of Europe* (New York: Macmillan, 1972), p. 17.

[17] *Die Zeit*, November 1, 1974.

[18] Also thanks to substantial assistance from the vilified West German government, which gives East Germany large credits and free access to the West German market. The Federal Republic has also paid about $250 million, 1961-1976, for the release of political prisoners, the recent minimum price being $20,000 per head. *New York Times*, December 4, 1976, p. 3.

[19] Thomas A. Baylis, *The Technical Intelligentsia and the East German Elite* (Berkeley University of California Press, 1974), pp. 262-263.

attracted to quasi-technocratic values than any liberal or democratic ideas.[20] The party was upheld as an agent of production: "The party is the engine of the plant, the cleanest, most progressive element."[21]   Planning and socialism were identified with rationality and progress, against the alleged moral degradation, inhumanity, and anarchy of the West.

Political socialization, aided by a very competent educational network, has been relatively successful.[22]   The departure to West Germany, from 1945 to 1961, of fifteen percent of the population temporarily placed the economy in jeopardy; however, the mass exodus did remove most determined opponents of the system and opened the social network for others to advance their status; it has been claimed that 75 percent of managers are of working-class origins.[23] There is also a widespread feeling of gratitude for the welfare state, and East Germans abroad are said to miss the supportive human relations of the collectivist society.[24]

Under the leadership of Walter Ulbricht, chief par excellence of the East German Communist ("Socialist Unity") Party, the state was totally conformist to Soviet policy. Only as detente came into vogue with the Ostpolitik of the West German Social Democrats and Soviet rapprochement with the U. S. did Ulbricht seemingly become somewhat disenchanted with Soviet leadership. He was forced out in 1971, perhaps because of his effort to brake the Soviet policy of relaxation;[25] he had been the fiercest opponent of "Western imperialism." He also seems to have become convinced, along with some other East German leaders, that they could develop a superior German socialism.[26] His successor, Erich Honecker (who pretended for a few months that the exit of Ulbricht was voluntary), realigned East German policy with that of the U.S.S.R. By a 1975 treaty East Germany bound itself even more closely to the Soviet Union, promising to concert in its foreign policy, to help militarily even in Asia, to coordinate its economy with the Soviet, and to cooperate with Soviet police agencies.

What was until the 1970s officially designated in West Germany as the "Soviet zone" has thus demonstrated how, with intelligent and capable leadership, Communism can be implanted and made to work under circumstances in most ways quite unpromising. In assessing East German success, it is impossible to separate the effects of the large Soviet military presence and the

---

[20] *Ibid.*, pp. 266-268.

[21] Putnam and Gohan, "East Germany," p. 322.

[22] Arthur M. Hanhardt, Jr., "East Germany: From Goals to Reality" in *Political Socialization*, I. Volgyes, ed., p. 87.

[23] Baylis, *The Technical Intelligentsia*, p. 47.

[24] Hanhardt in *Political Socialization*, Volgyes, ed., p. 87.

[25] Ludz, "Continuity and Change," p. 56.

[26] Lippmann, *Honecker*, p. 219; Henry Krisch, "The German Democratic Republic in the Mid-1970's," *Current History*, 70 (January 1976), 119.

awareness of narrow limits of Soviet tolerance for native impulses. But if the human material is favorable, as in the case of the orderly and hardworking Germans, Communism can show respectable results, no matter how unwilling the majority was at the outset.

Czechoslovakia

Occupied by Soviet forces since August 1968, Czechoslovakia rivals or excels East Germany in orthodoxy and official faithfulness to the Soviet protector; no other state is more zealous in adherence to "proletarian internationalism," because in no other state is the Communist rulership less representative of national feelings. Czechoslovakia also provides a good example that Communism backed by adequate force can be a workable and reasonably productive system in the face of general unpopularity, even abhorrence.

Before August 1968, however, Communism in Czechoslovakia was voluntary or at least largely native. In 1946-1947, under a multiparty but Communist led government, Czechoslovakia tried to act as a model of democratic socialism, an East-West bridge, retaining liberties at home while adhering to Soviet foreign policy. But Communist fear of forthcoming elections led to the coup of February 1948 and long years of Stalinism, purge trials, tightly reined economy dedicated to heavy industry, and closed borders. At the end of the 1950s, Czechoslovakia was perhaps the most Stalinist country of Eastern Europe. Dogmatic equalitarianism and party anti-intellectualism brought about an exceptional degree of levelling, such that unskilled workers earned more than skilled or white-collar workers and professionals.[27]

Liberalization. But economic growth came to a virtual halt, as investments were swallowed up in waste.[28] The country felt strangled in bureaucratism, and discontent grew. Fears of Germany wore off, admiration of Russia faded, and party morale declined.[29] Reform became essential, and the government began economic experimentation to restore capacity for growth. To get foreign currency, tourists were admitted in large numbers, and some Czechoslovaks were permitted to travel abroad. Nationality dissidence helped loosen controls, as the Slovaks, demanding better treatment, led the attack on the central authorities. The party still held all the instruments of repression but found itself unable to use them. In 1964 an International Jazz Festival was held in Prague, making it the hippy capital of Eastern Europe, and people developed a certain

[27] Otto Ulc, "Czechoslovakia: The Great Leap Backward," in *The Politics of Modernization in Eastern Europe*, Charles Gati, ed. (New York: Praeger, 1974), p. 95.

[28] Ota Šik, *Czechoslovakia: The Bureaucratic Economy* (White Plains, N.Y.: International Arts and Sciences, 1972), p. 61 and *passim*.

[29] Robin A. Remington, ed., *Winter in Prague: Documents on Czechoslovak Communism in Crisis* (Cambridge, Mass.: MIT Press, 1969), pp. xiii-xv.

case about expressing themselves freely.[30] Writers exercised substantial freedom, excellent movies were produced, and Prague became by 1967 a center of avant-garde culture.[31]

To some extent, Czechoslovak liberalization proceeded in sympathy with relaxation in the Soviet Union under Khrushchev; but whereas Soviet liberalization came to a halt in 1965, the Czechoslovak continued. Free discussion on broadcast media and in the press increased, and official censorship was even restricted in January 1967.[32] A writers' congress in June turned into a basic attack on the Communist state; one criticism emboldened another, until a writer (Ludvig Vaculik) could express such a sentiment as that political power "affects the ruler and the ruled and threatens the health of both. . . . ."[33] Sympathies for Israel in the June war, contrary to the official pro-Arab line (decreed by Soviet policy) contributed to discrediting the party. In December, deadlock in the Politburo put decisions up to open debate in the Central Committee. There followed a verbal storm, with Alexander Dubček, Slovak First Secretary, leading the attack on party boss Novotny over the Slovak question. Police brutality against university students protesting the irregularity of lighting aroused the liberals. Novotny tried to save himself by advocating socialist democracy and appealing to the workers against the "dictatorship of the intellectuals", [34] but he was overthrown by the erstwhile rubberstamp Central Committee in January 1968.

In parliamentary style, the leader of the opposition, Dubček, became the new leader of the government; and there began one of the most remarkable episodes of modern history, the spontaneous birth of freedom in a Communist state. The Communist elite no longer saw themselves justified in exercising total power, and everyone began to enjoy a freedom which was the more delightful as it was unaccustomed. The apparatus of control no longer knew what, if anything, should be prohibited. Censors advocated the end of censorship.[35] By March the press was free, and a flood of denunciations was gushing forth. Many popular organizations sprang up, no longer subject to party guidance, while the Communist youth organization, after twenty years' monopoly, collapsed.[36] The Stalinist rubberstamp parliament became real, abolished

---

[30] Staughton Lynd and Thomas Hayden, *The Other Side* (New York: New American Library, 1966), p. 25.

[31] Harry Schwartz, *Prague's 200 Days: The Struggle for Democracy in Czechoslovakia* New York: Praeger, 1969), pp. 26-27.

[32] *Ibid.*, p. 38.

[33] Z. A. B. Zeman, *Prague Spring* (New York: Hill and Wang, 1969), p. 61.

[34] *Ibid.*, p. 39.

[35] Remington, *Winter in Prague*, Document 8.

[36] Otto Ulc, "Czechoslovakia: From the Winter of Discontent to the Despair of Husak's Autumn," in *Political Socialization*, I. Volgyes, ed., p. 46.

censorship, and promised electoral reform for genuine elections. It subsequently even became a valiant defender of the nation in the face of the Soviet invasion.[37] There was tremendous popular interest in politics and endless discussion. Pent-up feelings were released; in the course of rediscovery of recent history, the Czechs let loose their dislike for the Russians and recalled their injuries, including Soviet annexation of eastern Czechoslovakia and the Hitler-Stalin pact which opened World War II.

The high tide of liberalization came with the intellectuals' manifesto, "2000 Words to Workers, Farmers, Scientists, Artists, and Everyone," which included a thorough critique of the absolutist state:

> Personal and collective honor declined. Honesty led nowhere, and there was no appreciation for ability. Therefore people lost interest in public affairs; they were concerned only with themselves and with money.... The apparatus decided what one might or might not do....No organization actually belonged to its members, not even the Communist organization.[38]

This naturally infuriated the Russians.

The Czechs did not, however, turn away from the Communist Party, but wanted it open and responsible to the people. They did not reject the socialized economy and basic Marxism but wanted these along with political democracy. Arguably, this was impossible. After some euphoria and experimentation, which would fail to bring happiness, tranquility, and prosperity, the party might have gone back to ruling much as before. But the Russians were too afraid that freedom would succeed and perhaps infect their own union, and so they brought it to a halt in the name of brotherly assistance to endangered socialism.

Soviet Intervention. The Russians claimed that they came invited, but they could point to no one of importance who had invited them. They were greeted only by a few hard-line Communists and some members of the political police, while the masses cursed and threw stones at the tanks. At first, however, the Soviet authorities treated the country fairly gently, spoke of temporary occupation to "normalize" the country, and left Dubček (after some harrowing experiences) nominally at the head of the government. Only after anti-Soviet riots in April 1969 did the occupiers step in to replace Dubček by the more compliant Gustav Husak and thoroughly tighten Communist controls.

In the Gleichschaltung, a large number of "liberals" were purged from the party and positions of responsibility in all walks. Some 40 percent of managers were removed.[39] In the interests of centralized control, the Soviet authorities demanded the reduction of party membership from 1,600,000 to 300,000[40] Virtually all Czech writers and members of the creative intelligentsia were either expelled from their positions or withdrew in protest; they have remained

[37] *Ibid.*, p. 110.

[38] Remington, *Winter in Prague*, p. 197.

[39] *Christian Science Monitor*, January 29, 1975, p. 3

[40] Ulc, "Czechoslovakia: The Great Leap Backward," p. 112.

remarkably noncooperative to this day despite the rewards offered for conformism. Even Czech science was beaten down.[41] In the hopelessness of resistance, some fifteen to twenty percent of the population were said to be active dissidents in 1975,[42] most of the rest being apathetic. The party fought apathy with indoctrination; even physicians must study Marxism-Leninism. But papers were so dulled by censorship that most people read only the sports page.[43] Corruption was reported to be extensive, with bribes used, for example, to secure good medical attention or to get children into higher schools. Samizdat was also widespread, probably much more so than in any other Communist state, as people sought a substitute for official writing.

A few convinced Communists staffed and supported the regime; many more acquiesced simply because this was the only way to material rewards and a career. Collaborationism was much more extensive than under the Nazis, no doubt in part because the present situation seems permanent. Many elderly people stood with the Communists because they were unwilling to admit that their lives and careers had been in error.[44] One section of the Communist Party, led by Vasil Bilak, head of the police, military, and foreign department of the Secretariat, pushed harder for Communist purity, strict controls, and punishment of those responsible for the "Prague Spring," in contrast to the more cautious approach of Gustav Husak, president of the republic and first secretary of the party.

In Czechoslovakia, too, Communism works. If no literature was produced this was not disastrous. There were slowdowns and work stoppages after the Soviet invasion, but the principal sufferers were the workers. People learned that there was no choice, they had to work to live, and the economy gradually improved. Life became materially as tolerable as in the other East European countries. The Russian soldiers stayed out of sight. The police were not very efficient, the dissenters were allowed to live quietly if they remained quiet, Czechoslovakia loyally mirrored Soviet policy internally as well as externally, and the schools taught Marxism-Leninism and the need for "proletarian internationalism." As in East Germany, much was made of the evils of American "imperialism." But the dominant mood was apolitical, well expressed by the statement of a member of the national assembly: "Never again must the parliament be allowed to degenerate into a political arena."[45]

By 1975, however, there were some signs that Czechoslovakia might adopt a more moderate line. The dogmatic "left" seemed to have lost some of its fear-based bitterness, and there was talk of economic reform. Since moderate

[41] František Janouch, "Science under Siege in Czechoslovakia," *The Bulletin of Atomic Scientists*, 32 (April 1976), 6-12.

[42] Karel Tynsky in *Christian Science Monitor*, January 7, 1975, p. 7.

[43] George S. Wheeler, *The Human Face of Socialism* (New York: Lawrence Hill, 1973), p. 118.

[44] Karel Synsky in *Christian Science Monitor*, January 7, 1975, p. 7.

[45] Ulc, "Czechoslovakia: The Great Leap Backward," p. 111.

changes could no longer endanger the ruling elite, it seemed possible that Czechoslovakia might follow the example of Hungary, where a Soviet-imposed regime gradually identified itself with the national interests within the limits permitted by the Soviet Union. Yet any evolution in such direction is very slow. In 1976, the government reaffirmed "class" criteria for admission to higher education, the key to a career, the undesired "class" being principally those associated with the 1968 movement. And musicians were still being imprisoned for playing rock music.

Poland

In Poland, as in East Germany and Czechoslovakia, the Communist government depends on the support of a disliked foreign power with forces stationed in the country so that it can intervene militarily whenever deemed necessary. But the Polish government has taken on the uncontestable virtue of standing for the defense of the nation against a possibly and allegedly revanchist Germany, particularly with respect to the large formerly German territories of western Poland. Fears for their security helped the Polish Communist regime very much during the first decades of its existence. The Poles, moreover, were probably justified in their fear that if they offended the Russians the latter might join with the Germans to dismember them as they did twice in the past.

Postwar Poland has never gone against Soviet foreign or military policy, and the Soviet leaders have had the reassurance of freedom to keep forces on Polish territory and bring in more. Perhaps for this reason, Khrushchev was willing, in October 1956, to accept as Polish chief the formerly imprisoned Wladyslaw Gomulka and to allow Poland considerable latitude in domestic affairs. This led to a period of liberalization, the "Polish October," when Gomulka had an opportunity to lead Poland toward a gentler brand of Communism.[46] He failed to do so, however. The political and economic situation gradually worsened until he was overthrown by a strike wave in December 1970, sparked by food price increases. His successor, Edward Gierek, again promised liberalization, more consumer goods, and greater use of democratic procedures; and he was able to keep much of that promise. The economy was loosened; and trade with the West grew to half Poland's total (by 1975), while trade with the bloc fell from almost two-thirds (in 1970) to well under half. There was an economic boom, and the standard of living rose sharply.

But gradually conformity crept back, conservative Communists asserted themselves, the press grew grayer, and the Church more troubled.[47] The boom came to an end as the foreign credits that had largely financed it ran out. New

---

[46] Erwin West, *Ostblock Intern* (Hamburg: Hoffmann u. Campe, 1970), p. 176.

[47] *New York Times*, June 13, 1975. Adam Bromke, "A New Juncture in Poland," *Problems of Communism*, 25 (September-October 1976), 1-6.

food price increases in June 1976 triggered another wave of riots. The government this time yielded immediately, and order was easily restored. But the workers had learned something of their power to influence the state.

The Polish Style of Communism. Poland has oscillated between a position at or near the liberal end of the Soviet bloc gamut and one nearer the middle. Its distinctiveness lies in the fact that the collectivization decreed in Stalinist days was undone, and a large majority of farmland is privately held. Despite Gierek's incentives for small farmers and a remarkable but short-lived rise in production, small farms are blamed for inefficiency, and the policy is still (and always has been officially) to go over to socialized agriculture, albeit gradually and voluntarily.[48] Peasants are given incentives to relinquish their land or to turn it over to the state upon retirement, and it was proposed to expropriate farmland not being efficiently worked—although state farms may be even less prepared to utilize it. From 1970 to 1975, the socialized sector of Polish agricultural land increased from sixteen percent to twenty percent.[49]

Polish Communism is also exceptional in that it has come to a modus vivendi with a very strong Catholic Church, which is a national symbol as well as a religious institution. It is said that 80 percent of Poles attend church.[50] Religious bookstores are conspicuous in Warsaw, and there are Catholic chaplains attached to the army. But the unequivocal official policy is to defeat the Church and destroy it so far as possible. Members of the party, the only means to an ordinary career, must subscribe to atheistic materialism. When, in the late 1950s, children who declined religious instruction in schools were subject to peer group pressure, it was discontinued, so the new generation grows up with formal education only in atheism.[51]

In many other ways the Polish state is less monolithic than the Soviet. The minor parties, especially the Catholic "Znak" group, have been allowed to express themselves to some extent. Some governmental positions are even reserved for them, so a man can make a political career of sorts outside the ruling party.[52] Elections have had some significance in showing the relative popularity of approved candidates. Since voters can express themselves in a negative way by scratching out names on the electoral list, less popular candidates suffer some loss of face. Trade unions have real functions, including influencing the removal of managers.[53] The press in Poland at its grayest sparkles beside the

[48] Robert W. Dean, "Gierek's Three Years," *Survey*, 20, no. 2-3 (Spring-Summer 1974), 66.

[49] Richard F. Staar, "Poland, the Price of Stability," *Current History*, 70 (March 1976), 102.

[50] *New York Times*, June 9, 1975, p. 10

[51] J. Fiszman, "Poland: Continuity and Change," in *The Changing Face of Communism in Eastern Europe*, Peter A. Toma, ed. p. 74.

[52] *Ibid.*, p. 65.

[53] Howard T. Ludlow, "The Role of Trade Unions in Poland," *Political Science Quarterly*, 90, no. 2 (Summer 1975), 324.

Soviet. A censored but rather bold theater gives some sense of freedom and acts as safety valve for a few intellectuals.[54]   A small independent Catholic weekly provides a forum for free and pungent discussion unique in the Communist world. Poles could openly criticize a draft constitution presented in December 1975, and earnest discussions in and outside the party led to real modifications.[55]

Poland has preserved a good deal of its own personality under Communism, while the system has offered the same advantages as elsewhere, industrialization, education, and the shedding of an inferiority complex.[56]   However, Poles grumble, and true believers seem to be fewer than in East Germnay, where the regime feels forced to prove itself as genuinely socialist. As a Polish Communist remarked: "Everything in Poland today is purely tactical and purely pragmatic and everybody knows it . . . a young man who has his own ideas knows he has no possibilities. He has learned from the beginning that he has to be politic in every sector of life, including his own way of thinking."[57]   As a Polish writer expressed it, "the goal is acceptance—not of the system (the party does not depend on this)—but of one's own impotence."[58]

Hungary

Like the Poles, the Hungarians have a historical tradition of hostility to the Russians; unlike the Poles, the Hungarians have little reason to accept the Russians as protectors against Germany. Presumably for this reason, the Hungarians, who had been under a thoroughly Stalinist regime, rebelled against Soviet domination in 1956. The party apparatus dissolved, and Imre Nagy, who had previously been ousted by the Stalinists because he tried to broaden the appeal of the state, took the helm in an effort to lead Hungary back to an open, pluralistic society. When the effort was brutally suppressed by Soviet forces, many thousands escaped the country; those who stayed had perforce to accept an imposed government.

But the government of Janos Kadar, who had been jailed in 1950 and castrated by the Stalinists, proved much less oppressive than expected. Facing a sullen population, Kadar tried to reconcile obedience to the Russians and satisfaction of popular needs. The principal requirement of the Russians is fidelity to the Soviet position in international relations, and the Hungarians have not deviated an inch from the line. They even sent token forces to participate in the 1968 invasion of Czechoslovakia, contrary to their feelings. In return for

---

[54] Jeffrey Goldfarb, "Students' Theatre in Poland," *Survey*, 22 (Spring 1976), 155-178.

[55] *New York Times*, March 19, 1976, p. 7.

[56] As claimed by the editor of a leading paper, *Polityka. New York Times*, October 16, 1974, p. 43.

[57] *New York Times*, June 13, 1975, p. 6

[58] Quoted by Walter D. Connor, "Generations and Politics in the USSR," *Problems of Communism*, 25 (September-October 1975), p. 25.

cooperation in foreign and defense matters, the Soviets have allowed the Hungarians a modest degree of internal freedom.

Easing has proceeded in several directions. Party guidance has been less close, and it is recognized that not only state and party but individuals and groups have legitimate interests. In elections, a few more (approved) candidates have been presented than there were posts to be filled, although hardly anyone shows up for electoral meetings.[59] The parliament has been given some role in the discussion of national policies, although it may be bypassed.[60] Propaganda is relatively muted. Censorship is mild by Soviet standards, and people are fairly free to criticize anything except the Soviet Union and the role of the Communist Party. Apathy is acceptable or even encouraged, as the state's hopes are focused on bringing up the children as good socialists.[61] Hungary is probably the openest of Communist countries except Yugoslavia, and Hungarians travel abroad with little difficulty. Church–state relations have been normalized, somewhat as in Poland. Modern or abstract art is permitted, and imported blue jeans became an almost obligatory status symbol for youth.

The chief deviation of the Hungarians, however, has been in the direction of much more economic freedom than the Soviet Union and other Communist states (except Yugoslavia). Although the Hungarians, unlike the Poles, were not allowed to drop collectivization, controls over the farms were loosened. The Hungarian economy is (followed by the Polish) the most consumer-oriented in the bloc, with a third of industry classified as "light" against a fourth in the Soviet Union and other vassal states. Hungary, alone in the Soviet bloc, showed a higher growth rate for consumer than producer goods in the years between 1961 and 1975. Centralized planning has been slackened, and 1968 saw the introduction of the "New Economic Mechanism" (NEM), allowing much more flexibility in management and a semi-market economy with stress on monetary incentives. Governmental planning controls were restricted to indirect levers, prices, taxes, credit, and management of foreign trade. In part as a counter to managerial independence, the trade unions were given real authority, including veto power over investments and some other management decisions.

The reward has been a steady growth of productivity, especially in the quality and quantity of consumer goods. But the NEM has come under pressure. Economic uncertainties, a threat of unemployment and inflation, and the lurking shadow of Communist ideology give ammunition to the centralizers who would like to concentrate power more firmly in the proper hands. It would be impossible to go over to a market economy (if the Soviet Union would allow

[59] Ivan Volgyes, "Limited Liberalization in Hungary," *Current History*, 70 (March 1976), p. 110.

[60] Roger E. Kanet, "Modernizing Interaction within Western Europe," in *Politics of Modernization*, C. Gati, ed., p. 293.

[61] Ivan Volgyes, "Hungary: From Mobilization to Depoliticization" in *Political Socialization*, I. Volgyes, ed., p. 97.

this) without sacrificing ideology, and it seems necessary for the regime to keep repeating that Hungary is socialist and socialism is better than the degraded system of the West. Change is restricted by the necessity to deny the reality of change.

Romania

For a decade Romania was a conformist satellite like Bulgaria. But in 1958 Khrushchev, as a reward for Romanian fidelity or other reasons unknown,[63] withdrew Soviet forces from Romania, a step doubtless much regretted later. There remained and remains the threat of Soviet military intervention, since Soviet forces stand on most of the borders; but Romania acquired room for maneuver and grounds for hope: if it shows itself sufficiently orthodox to avoid provoking the hegemonic power and also remains strong, both in political cohesion and economically and militarily, it can hope to stave off intervention and go its own way.

A strong Communist government thus became necessary to protect independence and was justified by its success in doing so. Whatever the costs in terms of dictatorship, bureaucratism, or censorship, the leadership can always contend that there is no alternative which will keep the Russians at bay. National pride, as a Latin island in a Slavic sea, joins with a feeling of need for rapid industrialization of a formerly poor agricultural land to call for a more or less authoritarian rulership, which under the circumstances can only be called "socialism" and structured in the Soviet way.

The Romanian Nationalism. Romania began in 1952 to steer toward independence with the ouster of many persons belonging to the Muscovite branch of the Communist party, mostly those of Jewish or Hungarian background. Stalin did not object because of the fulsome subservience of the Romanians. After Stalin's death, the Romanian leader, Gheorghiu-Dej, with Balkan cunning sought to secure bits of freedom while making demonstrations of loyalty; his patriotic approach was probably reinforced by fears that de-Stalinization might be applied to Romania. Khrushchev's desire to ease relations with the satellites helped, as did the developing split with China, during which time the Romanians remained carefully neutral. After the 1958 withdrawal of Soviet forces, the major landmark was the Romanian refusal, 1961 and after, to accede to further economic integration in Comecon, integration which seemed to condemn Romania to be purveyor of raw materials for other countries' industry. This was inadmissible for a Communist state, offensive to pride as well as injurious to the economy. Since then Romania has been the backward-leaning member of Comecon, never quite bringing the Russians to desperation but usually

---

[62] The growing apprehensions of Khrushchev regarding China may have been an important factor. Stephen Fischer-Galati, "The Socialist Republic of Romania," in *The Changing Face of Communism in Eastern Europe*, Peter A. Toma, ed., p. 25.

braking, sometimes forcing the Russians to carry out projects with more amenable members outside the Comecon framework. Romania also gradually diversified its foreign trade, which had been almost entirely within the bloc, until over half was with "capitalist" states.

Beginning in 1962-63, Romania symbolically declared independence by erasing many of the evidences of Russification dating from the Stalinist era. Tokens of Russian influence, such as street names, were removed; Russian ceased to be an obligatory language in schools; Soviet cultural institutions were closed. The slavicization of the Romanian language was reversed, even to the exclusion of old words of Slavic origin. The national history, which had been rewritten to make Romania always dependent on Russian help and enlightenment, was re-rewritten.[63] "Socialist realism" in art was abandoned. Jamming was shifted from Western to Soviet broadcasts.[64]

It also became possible to mention the fact that the Soviet Union held a large territory inhabited mostly by ethnic Romanians; Romania is the only Eastern European country to have an important irredenta in the Soviet Union. The Bessarabian question kept relations between the Soviet Union and Romania tense in the interwar period, and it was the prime reason that Romania willingly joined Hitler's anti-Bolshevik crusade in 1941. The Romanians could not raise their claim openly, but they published Karl Marx's writings on the subject. The Romanian radio continually reminded the people between the Prut and the Dniester of their Romanian background, while the Soviets insisted that Moldavian was a very different nationality.[65]

Romania also asserted a limited independence in defense and foreign policy. It declined to permit joint WTO maneuvers on Romanian soil and restricted military integration, all the while emphatically protesting loyalty to the Soviet alliance. The critical turn came in 1968, when Romania refused to join in the Soviet criticism of Czechoslovak independence and in the subsequent invasion. It was then feared that Romania would be similarly reduced to conformity. Nicolae Ceauşescu, who had succeeded the deceased Gheorghiu-Dej in 1965, proclaimed to the multitude in Bucarest that Romania would forcibly resist invasion; the Communist Party thereby became truly popular and the cult of the personality of Ceauşescu was born.[66]

There has thus emerged a nationalistic, authoritarian Communism; reversing Lenin's motto, it is socialist in form and nationalist in content. Romanians saw Soviet policy as directed to the economic exploitation and political extinction of their nation; in the reaction, nationalism became almost an obsession.[67]

---

[63] George Schopflin, "Romanian Nationalism," *Survey*, 20, no. 2-3, (Spring-Summer 1974), 84, 86, 88.

[64] Ivan Volgyes, "Political Socialization in Eastern Europe" in *Political Socialization*, I. Volgyes, ed., p. 21.

[65] Schopflin, "Romanian Nationalism," p. 102.

[66] Julian Hale, *Ceauşescu's Romania* (London: Harrap, 1971), pp. 11, 92.

[67] Schopflin, "Romanian Nationalism," p. 77.

Otherwise, ideology is of secondary importance, and it is appropriately shaded; by the Romanian interpretation, the nation can progress only under socialism, and the party represents not the international working class but the nation.[68] It may be said that the Romanian leadership for its own purposes and national pride has adopted Stalinist methods of rule, somewhat as Romanians once embraced Turkish methods.[69] Party membership requires little knowledge of Marxism-Leninism, only loyalty to the leadership. The glories of socialism are mixed with the glories of Romanian history, its heroes and victories. Michael the Brave, who united Romania in 1600 and was degraded in the 1950s as a feudal conqueror, by 1976 was a grand symbol of the Communist government.

Nationalistic Communism. Nationalism and authoritarianism come together in forced industrialization in the Stalinist manner; socialism for Ceauşescu seems to consist in the devotion of the maximum percentage of the national product to investment—nearly a third, a percentage much higher than in the Soviet Union and other supposedly energetically industrializing Communist countries. There is also strong emphasis on heavy industry.

This has meant no liberalization; it has seemed that relative freedom from Soviet domination has been compensated by greater discipline at home. There has been no retreat from centralized planning in industry or agriculture. The economy is the most highly centralized of European Communist states, with managerial decision making at the ministerial level if not higher, enterprises being permitted only about as much autonomy as ordinarily permitted to shop foremen in the West.[70] This system of management, possible only for a relatively primitive and producer-oriented economy, has yielded a higher rate of industrial growth over the past two decades than in any other Soviet bloc state—a rate projected to continue through the 1976–1980 plan period.

In cultural affairs, there have been periodical fluctuations, as in other Communist states, from slackening to tightening; in 1971 there was "Little Cultural Revolution," with reemphasis on ideological verities and demands for conformity from writers and artists who had been permitted some latitude since 1968.[71] Contacts with the West have at times been welcome, but more often feared as subversive. On the whole, Romania remains one of the most closed regimes of Eastern Europe.[72]

One important development has been a reduction in the role of the party; from a hierarchy standing over the state and society, it has become a mass

---

[68] *Ibid.*, pp. 92-93.

[69] Hale, *Ceauşescu's Romania*, p. 188.

[70] David Granick, *Enterprise Guidance in Eastern Europe* (Princeton: Princeton University Press, 1975), p. 476.

[71] Trond Gilberg, "Romania in Conquest of Development" in *Political Socialization*, I. Volgyes, ed., p. 183.

[72] *Ibid.*, p. 148.

organization subordinate to the state.[73]   Party and state functions have been much more extensively merged than in the Soviet Union. Central Committee departments are joined to the corresponding ministries, the local party secretary is head of the local government council, etc.[74]   Romanians must swear loyalty to both state and party.

The strongest fusion is at the top. Ceauşescu is at once General Secretary of the party, president of state, president of the State Council, Chairman of the National Defense Council, head of the Ideological Commission, chairman of the Supreme Council on Socioeconomic Development. . . . ad infinitum. His personality cult is the strongest in the Communist world except that of Kim Il-song.[75]   As center of a small elite of loyalists who run the country, his image is everywhere, and the banners proclaim not only, or not primarily, the Communist Party but the name of Ceauşescu.[76]

The Russians thus have no cause to complain about liberalism within the Romanian regime or of possible contagion. Nonetheless, Romania may be living dangerously in seeking something near to nonalignment, minimizing cooperation with Comecon while forming links to the European Economic Community, maintaining good relations with China, showing more warmth toward the U. S. than any other Soviet-allied country, and paying minimal attention to WTO. The Hungarian desire to withdraw from the Soviet alliance was sufficient to provoke armed intervention in 1956, and the Soviet Union has never renounced the Brezhnev doctrine of the priority of "class" interests over "bourgeois" international law. Knowing that no one is likely to rush to help them, the Romanians must remain very cautious.[77]

Yugoslavia

Like Romania an advocate of national Communism and a rebel against Soviet domination, Yugoslavia is in some ways in a parallel situation. Yet conditions are importantly different. Yugoslavia rebelled not against Khrushchevian semiliberalism but against the effort to extend Stalinist controls to Yugoslavia. Yugoslavia is not in a Soviet military vise and has felt little danger of Soviet invasion since the consolidation of Western defenses under NATO in 1949. The threat to Yugoslavia is more ideological and political, although the specter of invasion reappeared in the aftermath of the invasion of Czechoslovakia and

---

[73] Francois Fejto, *A History of the People's Democracies: Eastern Europe since Stalin* (New York: Praeger, 1971), p. 246.

[74] Robert R. King, "Reorganisationen in Rumänien," *Osteuropa*, 24, 1 (January 1974), 36-46.

[75] Trond Gilberg, "Ceauşescu's Romania," *Problems of Communism*, 23, no. 4 (July-August 1974), 29-30.

[76] *New York Times*, April 29, 1975, p. 4.

[77] Graeme J. Gill, "Rumania: Background to Autonomy," *Survey*, 21 (Summer 1975), 109-110.

Yugoslavia has never been exempted from the applicability of "proletarian internationalism." Romania can be simply nationalistic, but Yugoslavia has to accommodate to a complex and difficult problem of self-aware nationalities; this is its chief vulnerability to Soviet pressure.

Undoubtedly the Soviet Union would be well pleased to eliminate Yugoslav deviationism from the Marxist-Leninist world because it is a perpetual challenge to conformism, especially in Soviet-dominated Eastern Europe. It is an alternative model in many ways more attractive than the Soviet, an example of dissent which has had incalculable if mostly invisible consequences for world Communism. The Sino-Soviet division was probably inevitable in any case, but the disobedience of Tito and the Yugoslavs was the first fissure in Stalinist monolithicism; all subsequent breaks came easier because of it.

Origins of Yugoslav Deviation. Stalin's conceit and foolishness drove the faithful Yugoslavs to break away. It had been taken for granted that to be Communist meant to be unconditionally loyal to the Fatherland of the Workers, the world's great proletarian socialist state; indeed, it was widely believed that to become Communist implied joining the Soviets' international union of socialist republics. At the very least, the Yugoslavs wished nothing better than to take the great Soviet Union as their guide and model.

Yet the Titoists were self-reliant; and when they came to power they almost immediately found that they had their own interests with which the Russians, for reasons of their own, did not sympathize. Having done very little for Tito during the war, Stalin urged him to collaborate with the royalists for the sake of Soviet relations with the Western Allies. Realpolitik again figured in Stalin's decision not to back Tito's ambitions in the Trieste area in 1945, and friction also arose over the misbehavior of Soviet forces in Yugoslavia.

As the Soviet sphere in Eastern Europe took shape, Stalin seems to have assumed that he could manage and exploit all the Communist countries in the same fashion. But the Yugoslavs, proud of their war record, disliked the domineering Soviet agents, especially the police. They also wanted to industrialize in their own way without gearing their economy to the Soviet,[78] and they declined to subordinate the Yugoslav army. As early as May 1945, when victory bells were still ringing, Tito publicly rejected the idea of being in anyone's sphere of influence.[79] Another cause of misunderstanding was Tito's somewhat naive hope that Stalin would approve a Balkan federation to unite good Communist countries but impede Soviet domination. Not least, perhaps, was the disharmony between a hierarchic, bureaucratized Communist state (although somewhat rejuvenated by the war) and a fresh, youthful, idealistic one.

---

[78] Charles P. McVicker, *Titoism: Pattern for International Communism* (New York: St. Martin's Press, 1957), p. 9.

[79] George W. Hoffmann and Fred W. Neal, *Yugoslavia and the New Communism* (New York: Twentieth Century Fund, 1962), pp. 113-114.

Complaints and charges went back and forth and escalated as leaders on both sides became aware of the issues involved. Tempers boiled in the beginning of 1948. Stalin forced the issue by withdrawing Soviet advisors. When this produced no contrition, he had Tito expelled from the movement. The Soviet Union, together with its satellites, broke off all relations—military, diplomatic, cultural, and commercial—in the hopeful conviction that the loyal mass of Yugoslav Communists would break away from the traitorous leaders. But Tito correctly summed up the situation for Stalin, "No matter how much each of us loves the land of socialism, the U.S.S.R., he can in no case love his country less, which is also developing socialism."[80] Only two men in the higher echelons of the party preferred adherence to the Soviet cause, which they had long upheld as the acme of political excellence; virtually all of the lower ranks out of a party membership of 400,000 displayed an unflinching loyalty to the national cause and leader—a loyalty possible because there were few Moscow-trained men in the party[81] and nearly all were veterans of the common fight. The violent attacks of the Stalinists made Tito popular as never before.[82]

Titoists React to Expulsion from the Movement. Nonetheless, such was the strength of conflicting loyalties that many in the Titoist leadership were made not only emotionally but physically sick by the quarrel.[83] The first reaction of the Titoists to expulsion from the movement was to demonstrate their Communist orthodoxy, so to prove their rightness in the dispute and convince Stalin of his error. Thus they kept up an anti-Western stance even while being execrated by the East, still seeing the Soviet Union as their protector against Western imperialism. Despite peasant resistance they stepped up agricultural collectivization, in which they were already well ahead of other satellite parties.

But Tito failed to realize that Stalin wanted not correctness but obedience. As it became apparent that Stalin was committed to the thesis that Tito was a fascist and would not bend, Tito began to popularize his revolution; he needed broad support to survive in Communist isolation. Collectivization was slowed, then undone; Yugoslavia remained, alongside Poland, a Communist country with predominantly private agriculture.[84] The Titoists began criticizing Stalinism for centralization and dictatorship and promising that they, in purer Marxism-Leninism, would rule *with* instead of *over* the people.

---

[80] Phyllis Auty, *Tito, a Biography* (New York: McGraw-Hill, 1970), p. 252.

[81] Adam B. Ulam, "Titoism," in *Marxism in the Modern World*, Milorad M. Drachkovitch, ed. (Stanford: Stanford University Press, 1965), p. 143.

[82] McVicker, *Titoism*, p. 20.

[83] Hoffmann and Neal, *Yugoslavia and the New Communism*, p. 140.

[84] About 85 percent of arable land is in private holdings, limited to 10 hectares. Although large cooperative and state farms contribute disproportionately to marketings, there has been less pressure than in Poland to increase the socialized sector.

The Yugoslavs Develop Their Own Brand of Communism. The uncertainty and demoralization by the discrediting of universalist-Communist loyalties demanded an ideological reorientation and the development of a unique Yugoslav variant of Communism. This was largely accomplished by the end of 1950.[85] It was discovered that "socialism" and "capitalism" were not black and white, and that there could be cooperation with elements of the "capitalist" world. Marx subsequently shrank from lofty prophet setting forth the course of history to a scholar-philosopher with no particular prescriptions for the present, and Marxism became welfare statism with a touch of Communist idealism.[86] Trade with the former partners of the Communist bloc was replaced by increased commerce and aid from the West, especially the U. S. Many privileges of the party elite were eliminated.[87] Most important, the Yugoslavs, to justify their revolution as both socialist and libertarian, took up the idea of "self-management," autonomy for national republics and communes and workers' councils to manage enterprises in fulfillment of Marxist ideals.

Socialism by persuasion was to come primarily through "workers' councils" originally provided for by a law of June 1950. The workers in an enterprise were to elect councils, which in turn elected a management committee. The workers' council was given broad powers over policy, including the distribution of profits, while management committees in the regional association named directors.[88] Direct central planning was ended, trade unions gained independence, and strikes were permitted—became in fact rather frequent. At first there was considerable confusion about the extent of freedom permitted the enterprises governed by workers' councils; party leaders did not know how far they should surrender power and workers hesitated to grasp levers thrust into their hands. But nominal autonomy tended to acquire reality through the 1960s, managers took over from party cadres, and the idea spread to many nonindustrial institutions such as banks, even governmental agencies. A reform of 1965 went further in reducing central controls and subjecting enterprises to market competition.

The purpose was partly ideological, an answer to Stalinist "state capitalism," a conversion of the theory of workers' ownership into a reality of workers' control and a step toward the presumptive withering of the state, in the Yugoslav view an essential part of progress toward socialism.[89] It was also economic, to permit profitable and efficient enterprises to prosper to the benefit of their

---

[85] For a discussion of doctrinal change from 1948 to 1953, see A. Ross Johnson, *The Transformation of Communist Ideology: The Yugoslav Case*, 1945-1953 (Cambridge: MIT Press, 1972).

[86] Dennison L. Rusinow, "Marxism Belgrade Style," in *Comparative Communism: The Soviet, Chinese and Yugoslav Models*, Gary K. Bertsch and Thomas W. Gauschow, eds. (San Francisco: W. H. Freeman, 1976), pp. 169-171.

[87] McVicker, *Titoism*, p. 30.

[88] Sharon Zukin, *Beyond Marx and Tito: Theory and Practice in Yugoslavia* (New York: Cambridge University Press, 1975), p. 57.

[89] Hoffmann and Neal, *Yugoslavia and the New Communism*, pp. 163-165.

workers, rewarding skill and effort and forcing inefficient enterprises to improve or go under.[90] There were negative aspects: economic freedom led to un-Marxist enrichment of some ahead of others; workers' councils, interested in job security, tended to resist innovation;[91] and Yugoslavia suffered a good deal of the instability familiar to market economies, with inflation as high as 30% yearly and unemployment alleviated only by the export of hundreds of thousands of workers to Western Europe. But results were excellent in terms of consumer goods; the Yugoslav standard of living, in 1948 well under that of the Soviet Union, by 1970 was perhaps ahead, variety and quality of goods being incomparably better. By 1975, Tito could boast that one Yugoslav in five had his own automobile, a figure about ten times better than in Romania and Bulgaria.

Workers' councils were only the most striking and most ideologically mandated aspect of the broader loosening of central direction. Yugoslavia has a nationality problem not unlike that of the Soviet Union: Serbs make up 41 percent of the population and were generally dominant in the old Yugoslavia; the wealthier Croats comprise 23 percent; and there are several other more or less mutually antagonistic groups mostly at lower levels of development. The federal division into six republics and two regions, originally decreed by a partisan congress in 1943, was at first more nominal than real, like the workers' councils; but administration was gradually devolved to them, and they acquired a share of the governmental budget.[92]

The minorities, whose separatist feelings had been repressed by the world war, became more self-assertive in the 1960s, and a constitutional reform of 1970 rounded out their powers. They could block most changes which they disliked and to a considerable extent control the federal regime through representation in the administrative branch and a collective presidency. The central government was practically limited to defense and foreign relations, and to preserving the unity of the market and the basics of socialism.[93] The principal problem plaguing relations between brother republics was the allocation of resources. The richer, specifically Croatia and Slovenia, wanted to keep more of what they felt they had produced; the poorer demanded more assistance from the center. As a result, the former favored more decentralization, the latter, a tighter structure.

Equating centralization with Stalinism, the Yugoslavs developed many more or less autonomous agencies under the autonomous republics. With considerable inventiveness, there have been established a multitude of elected

[90] Zukin, *Beyond Marx and Tito*, p. 73.

[91] Fejtö, *A History of the People's Democracies*, pp. 278-279.

[92] W. M. Fisk, "The Constitutionalism Movement in Yugoslavia," in *Communist Systems in Comparative Perspective*, Leonard J. Cohen and Jane P. Shapiro, eds. (Garden City, N. Y.: Doubleday & Co., 1974), p. 175.

[93] Paul Shoup, "Yugoslav Nationalities," *Problems of Communism*, 21, no. 1 (January-February 1972) 18-29.

councils and boards.[94]   Local government is in the hands of 501 putatively independent communes, which are close to the workers' councils. They, unlike Soviet local governments, have their own financial base and frequently oppose the wishes of their republic.

The court system was also given a larger measure of independence than usual in Communist countries. As an innovation, constitutional courts were given a power of legislative review in the interests of constitutionalism.[95] The courts not infrequently decided against the wishes of party magnates; in 1965, despite the anger of Tito himself, the writer Mihajlo Mihajlov was virtually acquitted.

The Communist Party (renamed in 1952 "League of Yugoslav Communists" to separate it semantically from the Stalinist parties) also diverged from the Soviet model by being relatively loose and non-dogmatic. Its Marxism consisted mostly in a vague commitment to equalitarianism, and the role of the members was defined (1969) mostly in terms of productivity.[96] Members were officially permitted to dissent and to criticize superior officials. There has never been a party blood purge. Before the break, the party was exceptionally secretive, hiding even the names of party officers.[97] Afterwards, party meetings were opened to the public. Policy formation was partly shifted from party councils to the government—including the parliament, which held significant debates and registered opposing votes. No party official (except Tito) was permitted to hold a government post. The party was not to supervise and control but only to exercise general leadership.[98]

Yugoslavia has also disengaged itself from the Communist model in its relations with the outside world. The borders are open; almost anyone can leave, and multitudes are exposed to Western societies. The remittances of hundreds of thousands of Yugoslav workers abroad, mostly in West Germany, have been essential to the Yugoslav balance of payments. Foreign trade is largely with the West, and it has become a relatively large percentage (about a quarter) of national income. Yugoslavia belongs to such Western economic groups as OECD and IMF. In the past, aid from the U.S. has been essential; at present, the Yugoslav economy is dependent upon and fluctuates with that of the West. More than any other Communist country, Yugoslavia has permitted foreign investment (up to 49 percent), and there have been many joint ventures, mostly with West German capital. In diplomacy, Yugoslavia commonly takes a position similar to that of the U.S.S.R., but it especially tried

---

[94] H. Gordon Skilling, *The Governments of Communist East Europe* (New York: Crowell, 1966), p. 161.

[95] Fisk, "Constitutionalism Movement," p. 188.

[96] Zukin, *Beyond Marx and Tito*, p. 64.

[97] McVicker, *Titoism*, p. 17.

[98] Fisk, "Constitutionalism Movement," p. 171.

to make itself leader of the non-aligned nations, raising the prestige of Yugoslavia much beyond its material strength.[99]

Limits of Liberalization. One could thus picture a Yugoslavia well on the way, under the guidance of a liberal Communist Party, to an open, plural society. One might also contend the concessions are only a facade, more of a democratic facade than tolerated in other Marxist-Leninist countries but nonetheless only a cover for the rule of the self-selected party elite. It may reasonably be argued that because of the quarrel with the Soviet Union and need to get along with the Western world, the Yugoslav leadership developed more trappings of liberalism, but that the essence of the dictatorship is unchanged. The case for a liberal evolution was more convincing through the 1960's; the contrary case against has been easier to make in the 1970s, when the rulership, under the direction of Tito, began reimposing discipline.

It is undeniable that the people in charge at the center are the same, with few changes, who were in charge in 1945-1947, when they were enthusiastic Stalinists and dogmatic centralizers. The partisan coterie around Tito—who was named life president at 82 in 1974—have never really shared power, only relaxed the exercise of it. They show no intention of withdrawing, and many of them, now in their fifties and sixties, may dominate the stage through the 1980s. There is no real pressure against them. The most important figure to lose power, police director Alexander Rankovich, fell in 1966 not because of anything said or done by public or press but because Tito so decided.[100] Tito personally enjoys a royal position and a cult many a Communist leader might envy;[101] towns are named after him, and schoolchildren sing about him.

In 1953-54, one of the top Yugoslav leaders, Milovan Djilas was led by disillusionment to launch an attack on what he saw as the self-serving elite. Although it evoked an enthusiastic response, when Tito and the inner circle felt themselves under fire they counterattacked and Djilas was eventually imprisoned. The "New Class" of which Djilas wrote is something of an exclusive and aristocratic club with its informal rules, membership in which requires above all total loyalty.[102] Supported by a party bureaucracy which is increasingly professional and has less and less to do with the workers, it is anti-intellectual in temper and close to the Soviet elite in mentality.

---

[99] Cf. Alvin Z. Rubinstein, *Yugoslavia and the Nonaligned World* (Princeton: Princeton University Press, 1970).

[100] Fejto, *People's Democracies*, p. 236.

[101] Cf. Anatole Shub, *An Empire Loses Hope: The Return of Stalin's Ghost* (New York: Norton, 1970), p. 59.

[102] Nenad D. Popovic, *Yugoslavia: The New Class in Crisis* (Syracuse: Syracuse University Press, 1968), p. 22 and *passim*.

Sympathizing with the Soviet party leaders because they are the same kind of people with similar problems, the Yugoslavs divorced themselves from Stalin essentially because (one may conclude) Stalin threatened their independence and privileges, and relations have continued after Stalin to be variably cool because the Soviets always want Soviet-led Communism. But the Titoists have never really been repelled by Soviet authoritarianism, and they have desired to be as close as possible without injuring their autonomy. In 1956, Tito scoffed at tales that the Hungarian revolution had been ignited by external reactionaries, yet he justified Soviet intervention to preserve Communist power.[103] Similarly in 1975 he warmly applauded Indira Gandhi's squelching of political freedoms in India.[104] It has been a great joy for Tito to be welcomed in Moscow and to greet Soviet delegations as fellow-socialists. In May 1974, Soviet representatives were seated at the Tenth Congress of the Yugoslav party. The Yugoslav press frequently speaks of the "crisis of capitalism" or finds reason to denounce the U. S. as aggressive and imperialistic and a menace to Yugoslavia (as regards, for example, naval maneuvers or harboring anti-Titoists).[105] Although nearly everyone sees the chief threat to Yugoslav independence in the East, this is seldom mentioned and usually only in veiled terms.

The Yugoslav New Class in any case does not seem threatened by the electoral process. Authentic democracy exists only in areas of no political importance, such as social security and public health;[106] and the Yugoslavs, like the Russians, like to think of "democracy" as lower-level citizen participation in administration, so-called "output" participation, in lieu of permitting a popular input to major choices of leadership or policies. In the elections, which are festive civic occasions somewhat in the Soviet manner, there are many more candidates than positions to be filled, but the party considers itself qualified to determine who may be proposed as candidates. The party, after all, claims to represent the will of the majority.[107] Potential difficulties are further avoided by indirect elections to higher bodies, permitting pressure and manipulation at each level; delegates to the federal assembly are chosen by three-stage elections. Then, too, the party nominates production workers, who are unlikely to have the sophistication or free time to oppose directives.[108] Even the value of lower-level direct democracy is qualified; for example, in the meetings of the communities into which communes are divided, only about one percent of voters are likely to attend, because decisions are devoid of consequences.[109]

The self-denying ordinance of the party to limit its role to general and ideological guidance did not last very long either; by 1958 it had returned to

---

[103] Hoffmann and Neal, *Yugoslavia and the New Communism*, p. 440.
[104] *New York Times*, July 31, 1975, p. 27.
[105] *New York Times*, March 4, 1975, p. 2.
[106] McVicker, *Titoism*, p. 316.
[107] *New York Times*, February 5, 1974.
[108] *New York Times*, May 17, 1974.
[109] Zukin, *Beyond Marx and Tito*, pp. 158, 165, 174.

"effective control over the direction of society."[110] The reality of federalism is diluted by the fact that republic parties are regarded as integral components of the central party and obliged to conform to its policies, much as is the case in the Soviet Union; autonomy of the governmental division is thus something of a formality if the party insists upon its will.[111] By means of party authority, Tito had fully quashed vocal Croatian nationalism by 1974. Votes in Yugoslav legislatures are normally nearly unanimous,[112] a result difficult to achieve without party guidance. Workers' control has some reality, but it is no threat to the elite, and it has been muted by reasserted party guidance in the enterprises. Council members and delegates are usually party members.[113] Workers' control has also been considerably circumscribed by state controls upon the economy, the fixing of wages and prices, and sundry bureaucratic meddling. As previously noted, directors must be approved by the party.

The Yugoslav party's stance is thus unique: it maintains basic Communist positions and requires uniformity of ideology without expecting uniformity of views.[114] The socialization of agriculture, a theoretically viable goal, continues to account for most agricultural investment. From time to time there are attacks on "bourgeois" profiteering and money-making, as though in fulfillment of ideals of socialist equalitarianism and in extenuation of the enjoyments of the party-privileged.[115] Atheism has also remained official policy and has claimed its share of party attention with the enactment in 1975 of new laws severely limiting religious activities.

The Yugoslav rulership was evidently willing to yield a considerable degree of freedom—much appreciated and generally rewarding—but without surrendering any real elements of power. It felt able to do so because of broad popular support.[116] But even when mildly threatened, it has reaffirmed its dogmatic self. There is to be autonomy and self-government everywhere except in the ruling party, which must be hierarchic and monolithic.[117]

From early 1970, Tito began calling for strengthening the role and unity of the party and for ideological purification, and he assailed liberal tendencies and the free-wheeling press. In September 1972, an angry and frustrated Tito issued a letter assailing disunity and calling for revolutionary spirit and purge of the party.[118] Independent-minded or potentially independent leaders were purged

---

[110] Skilling, *Governments of Communist East Europe*, pp. 64-65.

[111] *Ibid.*, p. 61.

[112] M. Fisk, "The Constitutionalism Movement," p. 187.

[113] Jacob Walkin, "Yugoslavia after the Tenth Party Congress," *Survey*, 22 (Winter 1976), 71.

[114] Walkin, "Yugoslavia after the Tenth Party Congress," p. 70.

[115] Zukin, *Beyond Marx and Tito*, p. 221.

[116] Hoffmann and Neal, *Yugoslavia and the New Communism*, p. 185.

[117] Walkin, "Yugoslavia after the Tenth Party Congress," p. 70.

[118] *Yearbook on International Communist Affairs, 1973*, ed. Richard F. Staar (Stanford: Hoover Institution Press, 1973), pp. 101–102.

in all republics. The prohibition against combining party and government posts
was derogated in 1974. Freedom of expression, the cornerstone of political freedom, came to seem decidedly conditional. A 1951 law prohibiting propagation
of "ideas hostile to the people and the government," and another of 1968 that
banned publications which "upset the citizenry" were more sternly enforced;
a 1975 law made even private criticism of the state a crime.[119] Mihajlov, who
had been gently treated in 1965, was repeatedly harassed until he was sentenced
in 1975 to seven years for having written articles for the *New York Times*.[120]
It was alleged that he had slandered Yugoslavia by stating that there was no freedom of speech in the country. About the same time fifteen persons, whose
leaders were professors and students, received terms up to thirteen years for
allegedly plotting the separation of Croatia.[121] Eight philosophy professors of
the University of Belgrade, who had been in the bad graces of the party for their
deviant Marxism, were ousted although, in view of the general support of their
colleagues, it was necessary to quash university autonomy to do so. One tactic
used against them by the party was to insist that sweepers and janitors have
equal voice with instructors in university self-government.[122] The scholarly
journal *Praxis*, long a vehicle of independent Marxism (principally tending to
criticize the "new class" in socialist society), was spared for many years because
of its international reputation but was finally closed in February 1975. Tito
ordered the courts not to "latch onto paragraphs like drunks clutching a rail-
ing," and his second in command and chief ideologist, Edvard Kardelj, stated
it pointedly: "Where we are weak, we must not hesitate to have recourse to
methods of revolutionary violence."[123] The party magazine *Kommunist* spoke
of "anarcho-liberal prattle about the so-called benefits of bourgeois freedoms."[124] Political prisoners, including liberals, minority separatists, and
pro-Soviet Communists, number in the thousands and are perhaps as many as
in any East European country.[125]

Judgment of the Yugoslav variant of Communism must consequently be
qualified. There are few banners, statues, or prominent displays such as commonly adorn Soviet streets, although portraits of Tito are visible enough; and
propaganda is usually muted in the press. Most art and literature are apolitical,
and artists and writers are free to create so long as they do not criticize sharply.
There is no a priori censorship, only the possibility of subsequent ban by court
order; and private publishers produce nearly as many titles as official publishing

[119] *New York Times,* March 4, 1975, p. 2.
[120] *New York Times*, March 1, 1975, p. 2.
[121] *New York Times*, February 18, 1975, p. 6.
[122] *New York Times*, February 6, 1975, p. 12.
[123] *Die Zeit*, March 14, 1975, p. 5.
[124] *New York Times*, January 22, 1976, p. 15.
[125] *Ibid.*

houses.[126] Newspapers are nearly uniform, but they are very informative in comparison with those of other East European Communist states, not to speak of the Soviet Union. The foreign press is freely available. Party spokesmen denounce Western influences in the press, but magazines continue to carry sensationalism and nudes, quite contrary to Communist morality.[127] Perhaps fifteen million persons cross the borders yearly. There is freedom of association so long as it is not anti-party. Tito has never shot and seldom jailed his opponents; Djilas, for example, could retire on pension and meet freely with foreign reporters. The workers' councils are a real source of pride.

It is questionable whether the party can manage so well in the absence of its lone great figure, Tito. Yet the country seems securely ruled by a small group which ordinarily exercises arbitral rights and whose power is undoubtedly decisive should it need to be invoked. Because of slackness of controls and appearances of autonomy, the Yugoslav League enjoys more genuine legitimacy than most ruling Communist parties; the democratic facade is more convincing. It may be questioned whether the usual Communist insistence on a grand panoply of controls and near-total conformity does not mix paranoia with political calculation.

Albania

The most hostile to the Soviet Union of all European states, non-Communist as well as Communist, is Albania. Like Romania, it pulled away not from Stalinist but from Khrushchevian Russia; and it still reveres Stalin as a leading saint of "scientific socialism." Moreover, the direct threat perceived by Albanian leaders is from Yugoslavia, which has made much of its softening of Communism. The Albanians consequently pull in the opposite direction and have the most unqualifiedly regimented state of Europe. Isolated from the West before the split, Albania completed its insularity by renouncing contact with the Soviet sphere and neighboring Yugoslavia as well. A mountainous backcountry on the road to nowhere, it is also the most backward country of Europe.

The first step in Albania's withdrawal from Communist patronage was its break with Yugoslavia. Formed during the war under the aegis of Yugoslav partisans, the Albanian Communist Party grew up as an appendage of the Titoist movement. There were Yugoslav advisors, joint Albanian-Yugoslav corporations, and a Yugoslav economic assistance program.[128] The Tito-Stalin divorce of 1948 set

---

[126] Zdenko Antic, "Private Publishing in Yugoslavia," Radio Free Europe *Background Report*, January 11, 1976.

[127] *New York Times*, June 23, 1975, p. 6.

[128] Hoffmann and Neal, *Yugoslavia and the New Communism*, p. 101.

Albania loose; to assert independence from the nearer menace, Albania adhered to the Soviet connection. Enver Hoxha took advantage of the rupture to purge the pro-Yugoslav faction of the party. Small-scale attempts at subversion by U.S. and British intelligence agencies during the years 1949 through 1953 helped keep Albania on an anti-Western course.[129]

After Stalin's death, the Albanian leaders, untroubled by Stalin's excesses, saw De-Stalinization as a betrayal of Communism and a threat to themselves. Consequently, they remain faithful to the dictator, whose statue still smiles down on squares all over Albania. Contrary to Soviet wishes, they also refused reconciliation with Tito; and, as in the case of Romania, they saw their industrialization plans menaced by Soviet schemes for economic coordination.

Total divorce from Moscow came with the Sino-Soviet split, which provided both an alternative model and a suitably distant and hence harmless source of support. As Albania took the Chinese line in the polemics beginning in 1960, the Russians tried to exert pressure on Albania much as they did on China about the same time, by reducing aid and trade, intriguing in the Albanian party, and trying to overthrow Hoxha. The effort was counterproductive, partly because the Chinese kept their small ally afloat. The frustrated Russians expelled Albania, 1961-62, from the bloc and their Communist movement.

Having become a distant satellite of Maoist China, Albania launched a Communist Education Campaign to eliminate divergent and non-Communist thinking, especially religion; and there were movements to cleanse the land of revisionism and bureaucratism. Artists and writers were sent to the villages to learn from the peasants, Chinese style.[130] This was followed by the Albanian Cultural Revolution, which ran its course in synchrony with the Chinese. Like the Chinese, the Albanian version was equalitarian, sending the cadres "back to the masses." It reduced salary differentials, mobilized the youth and damned individualism and leftovers of capitalism, in particular the household plots that had been permitted the collectivized peasants. It virtually eliminated foreign contacts and the publication of foreign books. Likewise it assailed religion and closed all churches; by 1969 Albania claimed to be in the vanguard of the world by virtue of having abolished religion. The Cultural Revolution also exalted workers over technical specialists, mixed more ideology with production, and demanded volunteer labor.

The Albanian Cultural Revolution was, however, an artificial echo of the Chinese. There was no attack on the party and state apparatus; youth was mobilized but only under close party leadership. There was some decentralization,

---

[129] Nicholas C. Pano, "The Albanian Cultural Revolution," *Problems of Communism*, 24, no. 4 (July-August 1974), 46.

[130] Peter R. Prifti, "The Albanian Party of Labor and the Intelligentsia," *East European Quarterly*, 8, no. 3 (Fall 1974), 320.

and communes were introduced, but the chief purposes were not renewal of spirit, Chinese style, but discipline and production.[121]

After 1969-1970 there was a slight relaxation, as trade with Balkan neighbors and some smaller Western European countries was resumed; Hoxha even spoke of "democratization." The Chinese alliance weakened as China steered toward detente with the U. S. and wound down its assistance program for the Balkan client. But by 1973, Hoxha, apparently apprehensive of loss of control, reversed gears and instituted a campaign against foreign influences.[132] Bristling against suggestions of detente, the Albanians brushed aside suggestions for normalization from both the Soviet Union and the U. S. and warned bitterly of the dangers of imperialist-revisionist encirclement. A decree of September 1974 ordered all Albanian citizens whose names were inappropriate by "political, ideological, and moral standards"—presumably referring to minorities—to change their names.[133] Exceptionally, in 1975 Albania asked for Western tenders of oil drilling equipment;[134] but the country remained remarkably isolated, untempted by tourist earnings, not greatly interested in foreign trade, and economically stagnant.

Like the East German rulership, the Albanian Communists seem to act under compulsions of insecurity. Their country is weak and has suffered direly in the past from Turkish and Italian occupation, and some nervousness is understandable. Worse, it is difficult to see how Communism can be permanently sustained in such a small country without external supports. It is probably a reflection of insecurity that Albanian politics are peculiarly cryptic and rather unstable. The real power structure is little known, beyond the chieftainship of Hoxha, party boss for over thrity years, assisted by Mehmet Shehu, head of the administration since 1954. There have been repeated mini-purges. In 1974, the minister of defense and aides were purged (as became known outside only months later), and in 1976 there was a major shakeup of the government and Central Committee.

The basic problem is ideological. Relations with the intelligentisia are especially difficult.[135] To insist on orthodoxy in art and literature, as well as in education, is to accept primitiveness and backwardness; at the same time it is impractical because of the ease with which Albanians who have receivers can tune to Greek, Italian, or Yugoslav television. Communism must promise

[131] Nicolas C. Pano, "Albania in the Sixties," in *The Changing Face of Communism in Eastern Europe,* Peter Toma, ed., p. 266.

[132] Ramadan Marmullaku, *Albania and the Albanians* (London: C. Hurst & Co., 1975), p. 65.

[133] *New York Times,* February 27, 1976, p. 3.

[134] *Business Week,* July 7, 1975, p. 34.

[135] Cf. Prifti, "The Albanian Party."

modernization, but to fulfill the task of raising the country from backwardness and inferiority vis-à-vis its neighbors, it must open up and accept interdependence and extensive contacts that would undermine an ideology seemingly to be retained at all costs. It is difficult even for a very large country such as Russia to keep up a faith of its own in a pluralistic and varied world—the Albanians must implausibly insist that everyone else is out of step.

Other Asian Communisms

North Korea

Communist rule in the northern part of Korea, as in Romania, was established under the direction of the Soviet Union in a land where there was practically no native Communist movement. Yet Korean Communism, like Romanian, has developed a strongly nationalistic character under a vigorously self-assertive leadership.

Soviet occupation forces were withdrawn at the end of 1948, probably to strengthen the position of North Korea in pushing for reunification, and perhaps because there was little to gain economically from control of the area. Soviet influence was clearly dominant, however, up to the Korean war, and the government north of the 38th parallel had every appearance of puppetry. But the Koreans became embittered because the Soviet Union supplied only equipment while the Chinese sent men.[136]

The Evolution of Ch'uché. In 1955 Kim Il-song still spoke of love for the Soviet Union and the "socialist camp" as equivalent to love of Korea.[137] But Korea was setting out on its own road, stressing independence and self-identity, the ideological expression of which was Ch'uché. This vague concept, which came to be the regnant philosophy of North Korea (and to a considerable extent of South Korea as well),[138] may be seen as a response to Korea's long history of subservience to China and Japan. It means almost everything good: independence, socialism, and the happiness of the people, with the accent on independence.[139]

Political independence was to be based on economic self-sufficiency. As early as 1948, Kim Il-song was speaking of economic independence.[140]

---

[136] Joungwon A. Kim, *Divided Korea: The Politics of Development 1945-1972* (Cambridge: Harvard University Press, 1975), p. 287.

[137] Chong-sik Lee, "Stalinism in the East," in *Communist Revolution in Asia: Tactics, Goals, and Achievements,* Robert A. Scalapino, ed. (Englewood Cliffs, N. J.: Prentice-Hall, 1965), p. 125.

[138] B. C. Koh, "Chuch'esong in Korean Politics," *Studies in Comparative Communism,* 7, no. 1-2 (Spring-Summer 1974), 85.

[139] *Ibid.,* pp. 83-97.

[140] Robert R. Simmons, *The Strained Alliance* (New York: Free Press, 1975), p. 30.

Despite dire need for assistance for reconstruction after the almost total devastation of the war, North Korea set out at high cost to make itself totally self-reliant.[141] There were, of course, the justified suspicions that the Russians wanted to keep Korea a supplier of raw materials. A turning point came in August 1956, when a group of leaders tried to use Khrushchev's denunciations of Stalinism and the cult of personality to push Kim aside. Having defeated and expelled his critics, Kim raised his own cult and much reduced Soviet influence.[142]

In 1958, the Koreans undertook the "Flying Horse" movement in imitation of the Chinese Great Leap Forward.[143] Previously the peasantry had been gathered into Soviet-style collectives; now they joined communes similar to the Chinese although smaller and less equalitarian–utopian. There was an industrial push at the same time, with stress on "moral incentives." Thereafter Chinese influence was usually more apparent than Soviet; and the Koreans, fervent revolutionaries, were apt to side with the Chinese on international issues. After the ouster of Khrushchev in October 1964, relations with the Soviet Union were normalized; but they have never returned to the earlier intimacy and at times have been barely correct. As Kim Il-song said, they would adhere to neither side: "Although certain people say the Soviet way is best, have we not reached a point where we can construct our own way?"[144]

Chinese and Korean Communism. Korean conditions are much more like Chinese than Soviet, and the North Korean world view is closer to that of Mao than to that of Khrushchev or Brezhnev.[145] Consequently, although Kim has been little influenced by Maoist ideology (perhaps because of personal rivalry as well as the vagueness of the message), Korean practice has owed a good deal to Chinese examples,[146] as in the Flying Horse movement and stress on cadres "going down to the masses." The Kim method is for the leader to visit a village or factory, talk with workers, solve the problems, and use it as a general model. For Koreans as for Maoists, "proletarian" is largely a mental condition;[147] and the Koreans, like the Chinese, welcomed to the United Front

---

[141] *Ibid.*, pp. 123–124.

[142] Chin O. Chung, "The Government and Political Structure of North Korea" in *Government and Politics of Korea*, Se-Jin Kim and Chang-Hyun Cho, eds. (Silver Spring, Md: Research Institute on Korean Affairs, 1972), pp. 186–187.

[143] Ilpyong J. Kim, "Changing Perspectives in North Korea," *Problems of Communism*, 22, no. 1 (January, -February 1973), 45–46.

[144] *Newsweek*, December 6, 1965, p. 59.

[145] Robert Scalapino, "The Foreign Policy of North Korea," in *Communist Revolution in Asia*, R. Scalapino, ed., p. 46.

[146] Robert Scalapino and Chong-sik Lee, *Communism in Korea*, (Berkeley: University of California, 1972), Vol. 2, p. 868.

[147] *Ibid.*, p. 861.

all those willing to support it, including "capitalists."[148] Kim, like Mao (and Stalin), sees contradictions continuing under socialism and justifying corrective measures. The Koreans share some of the Chinese distrust of the city. Both claim to believe in general revolution, desire to be leaders of the Third World, and make some effort to propagate their revolutionary views.

There are marked differences, however. The North Koreans have no feeling for spontaneity among the masses and have no idea of calling upon the people to set right the party apparatus, which is a tool in Kim's hand. On the contrary, their frank espousal of the "core" guiding the relatively large party is super-Leninism.[149] Any popular movement in Korea is to be closely controlled, and the peasants have not been adulated or called upon to educate anyone. Neither has the Korean army been tempted to do away with insignia or to make officers look like rank and file and live with them. The Koreans, with considerable industrial development, have also been more disposed to rely on technology, not allowing ideological clouds to obscure the need for expertise. Finally, the Chinese have often given an impression of joviality beneath their Communist commitment, at least a willingness to seem occasionally human; the visage of North Korea is unblemished in its grimness. The two Communisms are sufficiently disparate that the Chinese deprecated Kim, like all other foreigners except Albanians, during their Cultural Revolution.

The Cult of Kim Il-Song. In North Korea, the cult of the leader has even more than in Maoist China taken the place of ideology in a scholastic sense. Kim was no great hero of war or revolutionary struggle and his position was weak in the disorder of 1945–46; but his cult gained noticeably in the aftermath of the war, especially since 1955-56[150] when his works were first published. Having attained full power only in 1961 after successively eliminating rival groups à la Stalin, the Kim regime subsequently equated the infallibility of the leader with the essence of Communist ideology.

There is little evidence of Kim's having read Marxist-Leninist literature. His writings are filled with mundane verbiage, with little pretense to theoretical invention and without the pithy sense that often graces Mao's utterances. Yet, whether because of Kim's strength of personality and vanity or because of Korea's need for a central symbolic figure, few individuals have ever made themselves so worshipped.

The cult of the Kim personality surpasses that of such eminences as Stalin and Mao.[151] In front of the Museum of the Korean Revolution stands a statue of Kim high as a six-story building; inside are 95 monumental rooms devoted

---

[148] Simmons, *The Strained Alliance*, p. 31.

[149] Bruce G. Cumings, "Kim's Korean Communism," *Problems of Communism*, 32, no. 2 (March-April 1974), pp. 27-41.

[150] Ilpyong J. Kim, *Communist Politics in North Korea* (New York: Praeger, 1975), p. 28.

[151] Cf. Harrison Salisbury, *To Peking and Beyond: A Report on the New Asia* (New York: Quadrangle Books, 1973), pp. 213-214.

to Kim Il-song, glorifying even his ancestry to the third generation. In Confucian fashion, his whole family is exalted as model revolutionaries. There is hardly a song or art work that does not allude to him.[152] He is credited with revolutionary heroics from boyhood and is treated as single-handed victor over Japan in World War II. His biography makes him sole liberator of Korea, with no mention of the Soviet Union; he likewise was the victor of the Korean war, his glory unshadowed by mention of the Chinese who rescued him from total defeat.[153] He is the greatest of Communist (or other) leaders, outdistancing all: "He first made it possible for a Marxist-Leninist party, after the establishment of the socialist system, to direct all its lines and policies to one clear class object, and taught how to go straight on to socialism."[154]

Kim's writings take precedence over the classics of Marxism-Leninism, and everyone is required to read them—indeed, Koreans are expected to devote two hours' daily to them, more on weekends.[155] Bride and groom at weddings swear loyalty to the unique genius with unexampled love for his people. He must be something of a god, because "In Chullima Korea, miracle is an everyday occurrence."[156] According to a North Korean statement, "Should any thought other than that of the leader exist, the Party would end up as a club-like organization," and "Boundless loyalty to the great leader forms the central core of our revolutionary world view."[157]

The Epitome of Autocracy. Everything is done to preclude variant thinking and to assure boundless loyalty in an autocracy virtually or quite without equal in history. The practice of religion, Buddhist, Christian, or Confucianist, has been suppressed. Lineage records have been destroyed to weaken family structures. Even other Communist countries threaten contamination; beginning in 1961, students were withdrawn from the Soviet Union and Eastern Europe, and only a few specialists have been permitted to study in Communist countries.[158] Cultural imports from China and the Soviet Union have been severely restricted. In 1973, North Korea boycotted the University Games in Moscow on grounds that South Korea was invited.[159]

Control of behavior is severe, with more reliance on the police than in China, less on persuasion. There is little pretense to democracy; since 1962, it has been impossible to cast a negative vote in elections, and results have always been 100 percent. Neighborhood committees oversee all aspects of life.

---

[152] H. Edward Kim, "Rare Look at North Korea," *National Geographic Magazine,* 146, no. 2 (August 1974), 256.

[153] Baik Bong, *Kim Il-Song: Biography* (Tokyo: Miraisha, 1970), Vol. II, chap. 4.

[154] *Ibid.* p. 368.

[155] Joungwon Kim, *Divided Korea,* p. 320.

[156] Note of Translation Committee, in Baik, *Kim Il-Song,* p. 623.

[157] Scalapino and Lee, *Communism in Korea,* Vol. II, p. 861.

[158] *Ibid.* p. 899.

[159] B. C. Koh, "North Korea: Old Goals and New Realities," *Asian Survey,* 14, no. 1 (January 1974), 41.

The peasants' work is regimented, and after a stint in the fields they relax with discussion of the thoughts of Kim..Workers march to and from the workplace. A plant manager told Harrison Salisbury that, since the workers own the country, it is up to the state to see that each one is in his proper niche.[160] There seems to be a high degree of conformity among whatever intellectuals there are, no doubt partly because there was only a feeble native intellectual tradition, partly because inducements are added to coercion; for example, university professors may even have automobiles.[161] Economic incentives are used to stimulate production, but controls and the priority of heavy industry are unremittingly Stalinist.[162]

The rationalization for national discipline is the permanent danger of imperialism along with the mission of reunification. Ch'uché means economic, political, and ideological mobilization. The struggle against capitalism, consecrated by Marxism, coincided with the struggle against the U. S., not only the obstacle to unification (and enslaver of the South in Kimist eyes) but enemy in a bitter war, the power that laid low the cities and might do so again. Hence the danger justified the demands of the state for selfless dedication and conformity, and the total state magnified those same dangers, justifying its own existence. As Kim Il-song said, "without educating the people in this spirit [of hatred for the U. S.] we cannot defeat the U. S., which is superior in technology."[163] North Korea became probably the most nationalistic country in the world.[164] It also became the most militarized, with the possible exception of North Vietnam while actively at war. Since 1966, the military has consumed over 30 percent of the national budget.[165] Even more than in most Communist countries, heavy and military industry receive priority. There is regular military training for men from 18 to 45, for women from 18 to 35, at least two hours weekly, with few exceptions. There is endless play of heroics and battle.[165] Kindergarten children act out battles against Japanese or Americans, and the greatest glory is to be a soldier.[166] Virtually all top leaders have a military background, the governing core being composed of Kim's fellows from Manchurian guerrilla days; and propaganda makes much of their combat experience.[167] Two-thirds of the Central Committee are either ex-guerrillas or active generals.[168]

---

[160] Salisbury, *To Peking and Beyond*, p. 202.

[161] Kim, *Divided Korea*, p. 262.

[162] Joseph Sang-Hom Chung, "Economic Development of North Korea, 1945-1947" in *Government and Politics of Korea*, Se-Jin Kim and Chang-Hyun Cho, eds. p. 231.

[163] Salisbury, *To Peking and Beyond*, p. 192.

[164] *Ibid.*, p. 195.

[165] Scalapino and Lee, *Communism in Korea*, Vol. 2, p. 919.

[166] Salisbury, *To Peking and Beyond*, p. 193.

[167] Glenn D. Paige, "Korea" in *Communism and Revolution: The Strategic Uses of Political Violence*, Cyril F. Black and Thomas P. Thornton, eds. (Princeton: Princeton University Press, 1964), pp. 218-219.

[168] Chin O. Chung, "The Government and Political Structure of North Korea" in *Government and Politics of Korea*, Kim and Cho, eds., p. 192.

There are obvious parallels to the nationalistic truculence of North Korea throughout the Communist world. Like Romania, North Korea feels it must fend off the domination of its big neighbors, and the cult of the leader is more palatable as a symbol of national independence. Like Albania, Korea feels its weakness as a small, relatively backward state. Like East Germany, it is aware that many of its citizens might choose the non-Communist part of the nation, and it must fear for the loyalty of its subjects. The respective elites have responded appropriately with a nationalistic turn to their Communism that fuses xenophobia and dogmatism with efforts to strengthen organization to the utmost and build a firmly integrated "socialism."

The truculence of Korean Communism also owes something to the national past. A proud, highly cultured nation with an isolationist tradition (the "Hermit Kingdom"), Korea was made a colony of the Japanese, who brutally maltreated their colonials and subjected them to intense humiliation. By comparison, Vietnamese Communism was tempered and "westernized" by the exposure to French influence for sixty years. Korea felt even less Western influence than did China and was far more abused, especially in its pride. There is reason for its Communism to be more violent and hate-filled.

Vietnam

The North Koreans rarely permitted Western journalists to view their country, even though they were engaged in no fighting after 1953. The North Vietnamese by contrast allowed many journalists and other relatively sympathetic individuals from the U. S. to visit, even though they were at war; and they made an impression of general good sense and openness.[169] In North Korea, contacts of foreigners with nonofficial persons were few and very controlled; there was heard nothing but the official propaganda line. In North Vietnam, visitors mingled rather easily, people joked and spoke fairly freely of their troubles as well as their victories,[170] and the police were little in evidence. In the middle of the war, in 1970, North Vietnam gave some scope to material incentives and permitted a free market in foods. At one time, from August to December 1956, open political criticism was sanctioned.[171] The regime subsequently undertook reeducation of the intellectuals, many of whom were put to manual labor, Chinese style;[172] but repression in North Vietnam has never approached the intellectual suffocation of North Korea.

---

[169] For a typical reportage, cf. Mary McCarthy, *Hanoi* (New York: Harcourt, Brace, 1968).

[170] *New York Times*, March 31, 1973, p. 16.

[171] Robert F. Turner, *Vietnamese Communism: Its Origin and Development* (Stanford: Hoover Institution, 1975), p. 152.

[172] P. J. Honey, "Ho Chi Minh and the Intellectuals," in *Vietnam: Anatomy of a Conflict*, Wesley R. Fishel, ed. (Itasca, Ill.: Peacock Publishers, 1968), pp. 161-165.

The politics of leadership have also been different. Ho Chi Minh was a genuine nationalist-revolutionary hero, respect and affection for whom came easily; he accepted the tribute modestly and had no inflated cult. After his death in 1969, the party chairmanship was not filled, and North Vietnam had as genuine and as stable a collective leadership as can be found in the Communist world. The quadrumvirate of Le Duan, party leader, Pham Van Dong, head of government, Chuong Tring, chief ideologist, and Vo Nguyen Giap, defense minister, has seemed very firm, with no dominant personality. Incredibly, there has been no visible leadership struggle since 1946. The leadership, solidified by the revolutionary struggle and shared sufferings—nearly all Central Committee members spent many years in jail—has been practically unchanged for many years. Not one of the thirteen members of the 1960 Politburo has been demoted.[173]

The differences of the two embattled Asian Communisms may be accounted for in part by the background of the one in Japanese, of the other in French colonialism. The French created an intelligentsia imbued with French culture[174] and imparted a respect for individualism and rule of law negated by the Japanese. North Vietnamese leaders had a French education; the Japanese hardly educated Koreans at all. Differences in personality no doubt also played a part, though what may be gleaned from Kim's personal life seems to indicate an easy-going temperament. Another factor is that the North Vietnamese were engaged in a genuine and popular war, in which the adherence of the people did not have to be forced. The North Koreans' situation, on the other hand, approximated that of the East Germans; originally installed by Soviet occupation forces, the Communists were none too well liked, especially as they lacked legitimacy either as national revolutionaries or as representatives of the majority of the nation. The regime was consequently constrained to shrill dogmatism and strict controls, like the East Germans. The Koreans' participation in their "war of liberation" was too brief to teach much realism; and foreign intervention, not their own efforts, was decisive. The North Vietnamese Communists, on the other hand, rose by their own efforts with wide popular support, and they shared with the masses the cause of national liberation—a cause intensified by the sufferings of war, French reprisals, and American bombings. In such a clear-cut situation, the leadership could afford to be flexible and reasonable,[175] much as Stalinist Russia was perforce rational in the well-understood and universally shared struggle for survival against Nazi Germany. The myth and the psychological compulsion became superfluous.

---

[173]David W. P. Elliott, "North Vietnam Since Ho," *Problems of Communism*, 24 (July-August 1975), 42-46.

[174]As in most other Communist parties, the elite is of middle-class origins; a 1953 study showed 1365 out of 1855 top posts held by persons of the "bourgeoisie" or "intelligentsia." Bernard B. Fall, "Power and Pressure Groups," in *North Vietnam Today*, J. P. Honey, ed. (New York: Praeger, 1962), p. 64.

[175]William S. Turley, "The DRV since the Death of Ho Chi Minh," in *Indochina in Conflict: A Political Assessment,* W. S. Turley and Allan E. Goodman, eds. (Lexington, Mass.: D. C. Heath, 1972), p. 26.

Party Mobilization since 1956. The North Vietnamese Communists have been stern enough on occasion. They ruthlessly eliminated non-Communist nationalists on the way to sole power, not scrupling to use French assistance when available. Although there have been no party purges, the rural population was thoroughly cleansed in the course of agrarian reform, especially in 1956. Peasants were classified somewhat arbitrarily into five classes, and kangaroo courts tried and sentenced many "landlords" who may have had only about two acres of land.[176] Excesses were sufficient to provoke an uprising in November 1956, which could be crushed only by the army. The Communists then proceeded to compulsory collectivization, which was virtually complete by 1963; but they have never tried Chinese-style communes. They do have huge state farms, run, like those of Cuba, by the army.[177] The party began an industrialization program in 1954 as soon as its position was relatively secure, with the usual Communist emphasis on heavy industry at the expense of living standards.[178]

Within the internationalist ideological framework, the Vietnamese Communists have taken pride in seeing "world contradictions," the historic clash of capitalism and socialism, coming to a focus in their battle and to view their victory as something even greater than the expulsion of French and American power from Vietnam. The feeling of a common cause with the "popular masses" of the U. S. and elsewhere has been helpful to morale; as socialists, Vietnamese Communists called upon the sympathies of Leftists everywhere. As in the Soviet Union and Czechoslovakia, Marxism-Leninism furnishes a basis for community with the various minorities who make up about fifteen percent of the population.

Communism has served in Vietnam its ordinary function of mobilizing formerly inert peoples. It told cadres, and cadres told peasants, that they had rights as people, even superior rights as "proletarians" against the rich and powerful, the French and Americans and those dependent upon them, and that they, the humble people, could defeat the wealthy.[179] Setting aside both foreign and traditional influences, the new doctrine brought millions into the stream of active endeavor, placing a new emphasis not only on the poor, the large majority, but on women, who were made fighters and producers alongside men, and on ethnic minorities. It created for all a supreme duty nourished by an equalitarian ethos. It was good for both the leaders and the led that the North Vietnamese army, like the Chinese, did away with visible emblems of

---

[176] Bernard B. Fall, *The Two Viet-Nams*, rev. ed. (New York: Praeger, 1964), pp. 155–156.

[177] Joseph Buttinger, *Vietnam: A Dragon Embattled* (New York: Praeger, 1967), Vol. II, p. 980.

[178] *Ibid.*, p. 898.

[179] Frances Fitzgerald, *Fire in the Lake* (Boston: Little, Brown, 1972), pp. 170-171.

status. As Ho said, "The national liberation revolution can be counted a complete success only if it develops into a socialist revolution."[180]

Communism in Vietnam remains relatively low-key. Members of the party are supposed to be chosen not by the insiders as per usual Communist practice, but by the workers themselves. Ho Chi Minh, who was always careful to steer pragmatically between Peking and Moscow, did not pretend to be a theoretician, made little use of Marxist language, and left no special dogmas.[181] It does not seem to be expected that the people in general should be steeped in Marxism-Leninism. It is obligatory for the cadres, but in the Vietnamese usage ideology remains vague and moralistic, and class categories are rather like abstractions to be given definite content as the occasion might require.[182] It is enough that the masses be patriotic—nationalism, not class consciousness, is the basis of real war. The North Vietnamese soldiers were extremely well motivated, but few regarded themselves as Communist.[183] As a North Vietnamese spokesman put it to a sympathetic American, "The young people only pay attention to things that are immediate and they forget the traditions, but it is the line of the party to restore all that is purely traditional Vietnamese."[184]

Vietnamese Eclecticism. In sum, Vietnamese Communism has been marked by relative flexibility and practicality. It has freely borrowed from all sides, e.g., party and state organization from the Soviet Union, and thought control techniques from Maoist China.[185] The 1959 constitution was in large part copied literally from the Chinese constitution of 1954.[186] Technology is freely borrowed from the West; in fact, the Chairman of the State Science and Technical Commission cited Britain, Japan, and the U.S. as examples of the successful application of technology, not mentioning the Soviet Union.[187] Vietnam has also laid out a welcome mat to foreign investment. It has been more oriented to economic growth than China and has strongly emphasized the training of technical personnel,[188] untroubled by the dilemma of "Red" versus "expert."

---

[180] Cited by Chalmers A. Johnson, *Autopsy on People's War* (Berkeley: University of California Press, 1973), p. 12.

[181] Jean Lacouture, *Ho Chi Minh: A Political Biography* (New York: Random House, 1968), p. 224.

[182] Fitzgerald, *Fire in the Lake*, p. 218.

[183] Konrad Kellen, "1971 and Beyond: The View from Hanoi," in *Indochina in Conflict*, W. S. Turley and A. E. Goodman, eds., p. 105.

[184] Lynd and Hayden, *The Other Side*, p. 101.

[185] Hoang Van Chi, *From Colonialism to Communism* (New Delhi: Allied Publishers, 1964).

[186] For articles, see Turner, *Vietnamese Communism*, pp. 195-201.

[187] William S. Turley, "The Democratic Republic of Vietnam and the 'Third Stage' of the Revolution," *Asian Survey*, 14, no. 1 (January 1974), p. 85.

[188] *Ibid.*, pp. 83-85.

By victory in the south, completed in time for the 1975 May Day celebration, the Vietnamese Communists doubled the territory and population under their sway. Here, again, they demonstrated exceptional pragmatism and more moderation than widely expected. There was no bloodbath but an extensive "reeducation" program, with long courses of indoctrination and self-criticism for higher officers and officials, briefer ones for common folk. Some private enterprise was allowed to continue as best it could in a land impoverished by the sudden withdrawal of American support. Numerous non-Communists, even merchants, were brought into the state structure.[189] Even the campaign to eliminate Western influences proceeded only gradually.

Yet men of Hanoi were entirely in charge in South Vietnam. After a transitional period,[190] reunification, the goal of the Communist Party for thirty years, was finally proclaimed on July 2, 1976,[191] with northerners holding almost all important positions.

Laos and Cambodia

The other countries of Indochina were of necessity involved in the long war, and a Communist victory in Vietnam overflowed and brought sympathetic regimes to power in the smaller states of Laos and Cambodia.

The Laotian Communists, the Pathet Lao, were closely allied to the North Vietnamese and followed rather similar but even more measured policies. They carefully took power by negotiation with minimal violence, leaving the civil service and army mostly intact.[192] The "patriotic bourgeoisie" was invited to cooperate. Only after several months was the king forced to abdicate. Songs and seminars were used to reshape the thinking of the people, and nearly everyone had to attend reeducation classes complete with manual labor. The "popular democratic" dictatorship moved to stamp out official corruption, decreed the equality of women, and began a literacy campaign. It also moved gradually to collectivize and nationalize, according to the official action program, "in order to abolish all economic bases of the comprador bourgeoisie, particularly those of the currently active bureaucrats, warlords and reactionaries serving as stooges of the U. S. imperialists."[193]

---

[189] Gareth Porter, "Vietnam's Long Road to Socialism," *Current History*, 71 (December 1976), 226.

[190] D. Gareth Price, "The Revolutionary Government of Vietnam," *Current History*, 69 (December 1975), 232.

[191] *New York Times*, July 3, 1976, pp. 1, 5.

[192] Richard Butwell, "From Feudalism to Communism in Laos," *Current History*, 69 (December 1975), 225.

[193] *New York Times*, December 16, 1975, p. 3.

Laotian Communism relied on Soviet assistance, perhaps because the country borders on China. The Cambodians, on the contrary, had nothing to fear from China but were potentially subject to Vietnamese domination. For such or other reasons, they turned sharply away from the Soviet Union and found friendship only in the Chinese.

The Cambodian Communists seem also to have felt more ideological sympathies for the revolutionary Maoists than for the sedate Soviets. Their state has shown itself perhaps the most coercive in the history of the Marxist-Leninist movement. One of the first measures taken after the Communists eliminated their enemies in the first months of 1975 was to empty almost entirely not only the war-swollen capital but all major cities, sending people to work the land in prescribed areas, far outdoing the Chinese rustication policies in their desire to eradicate the influence of the colonial-tainted centers. All private ownership, even of small peasant plots, was abolished; and peasants were put to work in brigades. Money was made worthless, as food and other goods were distributed by rationing. According to an officer, "Everyone must work. If not, we use the law, and the law now is the law of the soldier, the law of the gun."[194] Executions, perhaps of hundreds of thousands of persons associated with the old order or indocile to the new, replaced the reeducation campaigns of South Vietnam and Laos.[195]

Schools ceased to exist, except for meetings of children to sing revolutionary songs.[196] In the extremity of nationalistic xenophobia, contacts with the outside world were limited (up to 1976) to China, North Korea, and Vietnam; and offers of assistance (which their Laotian comrades eagerly sought) were rebuffed. Cambodia was to produce all its needs, even medicines from jungle herbs.[197] Foreign languages, foreign songs, foreign-looking clothing and haircuts were prohibited along with jewelry, cigarets, and alcohol.[198] No journalists were admitted, even from Communist countries.

The regime wrapped itself in extraordinary secrecy; to the peasants, it was simply *Angka*, the "organization," with a hierarchy extending down to leaders over groups of ten families. Westerners knew few names of leaders and hardly anything regarding their roles. Marriages were prohibited for a year, then promoted to increase the population for national greatness. "Comrade" was made the sole form of address. Reportedly, all but those at the top of the hierarchy were given new names to dissolve family relations.[199] All religions were virtually prohibited. In accordance with Communist patterns, however, elections

[194] *New York Times*, September 2, 1975, p. 2.

[195] *Time*, April 9, 1976, p. 65.

[196] *New York Times*, January 28, 1976, p. 4.

[197] *New York Times*, July 15, 1975, p. 10.

[198] Robert Keatling, *Wall Street Journal*, May 22, 1975, p. 14.

[199] *New York Times*, October 13, 1975, p. 1.

were held within a few months for a 250-member National People's Assembly.[200]

Thus, in nationalistic, anti-intellectual, anti-urban Cambodia, Marxism came almost full circle; the Cambodian version was antipodal to Marx's vision of a non-national society based on the highest technology and the fullest development of industry. One may conjecture that this phenomenal outcome is partly due to traits of national character, but the parallel with impoverished and backward Albania is at least suggestive. In both cases, a weak nation lying militarily at the mercy of a more powerful Communist state, strongly alienated from the West and determined to assert its national destiny—Cambodia looks back on the historical greatness of the Khmer empire—seemed determined to follow the logic of its convictions with little regard for human consequences or its reputation in the world.

Castro's Cuba

Communist victory in Cuba resulted not from efforts of a Communist party to incite a revolution but from the decision of a nationalist revolutionary reformer to use Communist ideas, methods, and support to achieve his aims. Even three years after the successful coup, the masses had not yet been socialized, by the admission of Cuban leaders.[201] Lenin began with an ideology, built a party, and overthrew a social order in gaining power. Castro won power and then sought an ideology and a party to apply it.

Castro's Style of Leadership. By corollary, Cuban Communism has focused strongly on the leader, although his cult has remained well below that of the less charismatic Kim Il-song. Ordinarily known simply as "Fidel," Castro is something of a folk hero, especially among the peasants, the good genius of the revolution not held responsible for errors and faults, inevitably the fault of others. Like the more idealistic of first-generation revolutionaries, he lives and dresses simply, at least in the public view, and mixes freely with the people in field and factory.[202] He has shown resistance to the corruption of power, although as years pass he has become more lofty and allergic to any hint of criticism.[203]

---

[200] *New York Times*, March 31, 1976, p. 2.

[201] Andrés Suárez, "Soviet Influence on the Internal Politics of Cuba," in *Soviet and Chinese Influence in the Third World*, Alvin Z. Rubinstein, ed. (New York. Praeger, 1975), p. 181.

[202] Herbert L. Matthews, *Fidel Castro* (New York: Simon and Schuster, 1969), p. 340; idem, *Revolution in Cuba: An Essay in Understanding* (New York: Scribners, 1975), p. 437.

[203] Maurice Halperin, *The Rise and Decline of Fidel Castro* (Berkeley: University of California Press, 1972), pp. 357, 360.

Castro's style has been in some ways more suggestive of the Latin American caudillo than of a Communist boss.[204]   Utterly resistant to any restraint or discipline, quite the opposite of the disciplined Communist Man,[205] he has seemed to regard Cuba virtually as his private estate, like a Trujillo in the Dominican Republic or Somoza in Nicaragua, personally inspecting and giving orders on how to plant or manage a store or government department, to build a bridge here or a dam there, commanding (as "Commander in Chief") the sowing of this crop or that, usually without much explanation.[206]   He is at once party leader, prime minister, commander of armed forces, president of the board controlling the economy, and president of the institute governing agriculture. The authority on almost everything, especially agriculture, he has confidence only in himself, and no one dares question or correct him.[207]

The Castro style of rule has been personal, with the delegation of particular responsibilities to trusted individuals, usually without benefit of regularized procedures.[208]   No constitution was found necessary for the first seventeen years of Castroite rule. Nor was it necessary to go through the formalities of elections. Castro would call a mass meeting and put a question to it; the roar of "si" was sufficient evidence of popular feelings.[209]   It is paradoxical that Castro, the only Communist leader to make a great point of free elections, is one of the few who dispensed with the charade.

The Roles of the Party and the Military. Just as it was superfluous to set down a fixed structure of government with pseudo-democratic institutions to gain legitimacy, the party was not made into a ruling elite but merely another transmission belt for Castro's personal power. Instead of overseeing administration, as in the ordinary Communist state, the Cuban party is subject to the executive, an arm of it, or intermingled with it; party and state functions are commonly (as in Romania) vested in the same individual.[210]   Not the party, with Politburo and Central Committee, but Castro's headquarters is the locus of decision making.

The top positions in the party are not occupied by expert Marxist-Leninist or old-time revolutionaries, a number of whom were purged in 1962

---

[204] Andrés Suárez, "Leadership, Ideology, and Political Party," in *Revolutionary Change in Cuba*, Carmelo Mesa-Lago, ed. (Pittsburgh: University of Pittsburgh Press, 1971), p. 14.

[205] Edward Gonzales, *Cuba Under Castro: The Limits of Charisma* (Boston: Houghton Mifflin, 1972), p. 11.

[206] René Dumont, *Is Cuba Socialist?*, (New York: Viking, 1974), pp. 57, 106.

[207] Dumont, *Is Cuba Socialist?* pp. 106, 108.

[208] For the grand informality of Castro, cf. Lee Lockwood, *Castro's Cuba, Cuba's Fidel* (New York: Macmillan, 1967), *passim.*

[209] Mohammed A. Rauf, Jr., *Cuban Journal* (New York: Thomas Y. Crowell, 1964), p. 76.

[210] Dumont, *Is Cuba Socialist?*, p. 52.

and 1968, but by those in Castro's favor.[211]   Only in 1975 were three "Old Communists" placed on the 13-man Politburo.[212]   And in the same year the party, which had gone through several reorganizations and name changes before emerging as the "Cuban Communist Party" in 1965, finally held its first elections and congress and acquired a regular set of rules. At the base, knowledge of Marxist-Leninist writings is not requisite for membership; candidates should be good workers of exemplary political purity.[213] They are supposedly chosen by the workers, but are in fact nominated by the party leaders.[214] In any case, they have no means even on paper of influencing higher party organs. Presumably because it did not have much to do, the party long remained small. Only 55,000 (in a population of 8,000,000) in 1969, membership was enlarged to over 200,000 in 1975; but it still represented the smallest percentage of popular involvement in the Communist world.

If the party is less important as a means of guiding society, the military is not surprisingly more so. The core of the regime is formed by men who were with Castro in the Sierra, the tight band of heroes who came to feel they could do anything,[215] much as the veterans of the Long March formed the nucleus of Mao's government. Second to the chief is brother Raúl Castro. The party itself is largely military in leadership; perhaps 80 percent of the Central Committee and a majority of the Politburo have had an army or guerrilla background.[216]

Courts are largely military, with officers as judges, and agricultural production has been mobilized, especially in 1968 and thereafter, under a hierarchy of "puestos de mando" (command posts). Farming is done by brigades, battallions, columns, etc., under army direction and organization.[217] All 28 agricultural and livestock institutes were placed under direct military supervision and control,[218] and all important agricultural enterprises were headed by army officers.[219] The army managed the sugar harvest, the great annual enterprise. As Castro had it, in November 1969, "The armed forces represent . . . the institution with the most experience in organization; they are the ones with most

---

[211] Suárez, in *Revolutionary Change*, C. Mesa Lago, ed., p. 12.

[212] Edward Gonzalez, "Castro and Cuba's New Orthodoxy," *Problems of Communism*, 25 (January-February 1976), 2.

[213] Halperin, *Rise and Decline*, p. 158.

[214] Dumont, *Is Cuba Socialist?*, p. 50.

[215] Draper, *Castroism*, pp. 219-220.

[216] Jaime Suchliki, ed., *Cuba, Castro, and Revolution* (Coral Gables, Fla.: University of Miami Press, 1972), p. 11.

[217] L. Nelson, "Changes in the Social Structure," in *Cuba, Castro, and Revolution*, Jaime Suchlichi, ed., p. 63.

[218] N. Valdés, "The Radical Transformation of Cuban Education," in *Cuba in Revolution*, Rolando Bonachea and Nelson P. Valdés, eds., (Garden City, N. Y.: Doubleday & Co., Anchor Books, 1972), p. 453.

[219] Dumont, *Is Cuba Socialist?*, p. 98.

discipline. They must contribute that spirit of organization and discipline [to the sugar harvest] . . . as well as their experience."[220] Soldiers in charge of work details carried revolvers, like bosses of old-time plantations.[221]

Cuban armed forces are the largest in Latin America after Brazil. Conscription was introduced in 1965, after the danger of U. S.-sponsored invasion had passed. Youths of sixteen were then made liable for a three-year period of service; as explained by Castro, this was more for discipline than for defensive needs.[222] The army is a mainstay of the economy, providing a great deal of cheap labor, especially for unskilled agricultural tasks, such as cutting cane and picking coffee. There is also a militia in which the majority of able-bodied adults have been enlisted.

Songs, textbooks, etc. are filled with the symbolism of struggle.[223] "Patria o Muerte" is written all over Cuban banknotes. Education is militarized, with brigades, campaigns, battles, marches, etc.[224] Uniforms are ubiquitous, and almost everyone who works must belong to the militia.

Out–Communizing the Soviets. It is correspondingly natural that most aspects of life are subject to close controls, in some respects more far-reaching than those of the Soviet Union. While children are engaged in "Pioneer" troops, youths are drafted for military duty, and adults are in the militia, about half of the entire population is politically mobilized in committees for the Defense of the Revolution.[225] These are in effect the lowest level of government, charged with control of the population, overseeing of distribution of goods, obligatory volunteer labor, and the like. Used in 1968 to carry out the nationalization of small businesses, the Committees are sufficiently effective that the services of regular or secret police are not much needed.

The Cuban revolution also surpasses the Soviet in that there is no pretense of farmers working cooperatively for the benefit of their particular group; cooperatives originally established were abolished on the ground, as Castro put it, that workers should work for the state, not for themselves;[226] Castro also desired the maximum control offered by outright state management.[227] About 30 percent of land was left to private growers because state management was impractical, but they were told what to grow, and their produce was taken

---

[220] Edward Gonzalez, "Castro, the Limits of Charisma," *Problems of Communism, 19,* no. 4 (July-August 1970), 20.

[221] Dumont, *Is Cuba Socialist?,* p. 98.

[222] Draper, *Castroism,* pp. 174-175.

[223] Cf. R. Fagen, "Mass Mobilization in Cuba: The Symbolism of Struggle," *Cuba in Revolution,* R. Bonaches and N. Valdés eds., especially pp. 201, 202.

[224] R. Paulston, "Education," in *Revolutionary Change in Cuba,* C. Mesa-Lago, ed., p. 392.

[225] By 1973. See Matthews, *Revolution in Cuba,* p. 15.

[226] *Ibid.,* p. 261.

[227] Lockwood, *Castro's Cuba,* p. 90.

by the state. In due time Castro hoped to bring them also under state control.[228] There was set up in the early 1960s a state monopoly of sales of foodstuffs, a degree of regimentation neither Russians nor Chinese have found practical.[229] Most foods and other consumer goods are distributed by rationing, which the Soviets abolished not long after the Second World War. Since 1968, nationalization has been total, including individual artisans, street vendors, etc., who were supposedly getting independent ideas and making too much money, because of the inefficiency of state enterprises.[230]

Labor is compulsory, a good deal of it with only nonmaterial, political, or psychological reward.[231] Students and schoolchildren are especially subject to the call to work, mostly agricultural. They put in three hours daily, and the contribution of the draftees is calculated at eight to twelve percent of all labor input.[232] Productivity is apt to be extremely low; however, labor is to be not merely materially productive but morally uplifting, an assist toward the making of "Communist Man."

It is not permitted to scrounge a living; "parasites" have been rounded up from time to time and put to work.[233] In 1971 an anti-loafing law provided penalties of up to two years at work farms. The Cuban on the job has little freedom. He (and everyone else) is unable to move far because his rations are available only at the particular store to which he is assigned. Like his Soviet counterpart, he must also carry a work book, detailing his employment record plus his political qualifications.

Undogmatic Castroism. In some respects, however, the Cuban style of Communism has been relatively slack. Castro has never seen fit to expound on art styles, modern painting has never been execrated, and impressionistic work has been welcome. Cuban posters are thus apt to show more imagination than Soviet.[234] Castro was also rather tolerant of unconventional, even mildly critical writing. In 1961, he uttered one of his celebrated aphorisms, "Within the revolution, everything; against the revolution, nothing."[235] To an American reporter, he claimed, "I especially am a partisan of the widest possible discussion

---

[228] *Ibid.,* p. 92.

[229] Rene' Dumont, *Cuba: Socialism and Development* (New York: Grove Press, 1970), pp. 80-81.

[230] Carmelo Mesa-Lago, "The Revolutionary Offensive," in *Cuban Communism,* Irving L. Horowitz, ed. (New York: Aldine, 1970), p. 74.

[231] Cf. C. Mesa-Lago, "Economic Significance of Unpaid Labor in Socialist Cuba," in *Cuba in Revolution,* R. Bonachea and N. Valdes, eds., pp. 304–412.

[232] *Ibid.,* p. 391.

[233] Dumont, *Cuba: Socialism and Development,* p. 131.

[234] David Caute, *Cuba, Yes?* (New York: McGraw-Hill, 1974), p. 200.

[235] Cited by Mario Bendetti, "Present Status of Cuban Culture," in *Cuba in Revolution,* R. Bonachea and N. Valdes, eds., p. 522.

in the intellectual realm."[236]   Such broad-mindedness harvested considerable sympathy among left-wing intellectuals, especially in France. This limited Cuban literary freedom was amputated, however, in 1971, when Castro lost patience with a deviant poet, Heberto Padilla, had him imprisoned, damned "ideological coexistence,"[237] and lost interest in cultivating left-wing intellectuals.

The relations of Castroism with the Catholic Church have also been mostly rather low key. Early on, Church property was confiscated, and Castro was angered by Catholic protests against the turn to Communism. Church schools were taken over, education was entirely secularized, and atheism was made a condition for membership in the Communist Party. But atheism has been little stressed and the Castroite policy has been mostly to ignore the Church in the apparent conviction that it will die out in due course.

The relatively undogmatic approach of Castroism to artistic expression and religion is related to the fact that it does not take ideology very seriously and has little dogmatic conviction. For Castro, Marxism is not doctrine but the revolutionary political will, *his* will. His speeches are filled with almost everything but Marxist-Leninist dialectics, and he has repeatedly changed opinions. The party has neither a glorious history nor a future program; given not to theory but exhortation, its chief role is to instill respect for authority.[238]

Anti-Americanism. The principal theme has been anti-Americanism, that antagonism to capitalism which made it possible for Cuba to become Communist. Castroism survived and was held in the radical track by the conflict of Cuban nationalism with ineffectual U. S. opposition. As Fidel said in 1963, "The revolution needs the enemy; the proletariat does not flee from the enemy, it needs the enemy."[239] At the commencement of the Kennedy administration, Castro probably had hopes for a settlement with the U. S.,[240] but any such hopes were smashed by U. S. support for anti-Castro Cubans during the next several years. That Castro was doubtless aware of CIA plotting against his life may have influenced his attitude. Equally important, in economic troubles he could effectively blame the "imperialist blockade." Anti-yankeeism also appealed to Cuban pride; defiance of the hemispheric giant put Cuba on the map as "liberated territory of the Americas"; and many Cubans unsympathetic to Communism were patriotically devoted to defense of the homeland. Castro could see himself as a leader and potential giant in the long-awaited Latin American revolutionary wave.

---

[236] Lockwood, *Castro's Cuba,* p. 129.

[237] Halperin, *Rise and Decline,* p. 359.

[238] Hans Enzensberger, "Portrait of a Party," in *The New Cuba: Paradoxes and Potentials,* Ronald Radosh, ed. (New York: William Morrow and Co., 1976), p. 104.

[239] Cited by Draper, *Castroism,* p. 217.

[240] Halperin, *Rise and Decline,* p. 117.

After 1965, when the U. S. began escalating the war in Vietnam, Cuba receded as an issue for American foreign policy. But for Cuba the issue of U. S. intervention in Vietnam and the concomitant emotion served the regime's radicalism very well and helped sustain it through a difficult period.[241] Long after any threat had disappeared, and even as detente was on the horizon, Cubans were loudly chanting, "Fidel, seguro, a los yankees dales duro!" ("Fidel for sure, hit the Yankees hard!").[242]

Anti-Americanism had an economic aspect, as well—the urge to remove foreign ownership and the foreign presense in Cuban agriculture, industry, and utilities; a sore point was the repugnance for the imperialistic aspects of the tourist industry, the reputation and reality of Havana as a center of gambling and prostitution. There was also revulsion against dependence on the American market for sugar. In the first years, down with imperialism meant down with sugar, and Cuba was misled into turning away from its best crop. Anti-yankee-ism also meant defense of, or restoration of native Cuban culture, which had been inundated by cheap imports, from Coca-Cola to TV serials. In brief, the revolution seemed to many to be a continuation of the Cuban struggle for independence stemming from the revolution of 1868 and aborted by U. S. patronage since 1898.[243]

Emphasis on confrontation was ideologized, by Castro's right-hand lieu-tenant, Ernesto "Che" Guevara, into a theory of guerrilla warfare as the means of overcoming capitalism. Seeing the success of the little band which escaped into the Sierra Maestra to emerge two years later as rulers of Cuba, Guevara (with Castro) postulated that bold revolutionaries could do the same anywhere by going to the peasants and organizing them. This was essentially Maoist, although Guevara claimed not to have been influenced by Mao, and it deviated widely from Leninism in frankly taking the peasants as the revolutionary class and making the guerrillas equivalent to the vanguard party. It left Marx behind in taking no account of the stages of history which Lenin telescoped, and it was opposed in spirit to the whole Marxist semi-deterministic approach. As Castro said, on May 1, 1966, "Communism can be constructed in a single country."[244] Revolution depended not on material conditions but on the spark which inflames the people. The Soviet Union, averse to stirring things up dangerously, disapproved of the general idea, which implied that Cuba was more revolutionarily virtuous than the Soviet Union;[245] and the tired Communist Parties of Latin America, for various reasons renouncing violence, declined to cooperate. Guevara, in turn, considered the U.S.S.R. nearly as degraded as the U. S. because the Russians worked for money, not from devotion to society.

[241] Matthews, *Revolution in Cuba,* p. 197.

[242] *New York Times,* October 4, 1974, p. 2.

[243] Gonzales, "Castro: The Limits of Charisma," p. 18.

[244] Dumont, *Is Cuba Socialist?,* p. 39.

[245] Andrés Suárez, "Soviet Influence on the Internal Politics of Cuba," in *Soviet and Chinese Influence,* Alvin Z. Rubinstein, ed., pp. 184-185.

But revolutionary Castroism in Latin American proved a non-starter, never involving more than a few hundred fighters.[246]   Guevarism had its trial in Bolivia, the only country where there seemed a possibility of applying its supposedly universal principles; and Che died in complete failure on October 9, 1967.

Return to the Soviet Fold. Castro thereupon began swinging away from his extra-radical course at home and abroad. There was no more serious effort to export revolution; instead, Castro found virtues in populist military dictatorships, such as the junta which took power in Peru in October 1968. He also moved closer to the Soviet Union, with which there had been friction from time to time. In August 1968, Castro indicated the abandonment of his earlier independent inspiration by supporting the Soviet invasion of Czechoslovakia. Chastened in 1970 by the failure of his grand goal of a sugar harvest of ten million tons, he geared the Cuban economy more closely to the Soviet and to Soviet aid, flowing in at the rate of about $400 million yearly.[247]   In 1972, Cuba was admitted as full member to Comecon. By 1976, cooperation with Soviet foreign policy had yielded considerable international e'clat, as Cuban armed forces stood in various nations of Africa and Arabia, Angola, Congo (Brazzaville), Equatorial Guinea, Guinea, Guinea-Bissau, Sierra Leone, Somalia, South Yemen, and Syria.[248]

Castro ceased to utter any criticism of the Soviet Union or to propagate independent ideas of Communism; Castroism lost most of its individuality as it settled down and became institutionalized in clientship, abandoning the notion of a quick leap to the higher order of Communism. The government ceased to operate from Castro's jeep or helicopter, and some effort was made to separate the functions of state, party, and army. The party was reconstructed more in the classic Communist style. In 1970 elections were held in trade unions for the first time since 1959. In 1976 a constitution finally furnished Cuba with a full set of pseudo-democratic institutions. The requirements of a stable rulership seemed to lead Cuba away from charismatic leadership toward reliance on patterns of control like those proved effective in Soviet and other Communist practice.

Differences remain. The Cubans are more equalitarian, less legalistic, and more given to mobilization. Striking is the greater Cuban emphasis on non-economic incentives. In the Cuban concept, it is practically the essence of the ideal society that people work for reasons other than money. The Russians soon practically forgot the goal of the non-monetary society; Castro has always exalted it and has done something to move toward it. Housing was made gratis for many, along with some meals, clothing, and services.[249]   Rationing has been

---

[246] Irving L. Horowitz, "Cuban Communism," in *Cuban Communism*, Horowitz, ed. (Chicago: Aldine, 1970), pp. 15-16.

[247] Suchliki, *Cuba, Castro, and Revolution*, pp. 3-4.

[248] *New York Times*, December 1, 1975, p. 2.

[249] Matthews, *Revolution in Cuba*, pp. 327-329.

retained for very many goods, not only for equalitarianism but to reduce the usefulness of money; non-rationed goods are often to be had only at much higher prices. For example, rationed cigarettes cost $.30, unrationed, $2.00. Many goods are not to be purchased but are reserved for especially meritorious citizens, presumably the most productive workers. For example, TV sets were not for the affluent but for the deserving.[250] "Moral" incentives thus become alloyed with material interests, but the transaction is pure because money is not involved.

An Assessment of Castroism. Partly renouncing revolutionism in its more moderate, pro-Soviet turn, Cuban Communism has prospered better than in the more experimental period. The economic results of the first decade were poor. Per capita income shrank considerably; very few countries shared this distinction in a time of generally rising economies. Agricultural production per capita was down in 1969 to 72 percent of 1959.[251] There was fearful mismanagement, all manner of bungling, confusion, and waste; Cuban workers in 1966-67 averaged only about four hours on the job—when they arrived at the workplace.[252] The effort to run everything from the center often simply broke down.[253] Since 1970, however, with better management and Soviet-blueprinted planning, more realistic targets, and progress toward mechanization of agriculture, the Cuban economy has taken off with broadly based growth at about the same rate as the Soviet, six to eight percent yearly—so far as can be judged in the virtual absence of statistical data.

There were still many shortages, however, in the mid-1970s.[254] But the Cuban people did not support Castro because he delivered more goods but largely because he appealed to patriotic and humanitarian sentiments; and the claims of success of the Cuban revolution rest not on the standard of living but on real or claimed successes in eliminating economic misery, in promoting education, medical care, and disease prevention for everyone, in the making of a more moral, more equal, and more just society. No one denies that the center of Havana has grown drab under Castro; this is compensated, one is told, by the elimination of the slums that make hideous large parts of most Latin American cities. The rich and middle classes have suffered—some 600,000 left the island, abandoning their possessions. Before emigration was entirely cut off in 1971, there was a waiting list of some 200,000, despite the fact that those who applied to leave the socialist land had to work on farms at least two years under

---

[250] *New York Times,* October 4, 1974, p. 2.

[251] Carmelo Mesa-Lago, "The Economic Significance of Unpaid Labor in Socialist Cuba," in *Revolution in Cuba,* B. Bonachea and N. Valdés, eds., p. 366.

[252] R. Bonachea and N. Valdés, eds., *Revolution in Cuba,* introduction, p. 372. On waste, disorganization, and indifference, see Dumont, *Is Cuba Socialist?, passim.*

[253] Dumont, *Is Cuba Socialist?,* p. 114.

[254] For example, see *New York Times,* October 4, 1974, p. 2.

conditions like those of nineteenth-century slaves.[255]   But the more numerous poor have gained both in self-respect and in economic security.

Critics have found many shortcomings. There are scores of thousands of political prisoners. Equality is qualified by a new inequality, as party leaders have special restaurants, stores, cars, etc.[256]   There is still racial inequality, blacks remaining de facto excluded from almost all good positions.[257]   If primary schooling increased thirty percent in the first decade, and secondary education by 83 percent, still the number of students in higher education decreased,[258] and only 22 percent of those who enrolled in the first grade in 1965-66 finished sixth grade.[259]

There is no doubt that many aspects of Communist Cuba, like Communist China, make a favorable impression on foreign observers, and for the same general reasons. They see Castro as the leader who built schools, clinics, and housing for the poor, who opened formerly exclusive beaches of the rich and luxury hotels to the masses. "Revolutionary Cuba has throughout enjoyed a quite new national spirit deriving from the heady experience of social revolution and international adventure."[260]

But the wave of enthusiasm has been receding since 1965, when Che Guevara, the animating spirit of revolution left Cuba for more promising fields of action. The original drive, a non-Leninist expression of Third World animosity mixed with hope, gives way to the organization of power, as the purpose of the party-state shifts from the remaking of the social order and power structure to its maintenance, from change to the prevention of change.

---

[255] Thomas, *Cuba,* p. 1482.

[256] Gonzalez, "Castro, the Limits of Charisma," p. 10.

[257] Nelson Amara and Carmelo Mesa-Lago, "Inequality and Classes," in *Revolutionary Change*, C. Mesa-Lago, ed., pp. 351–352; John Clytus, *Black Man in Red Cuba* (Coral Gables, Fla: University of Miami Press, 1970).

[258] Jorge I. Dominguez, "Is Castro's Cuba Good?" *Intellectual Digest,* 4, no. 3 (November 1973), 51.

[259] Bertram Silverman, "A New Direction in Cuban Socialism," *Current History,* 68, no. 401 (January 1975), 28.

[260] Thomas, *Cuba,* p. 1485.

Chapter five

Change in Communist Systems

From Faith to Dogma

In a mutable world, no political and social system can remain immutable. Not only do ways of life and interaction change with material conditions; perhaps more important, the values and expectations of people and elites change continually, and with them the meaning of institutions if not the institutions themselves.

Change in Communist systems takes on special dimensions because they are uniquely linked to a single event, the revolution and the violent struggle through which the structure was set in place. But the revolution cannot be repeated (Mao tried in vain)—it inevitably recedes. Its achievements come to be taken for granted, its failures accumulate, and its promises are either fulfilled or broken. A new generation comes along for which the ideals of the revolution are a matter of history, not experience, taught in school, not in action. The leadership, too, comes not from revolutionary struggle but from political intrigue.

Institutions change little; the government and party structure of the Soviet Union and other Communist countries (except the newest) are much as they were twenty, even forty years ago. The ideology, so far as it is more than rationalization of current policy, also changes little. Indeed, doctrinal evolution is impermissible. But attitudes have changed very much. The passion of the great renewal, for which men had staked their lives and from which they hoped everything, in China as in Russia, Vietnam, or Cuba, is worn out. The struggle to remake the world becomes a struggle for a better standard of living, and the efforts of the press to keep alive a transcendental mission become ever more hollow.

There are no exciting new ideas; indeed, controversy of any kind simmers down.. No latter-day prophet galvanizes the nation with a saving vision. There is not even a real attempt to square the inherited ideology with new reality. Khrushchev's espousal of peaceful coexistence in 1956 was the last real effort in the Communist world to update the canon.

Even if we assume that the elite has a genuine belief in the essence of Marxism-Leninism, Maoism, Castroism, etc., yet their emotional commitment has certainly lost fervor. The revolutionaries—Lenin and Stalin, Mao, Castro, Ho Chi Minh—were sincerely dedicated to the cause of social change. But their successors are less and less passionately devoted to change, more and more desirous of maintaining a system advantageous to themselves and which they do not know how to make more satisfactory. Their identification with the working class or social revolution comes to look more and more hyprocritical.

The result, in the Soviet Union as in other Communist states, is apathy. John Armstrong has perceived Communist ideology as "a conditioned reflex of bureaucratized oligarchy self-righteously proud of its own accomplishments and intensely motivated to legitimize its continuing grip on power."[1] Ideological campaigns seem to go largely unheeded—it would be remarkable indeed if many listened to what they have heard countless times before. "Socialist competition" and "moral incentives" arouse a tepid response unless accompanied by solid prizes. There is widespread questioning of the party role even in official circles.[2]

The decadence of ideological feeling is most advanced in the young people for whom the revolution is most distant and who have the least stake in the established order, since they have been spared the sufferings of the older generation.[3] They are widely reported to be politically apathetic and to be indifferent to organization of "social" and political activities.[4] In 1920, joining the Communist Youth League was an adventure and a dedication; now it is a boring duty. Finding truth elusive and lies omnipresent, Soviet youth in its devotion to eating, drinking, and sex, is said to be more hedonistic than most young Westerners.[5] Troubled by this indifference, Soviet leaders find no remedy but military-patriotic training.[6]

---

[1] John A. Armstrong, "The Soviet-American Confrontation: A New Phase?" *Survey,* 21 (Autumn 1975), 41.

[2] Moshe Lewin, *Political Undercurrents in Soviet Economic Debates: From Bukharin to Modern Reformers* (Princeton: Princeton University Press, 1974), p. 244.

[3] Georgie Anne Geyer, *The Young Russians* (Homewood, Ill.: ETC Publishers, 1975), p. 9.

[4] Cf. Mervyn Matthews, "Soviet Students—Some Sociological Perspectives," *Soviet Studies,* 27, no. 1 (January 1975), pp. 102-103; *New York Times,* December 23, 1974, p. 16; Geyer, *The Young Russians,* Chap. 4.

[5] George Feifer, *Russia Close-Up* (London: Jonathan Cape, 1973), p. 12.

[6] Leon Goure, *The Militarization of Soviet Youth* (New York: National Strategy Information Center, 1973), p. 11.

China has followed the same course, perhaps more rapidly. In 1957, the Chairman commented, "It seems that Marxism, that was once all the rage, is not so much in fashion now."[7] In the 1960s he was warning more pointedly that the Communist Party and the bureaucracy was becoming a self-serving "class" opposed to the proletariat.[8] He also lamented that youth had no experience of war, oppression, and revolution to make them good revolutionaries.[9] In Mao's view, the Communist state turns out to be self-limiting; if it is successful enough to bring peace and improvement of living standards, the people will no longer suffer and so lose the will and character needed to make the perfect society. As he said in 1965, "Our revolution cannot simply be a stabilization of the past."[10] That is, a revolution which stands still ceases to be a revolution. Thus, the Communist Youth League by 1966 was becoming an elitist organization.[11]

In his Cultural Revolution, Mao struck out against bureaucratism, gradualism, economism, neglect of ideology, and traditional culture; and he put himself at the head of the proletariat rising against their masters.[12] But little was achieved, and from 1969 the tide of revolutionism has steadily ebbed. Subsequent propaganda campaigns have seemed pallid and ineffectual. Normalization proceeded, probably contrary to the wishes of the Chairman, until it was climaxed by the purge of the leftists shortly after his demise.

In Eastern Europe there was never any comparable Communist fervor (except perhaps in Yugoslavia), yet even that has cooled. Fear of German revanchism is dying out and with it the longtime excuse for Soviet protection. The last of the old Comintern crew committed to the Russian Revolution and the Fatherland of Socialism, those who came in with the Soviet armies to do their duty for socialism, are disappearing. Even Bulgaria, next to Albania the least hospitable of the East European Communist states, would like cooperative agreements with the U. S. Tourism, preferably from the West, has become a major industry, indeed a vital necessity, for most of the countries. Many years of pro-Soviet propaganda have evidently failed. According to State Department Counsellor Helmut Sonnenfeldt, "There are almost no genuine friends of the Soviets left in Eastern Europe, except possibly Bulgaria."[13] It was said some

---

[7] Cited by A. Doak Barnett, *Uncertain Passage: China's Transition to the Post-Mao-Era* (Washington, D. C.: Brookings Institution, 1974), p. 7.

[8] Lowell Dittmer, *Liu Shao-chi and the Chinese Cultural Revolution* (Berkeley: University of California Press, 1974), p. 47.

[9] Stanley Karnow, *Mao and China: From Revolution to Revolution* (New York: Viking, 1972), p. 56.

[10] David Milton, Nancy Milton, and Frank Schurmann, eds., *People's China: Social Experimentation, Politics, Entry onto the World Scene, 1966-1971* (New York: Random House, 1974), p. 217.

[11] Shelah G. Leader, "The Communist Youth League," *Asian Survey*, 14, no. 8 (August 1974), 715.

[12] Dittmer, *Liu Shao-chi*, p. 46.

[13] *New York Times*, April 6, 1976, p. 14.

years ago that East European Communism has lost the battle against cultural pluralism and modernism, and that "proletarian internationalism is utterly discredited."[14] Youth has become fond of Western styles; long hair and the mod look have been as obligatory for young people in most East European countries as in the U. S.[15] A priest said of the generation raised behind the Berlin Wall, "They are lost to the revolution—all they want is to be left alone, to be able to buy blue jeans and enjoy Western rock music."[16] Even in doctrinaire East Germany, it is doubtful that courses in Marxism-Leninism produce more conviction than boredom.[17] People ordinarily respect the general idea of socialism but the rulership is seen as alienated from the people.[18] A major demand has been for the dropping of Marxism-Leninism from the curriculum.[19] Possibly the powerful parents sympathize, since offspring of top-ranking Communists are sent to the most prestigious academies in England or Switzerland.[20] The worst Western films are preferred to the best Soviet productions.[21]

This is not to imply that ideological education has not been successful or that any large number of citizens of any Communist country reject the state or its general interpretation of society, history, and politics. Many years of indoctrination without alternative views or experience of non-Marxist ways of thought suffice fairly well to shape minds. Apathy means noncommitment, not independence. The Communist-trained mind has no room for ideas of individualism or freedom, the contentions of pluralism, Western-style. As a Soviet scientist said, "The only thing Communism has prepared us for is more Communist rule."[22] The situation in Eastern Europe is more complicated than in the Soviet Union because of much more Western influence; but there too it appears that education and propaganda, while not making true believers, largely exclude alternative ideas of the organization of society.

The trend may be summarized as change from enthusiasm on the part of a committed minority to general acceptance by the majority. The Communist state has become the establishment, the fixed structure of society. There is no reason for anyone to sacrifice himself voluntarily to it or its purposes, but

---

[14] François Fetjő, *A History of the People's Democracies of Eastern Europe since Stalin* (New York: Praeger, 1971), pp. 288, 289.

[15] For Poland, cf. *New York Times*, October 28, 1974, p. 2.

[16] *New York Times*, April 5, 1976, p. 3.

[17] Thomas A. Baylis, *The Technical Intelligentsia and the East German Elite* (Berkeley: University of California Press, 1974), p. 55.

[18] Ivan Volgyes, in *Political Socialization in Eastern Europe: A Comparative Framework*, I. Volgyes, ed. (New York: Praeger, 1975), p. 127.

[19] Fejtő, *A History*, p. 294.

[20] Julian Hale, *Ceausescu's Romania* (London: Harrap, 1971), p. 113.

[21] Ivan Volgyes, in *Political Socialization in Eastern Europe: A Comparative Framework*, I. Volgyes, ed., p. 25.

[22] Observer, *Message from Moscow* (New York: Vintage Books, 1971), p. 347.

there is no point in opposing it or even bothering with dangerous thoughts. It is to be used by those who can, to be suffered by those who must.

The Loosened State

The tightness endemic to Communist states depends upon a special degree of support and wholehearted backing for Communist ideals, at least on the part of the rulership. The result of loss of ideological commitment is a loosening of the fabric, the growth of bits of independence and pluralism which in a Western country might seem trivial but which represent a transformation from the total and totalitarian Communism of the earlier days. Communist mobilization seems here and there, in a hundred petty and not so petty ways, to be demobilizing. Differently stated, "bourgeois" elements and traits seem to be arising, in the Soviet Union and other Communist countries, as authority is eroded by relaxation. Controls become less effective, more of life is privatized, and the capacity of party and state to move the country diminishes.

This has countless different aspects. Observers agree that there has been an upsurge of religiosity in the Soviet Union and in most East European countries since the mid-1960s. Soviet intellectual dissidents are few, and are not cowed by repressions. A sector of the Jewish community can also carry on an unending campaign for the right to emigrate; and police harassment no longer seems so effective. Despite arrests and multifarious intimidation, circulation of uncensored materials ("Samizdat") goes on. The volume reaching the West has increased every year for a decade, coming to about 6,000 pages in 1975.[23] It is mostly typed, with multiple carbons; however, there are some photocopies. There have also been some underground presses; a Latvian group claimed to be preparing 30,000 Bibles when uncovered by the police.[24]

As discipline and fear of the authorities decline, violations of Soviet law and policy increase apace. As the Chinese state, somewhat strongly, "A bureaucrat-monopoly capitalist class of a new type dominates all parts of life in Soviet society today. Corruption, degeneration and all the other social evils inherent in capitalism have spread like a plague to every part of the Soviet land under the rule of the clique."[25] In a society that tries to regulate everything, there are infinite ways of cheating, doing favors for friends or for a consideration. Sellers deliver goods if there are inducements; bosses who decide issues in favor of their underlings receive appropriate tokens of gratitude. The planning mechanism is riddled with effects of influence, as low quotas (meaning easy bonuses) are a very valuable commodity. A person with influence can buy a new car and

---

[23] *Radio Liberty Research*, RL 40/76, January 24, 1976.

[24] *The Samizdat Bulletin*, no. 25, May 1975.

[25] Ming Sung, "Dire Consequences of Soviet Revisionists' All-Round Capitalist Restoration," *Peking Review*, no. 42 (October 19, 1974), p. 19.

resell it immediately for a large gain. Then, too, measures aimed at cheating may actually increase it; for example, to control repair bills on TV sets under guarantee, the factory issued coupons to buyers; the store simply kept them and appropriated the full value.[26]

Black or gray markets have come to play a large part in the Soviet economy, despite laws against speculation,[27] and the authorities mostly acquiesce. This is partly due to the fact that factories have to resort to illegal or semilegal sources to procure materials needed but not furnished by the plan. There are also large amounts of goods diverted from official channels and even heavy machinery is put to private use; Soviet papers from time to time mention substantial percentages of shrinkage, which seems justified to workers by the wastage visible on all sides. It was found necessary to detail 750–800 guards to protect the Moscow railroad junction from pilferage.[28] Valuable furs seem to be mostly illegally taken and traded.[29] According to Soviet denunciations, only half of the New Year's trees (equivalent to Christmas trees) in Moscow were sold legally.[30] Nearly half of the industrial fishing catch on internal Soviet waters, it seems, was taken by poachers.[31] Most or perhaps all used car sales are outside the law, since official prices are much below what people will pay. A state agency cooperates on these sales, although the state is cheated of taxes.[32]

In many sundry ways the problem of law and order grows. There have been many stories of bought admissions to select institutes and faked diplomas. In Moscow, taxis are available at night only to the highest bidder, in open scorn of regulated fares. Gone are the days when hotel staffs upheld socialist dignity by declining demeaning tips.[33] Beggars, long abolished, have reappeared on Soviet streets.[34] Unauthorized radio transmitters, seldom with a message more political than the pleasure of doing one's own thing, have become a problem for official communications. According to a paper, "Over one thousand radio hooligans have been detained in Donetsk since the beginning of the year. . . .The owner of a transmitter enjoys prestige among his pals . . ."[35] The Soviet Union has joined the non-Communist world in having a drug problem, both as a result

---

[26] Murray Seeger, *Los Angeles Times*, October 16, 1973, p. 21.

[27] P. Osten and F. Kantowski, " 'Chaltura,' ein sozial-ökonomisches Phänomen," *Osteuropa*, 24, no. 2 (February 1974), 99–114; Steven J. Staats, "Corruption in the Soviet System," *Problems of Communism*, 21, no. 1 (January–February 1972), 40–47. See also Yuri Brokhin, *Hustling on Gorky Street* (New York: Dial Press, 1975).

[28] *Gudok*, February 6, 1973.

[29] *New York Times*, May 3, 1975, p. 8.

[30] *New York Times*, December 22, 1974.

[31] *Ekonomicheskaya gazeta*, no. 41 (1973), p. 22. Cited by *Radio Liberty Dispatch*, December 4, 1973.

[32] *New York Times*, October 25, 1974, p. 15.

[33] *New York Times*, June 26, 1975, p. 9.

[34] *New York Times*, May 24, 1975, p. 8.

[35] *Komsomolskaia pravda*, September 9, 1974; cited by *Radio Liberty Dispatch*, 384, no. 74 (November 22, 1974).

of imports from Central Asia and from manufacture in medical institutes or as prescribed in return for compensation.[36]

There is universal testimony of the growth of drunkenness, confirming statistical data that that country leads the world in consumption of hard liquor. Consumption of legal alcohol nearly doubled, from 4.85 liters per person over age 15, in 1957, to 9.25 liters in 1970; to this must be added moonshine, amounting to about a third as much as legal production.[37] The growth of alcoholism is generally attributed to boredom, satiation with official ideology, and the organized life. It is also part of the anti-work ethic which party and state have been vigorously combatting for over half a century. All exhortations, rewards, and compulsions to the contrary, Soviet workers do not labor very hard. As a Soviet emigré said of fellow emigrés, "Some of them are making a big mistake—if you want to live well without doing a stroke of work, there's no better place than the Soviet Union."[38]

Communist discipline is much laxer still in Eastern Europe. Perhaps nowhere is influence more influential than in Romania.[39] Black and gray markets thrive across Eastern Europe.[40] The expectation of payoffs is a problem for foreign businessmen, especially in Romania, followed by Bulgaria and Poland.[41] Thievery and pilferage of state property seem to occur on a very large scale, while factories are plagued not by organized strikes but spontaneous absenteeism. As in the Soviet Union, bureaucrats are likely to resent anyone's working too well. For example, when the manager of a tourist castle made such improvements as to produce a large income for the state instead of requiring a subsidy, ministerial officials were infuriated.[42]

The ability of governments to intimidate and coerce has generally decreased. The Poles have learned that they can force the leaders to retreat by strikes and protests, and the Church urges workers to demand their rights. Hungarians talk freely. Even East Germans, notably conformist since the building of the Wall in 1961, have taken the Helsinki accords as license for demanding civil rights and freedom to travel. Hundreds of thousands have boldly applied for permission to emigrate.

From China similarly, in 1975 and afterwards, there were many reports such as had not previously emerged of peculation, black marketeering, labor indiscipline, and other lapses more familiar on the Soviet scene. According to a Chinese broadcast, over ten thousand troops were sent into Hangchow because the

---

[36] *New York Times*, May 27, 1974, p. 2.

[37] Vladimir G. Treml, "Alcohol in the USSR: A Fiscal Dilemma," *Soviet Studies*, 27, no. 2 (April 1975), 163, 165.

[38] *Christian Science Monitor*, March 5, 1975.

[39] Hale, *Ceausescu's Romania*, p. 11; Trond Gilberg, "Romania in Conquest of Development" in *Political Socialization*, I. Volgyes, ed., pp. 185-189.

[40] *Business Week*, April 19, 1976, p. 41.

[41] *New York Times*, September 9, 1975, p. 8.

[42] George S. Wheeler, *The Human Face of Socialism* (New York: Lawrence Hill, 1972), p. 116.

workers had been "unable to increase production under the pernicious influence of the counterrevolutionary revisionist line and bourgeois factionalism and due to the sabotage activities of a handful of class enemies."[43] There have been factory slowdowns and factional fights.[44] And bank robbers seem to have been made folk heroes.[45]

It is not to be inferred that government shows any signs of breaking down anywhere, and the level of public order may well be higher in most or all Communist states than in a large majority of the countries of the world. But it is clear that the Communist states are losing, under the corrosive influences of ordinary life, much of the special drive and discipline that had set them apart.

The Problem of Power

A more serious threat to the Communist state than the inevitable relaxation of faith and discipline is the problem of allocation of power, the renewal of the rulership, both of the supreme leadership and the elite as a whole. The Leninists never had a positive theory of the state, beyond general ideas of the dictatorship of the proletariat as expressed by the party. They looked for ways of maximizing power, not of managing and checking it—which includes the advancement of suitable people and the prevention of the abuse of power.

In effect, the basic political theory of the Leninist state is the right of the holders of power to organize it and use it as they see fit, supposedly for the benefit of the masses, according to Marxist presuppositions, but without practical accountability. The basic political constitution is the rulership of an all-powerful, self-chosen elite acting partly for the good of the country, partly for its own benefit. The Communist Party is quite frankly holder of all political power, and it is the judge of its own membership—in effect a great club or brotherhood that rules without legal limitation, whose rules apply both to itself and the community at large. It has never been open; if it were, it would cease to be a Communist party. It is a closed ruling class such as no Western nation possesses and such as no modern nation possessed prior to Leninism. There is no information on the extent to which party membership and elite status within the party are hereditary, but it would be quite remarkable if party members did not favor their own offspring—perhaps with the plausible argument that they are the most reliable recruits. The weaker ideological drive becomes, the more the party evolves toward a closed group, a coterie that profits by the system and does not care to change it.[46] And the more privileges are involved, the less the inclination to share them with outsiders. The logical evolution of

---

[43] *New York Times*, July 29, 1975, p. 6.

[44] *Ibid.*, November 26, 1976, p. 3.

[45] *Ibid.*, August 22, 1976, p. 1.

[46] Robert Conquest, "A New Russia? A New World?" *Foreign Affairs*, 53 (April 1975), 486.

the Communist Party is from a revolutionary band to a new aristocracy, as foreseen by many revolutionaries, such as Bukharin in 1922[47] and Bakunin in 1875.[48]

The privileges of the elite are real and growing. Party members are expected to work hard; but they get special pay, special vacations, preference for scarce goods, dachas in exclusive settlements, and the like, even special hospitals. If they rise a little in the hierarchy, they may qualify either to buy an automobile ahead of the waiting list or to have that prized status symbol, a chauffeured limousine. They can titillate their senses with the Western cultural imports, including pornography, denied ordinary people.[49] They have better chances of travel abroad and are preferred for promotions. By wirepulling if not outright bribery (perhaps by coaching for entrance examinations), they can probably ease the way for their offspring into the universities which, along with party status, screen the Soviet elite; and they can feel confident that their sons and daughters will qualify for a diploma. In any case, according to Alec Nove, "The beneficiaries of such privilege live in a world of their own, to which ordinary mortals are denied access. Surely they have a sense of belonging to some separate and high 'class' . . ."[50]

There is similar evidence of the stabilization of the elite class and its separation from ordinary people in other Communist states; it would be phenomenal indeed if this did not occur in the absence of forces to compel opening and renewal of elites. High-ranking Chinese leaders live totally screened from the masses, and cadres in black limousines speed among the cyclists. East European parties are privileged corporations in the medieval sense. Typically, Poland is characterized as a land of cliques dedicated to self-aggrandizement.[51]

The obvious consequence to be expected is indefinite deepening of the gap between the "new class" and the masses, with further falsification of Communism's basic equalitarian tenet and a deep-seated corrosion of the values of the system. Less obvious is the stiffening of the system. Under Communism, one can advance oneself not by getting richer but by climbing a status ladder; consequently position on the ladder becomes the principal form of property and the most cherished possession. The mission of change having disappeared, the goal of the elite becomes the maintenance or improvement of status; and holders of valuable positions have an interest not only in their own security but in the principle of security of tenure.

---

[47] Alec Nove, "Is There a Ruling Class in the USSR?" *Soviet Studies*, 27 (October 1975), 620.

[48] David McLellan, *The Thought of Karl Marx* (London: Macmillan, 1971), p. 222.

[49] Hedrick Smith, *The Russians* (New York: Quadrangle/New York Times, 1976), pp. 45-46.

[50] Alec Nove, "Is There a Ruling Class in the USSR?", pp. 635, 637.

[51] Alexander Matejko, *Social Change and Stratification in Eastern Europe* (New York: Praeger, 1974), pp. 213–214.

A dictator can shake up, purge, renew elites, and break up cliques; but there are few remaining dictators in the Communist world able to do this. The Stalins, big and little, have mostly been succeeded by less forceful characters, and even Stalin in his old age found the apparatus getting out of his control. Stability seems almost everywhere to be the order of the day, China, Albania, and the newer Communist states of Indochina having yet to settle down. This is especially true of the Soviet Union, where admissions to and exclusions from the ruling circle have been few since the ouster of Khrushchev.

One result is that the average age of the elite, especially at the top, has increased markedly. Central Committee members of the Soviet party in 1976 averaged 60 years of age, whereas the norm in 1939 was 44 and in 1966, 56. The average age of Politburo members also climbs steadily, over the past decade nearly a year for each calendar year, to 67 in 1977. Very few in the upper echelons are dismissed or demoted; it seems to be the rule, in the absence of any civil service rules, that they stay on indefinitely as long as they are loyal to the group. Similarly, the Chinese leadership, at least up to the death of Mao in 1976, was ruled by veterans of the Long March of 1934-35. The Chinese Politburo members averaged 49 in 1945 and 66 in 1974; throughout the regime, there has long been a strong tendency to cling to positions and grow old in them.[52] Even the tumult of the Cultural Revolution brought no considerable rejuvenation.

The pattern holds true for other parties, although information is incomplete. As of Khrushchev's 70th birthday (1964), six of the top leaders of the thirteen Communist countries (Cuba excluded) were under 60; as of Brezhnev's (1976), only two, Ceauşescu (58) and newly elected Hau Kuo-feng (probably 57).

There is no ready answer for the renewal of elites. The only method suggested by the Communist ideology is revolution, an idea clearly at the heart of Mao's Cultural Revolution. But the more settled things become and the lower ideological fires burn, the more difficult to carry through anything like Mao's Cultural Revolution (which largely failed) or Stalin's revolution from above with mass purges. As the Communist state becomes fixed in its ways, a revolution can only portend the overthrow of Communism. Since no change of leadership is legally provided—a Brezhnev is not likely to follow Khrushchev's example and risk rebellion by at once allowing his colleagues considerable latitude and making them feel insecure—change can only be traumatic, discrediting past leaders and threatening systematic change.

The more centralized the system, the graver the problem of succession, and the Communists have no new or promising answer to this old crux of empire. Various logical remedies might be devised, but they would have to be written

---

[52] A. Doak Barnett, *Cadres, Bureaucracy, and Political Power in Communist China* (New York: Columbia University Press, 1967), p. 434.

into a constitution of sorts, and constitutional Communism is a contradiction of terms. It is in any case difficult for the leadership to devise reform, because reform would at any moment probably be disadvantageous for it. The regimes and their rulers are also handicapped by distrust. As they become older, feebler, and more fearful, they are likely to become more distrustful of suggested changes and of those beneath them who are probably hoping to succeed to power; and distrust may be expected to pervade and poison the system like a miasma creeping down from the summit. The perennial weakness of all authoritarian systems, lack of feedback, is also sorely felt. There is no critical journalism; there are no political analysts, or at least none in view. There is no criticism of high-level corruption and stupidity, except so far as those on top see fit to criticize themselves. The leaders do not even have the benefit of study of historical experience; by turning history into a chronicle of party victories, they have shut themselves off from knowledge of their own past.

In sum, the Communist system, which set out as something very special in the world, the maker of a new order, not surprisingly becomes less special as distance from the revolutionary struggle grows. The fervent dedication cools; the commitment to change is reversed; equalitarian feeling is choked by the establishment of a new ruling group; economic growth slackens; the grip of the state over all its citizens relaxes somewhat; problems of public order grow more bothersome, as in the rest of the world. In such ways, the Communist state faces troubles like those plaguing other states without demonstrably better answers. In another way the Communist state is worse prepared to advance into the future than constitutional states of the West—indeed, Communism may be at a disadvantage by comparison with traditional authoritarianism. The traditional tsar or monarch could name or change a ministry, and everyone knew who was to replace him. The Communist state has no such authority to permit change with stability.

The Life Cycle of Communism

A Communist revolution represents a mighty triumph, a cataclysmic assertion of political will over institutions, customs, and possession, the victory of the untried underdogs over all the most respectable. It is a magnificent and promising new beginning. But its strength lies in its beginnings, and it can continue strong only so far as it can maintain the morale and drive with which it was born.

The overthrow of the old order represents a promise of infinite improvement, everything after which is anticlimactic. It is the big upheaval in the lives of everyone, most of all the revolutionaries, who are transmuted from being the attackers, disadvantaged zealots of change, outsiders storming the palace gates, to possessors and rulers, the privileged builders and defenders of the new order. It changes the entire character of their lives; nothing they can possibly achieve subsequently can have comparable importance. It was their adventure, their self-fulfillment, and their success, after which the failures and frustrations begin.

The exacting and inspiring times are those of struggle. But when the revolutionary party has become a government and has done its work of expelling the foreigners, destroying the parasites, and reasserting the national worth, what then? What is the army to do after the victory?

It can continue the fight, perhaps, in threat and confrontation, or in preparation for the expected return of the attack. Stalin, for example, built up the industrial forces of Russia for the renewal, predicted by Lenin, of the capitalist onslaught. As the good cause loses its demoniacal opposition, propaganda can step in to keep up the image of conflict for a time. But enemies, at home and abroad, become less useful, and the revolution finds itself subsiding into the lassitude of peace. It is then that the peaceful goals of the good life must come to the fore—better clothes, more housing, better education, and the like. But these raise no hot enthusiasm and do not unite but divide, as everyone has his own priorities; the organization for revolutionary combat is not appropriate for the tasks of peace, and the failures are not long excused by the cunning of the foe.

The revolution that was the inspiration of youth becomes the property of oldsters. Revolution becomes established power, and those who fought for the poor become the super-rich, owners of the whole country. The revolutionary ethic becomes conservative. The anti-traditional movement increasingly bases itself on the traditions it builds up. Excitement wears away; there are no more big victories to justify faith and sacrifices. Ideas yield to enjoyment. The rulership looks to advantages at home and abroad, and the people seek advantages in dealing with one another. Communism for Lenin was internationalism; for Stalin it became nationalism; for his successors it has become a set of organizational principles for the maintenance of power.

Ideology is close to charisma which rises when traditional leadership breaks down or is discredited. It spells faith in what a leader says because he says it. "Lenin said" carries weight. But the heroes are followed by the clerks; "Brezhnev says," anyone knows, has meaning only so long as he hold the reins, aside from the fact that he has nothing exciting to say. The older the revolution, the more difficult for anyone to move people and change things, should he actually desire to do so.

Ideology fails also because of its success. It is a truth which must be pure, and as long as the Soviet Union was alone in the world, there was a single truth which could accommodate pretenses of internationalism to the substance of nationalism. But multiplicity of Marxist-Leninist states means multiple nationalisms, diversity, and degradation of truth to a vague common denominator. There is no longer any one true road. The faith rests no longer on conditions and natural passions but, so far as it lives, on teaching. It becomes verbal instead of visceral; habitual instead of passionate. "Struggle" is something in history or distant lands. The expectations of great change have been fulfilled or come to seem fulfillable only gradually; and the interests of the party can no longer be assumed to be the same as those of the people. So far as the revolution has succeeded, it has erased the conditions of oppression and inferiority which generated it; so far as it has not succeeded after a generation of sacrifices, the old slogans are empty.

War and violence, or their image and expectation, are necessary to keep alive the spirit of the Communist state, to make workable the centralized management of the economy, the party's monopoly of political power, and the control of communications, which are essential components of the system. Without conviction, indoctrination becomes training in cynicism. There is less rejection than indifference; people simply stop listening without bothering to deny. As the purposefulness of the party declines, there is no way to keep the party cadres honest and dedicated, hardworking and self-denying; and the party, once a guiding and inspiring body, becomes an aristocracy. Maoists accused the Soviet Union of failing to inculcate a revolutionary spirit among the young, that is, of failing to do the impossible. The Communists wait in vain for the "New Man" to emerge from the revolution. Tito wanted all retired office-holders to be political activists;[53] the pensioners would uphold the revolution.

Revolutionary conviction declines because of the passing of time and generations, the failure of promises, changes of leadership, changes in the world picture, and the economic maturation of society. As it declines, Communist society must become looser, less directed and less monolithic. In terms of physics, the first law of political dynamics is the increase of entropy in the absence of inputs of energy. As Weber said, charisma becomes routinization. The culture becomes, in Sorokin's terms, less ideational, more sensate. Spirit turns into organization, and organization decays. Although the world and the party are slow to realize it, the Communism of struggle becomes the Communism of possession.

The outcome may legitimately be called decay and not simply adaptation because it is movement away from the ideals of Communism, not only the ideals for which it was born but those to which it claims always to subscribe, of justice and equality. Government of the large state requires hierarchy, and the Communist state is the more hierarchic because government controls so much and because authority must be tightly centralized. The revolution becomes bureaucracy, and bureaucracy is self-centered and self-serving, unable to maintain high productivity more than a few years. In short, the establishment replaces purpose with procedures. It is saved from complete ossification only by feedback, of which the outsize bureaucracies of Communist societies receive least.[54] The best bureaucrats, and those who prosper most in the system, are

---

[53] Nenad Popovic, *Yugoslavia: The New Class in Crisis* (Syracuse: Syracuse University Press, 1968), p. 25.

[54] Anthony Downs, *Inside Bureaucracy* (Boston: Little, Borwn, 1967), pp. 160, 163-164.

those most devoted not to the whole community but to the organization of which they are a part. Authority leaks away from the governors. The middle and lower echelons gradually gain standing of their own and the ability, when terror is laid aside, to sabotage top-level decisions. One answer to the problem of bureaucratization is campaigning, concentrating attention on a single objective in order to override bureaucratic road blocks, but campaigns cannot last long. There may also be periodic shakeups, like Khrushchev's reorganizations or the Cultural Revolution; but rigidities return all too soon.[55]

The party becomes "tailist" in Lenin's sense, following instead of leading. It ceases to try really to move society but settles down to governing society, not initiating change but mediating demands. Leaders try to develop constituencies to support their careers; and the party becomes slightly representative. The single-minded elite becomes more like a coalition of interests and tendencies of the increasingly differentiated society. Bureaus develop their own ideologies.[56] Specialists must be heard to enable the state to function smoothly, and the complexity of society brings demands for autonomy. To retain the loyalty of their members, organizations must promote membership interests. The newly rising party mobilized for its holy purposes; the mature party answers the interests of its members and the demands brought upon it.

Hierarchy brings stratification as people become settled in their positions and networks of relationships are formed. The theoretical equality of socialism degenerates into inequality of power. Elite privilege and exclusiveness becomes an essential means of securing coherence of the rulers as the shared mission fades. Communist movements are always a mixture of idealists and self-seekers; when revolution turns into drudgery, idealists are replaced by careerists.

Corruption is more the misuse of power—the haughtiness and arbitrariness of authority—than misappropriation of money. But inequality of power is converted, as soon as the will to sacrifice dies, into inequality of material rewards. The way to wealth in any authoritarian society is through authority, that is, politics. The ruling class which does not take the best for itself has yet to be invented. There are all manner of legal and illegal advantages for the powerful. The overgrown system of controls, for which people lose respect as the necessity ceases to be apparent, furnishes countless opportunities to make political position profitable. The luxuries of the new rulers approach or surpass those of the monarchs and nobles whom they displaced. After only nine years of power, the Nazi elite was too corrupt to cut down its sumptuous and splendid life style even in a life-and-death war. Communist regimes have decayed more slowly.

Abuses are contagious; as the propaganda of the word weakens, the counter-propaganda of the deed gains force. As some have, others deserve no less and demand more. When so many decisions are political, more or less arbitrary and

---

[55] Downs, *Inside Bureaucracy*, pp. 164–165.
[56] *Ibid.*, Chap. 19.

secretly reached, with very little independent inquiry or fears of exposure, the system is practically engineered for corruption. People everywhere have to try to secure their interests by political means, and politics becomes a network of personal relations. The bosses may even prefer to do things irregularly, by nepotism, friendship, and rewards, for example, appropriating supplies to barter for desired goods without even trying to obtain them legally.[57] The system can work tolerably well only so long as there remains at least a scintilla of faith in doing something noble. The passing of generations deepens the spoilage, since the children of the elite have the easiest road to power, and they not only lack the tempering of their elders but take for granted the superiority to which they have grown up.

Such dissipation of inspiration has occurred countless times. Vigorous new dynasties in China and other empires always ran down, despite the most sophisticated efforts to avoid it, in profound putrefaction. Major religions, such as Christianity, Buddhism, and Islam have known it in different ways. Many a monastic order has begun in fervent dedication to equality, poverty, and piety, only to drift into elitism, wealth-seeking, and ritualism. Idealistic non-Communist political revolutions have similarly run down. The 1910 Mexican revolution, for example, has maintained itself, like the Russian Revolution, under the same political party; but a new ruling class has long ago set itself up, and the old idealism has long since faded. During the 1920s Kemal Atatürk revolutionized Turkish life, abolishing most Moslem institutions, giving women equal rights, changing the script, discarding Oriental clothing in favor of European, partially socializing the economy, etc.; but change slowed down well before his death in 1938 and practically halted for many years after. Many a revolution has started out to remake the world, has indeed brought some changes, then settled down in its achievements. The Communist revolution differs only in being more systematic and more ideologized.

No Communist state is exempt, so far as information is available, from the progressive change which may be called decay or normalization. The revolution has been maintained, apparently, in greatest purity in Vietnam, where war continued until April 1975. Here too, time does its work; the revolution was begun by youths; in 1977 the average age of the Politburo was 67. North Korea has tried very hard to maintain a state of near-war, but economic crime became a problem in the 1960's.[58] Kim himself warned that the younger generation would likely "forget the enemy, dislike the struggle, enjoy idleness."[59] Nepotism at high levels is a poor augur; Kim's wife is on the Central Committee and numerous other relatives sit in high office. His brother is on the

---

[57] Ulc, "Czechoslovakia: The Great Leap Backward," in *The Politics of Modernization in Eastern Europe: Testing the Soviet Model,* Charles Gati, ed. (New York: Praeger, 1975), p. 109.

[58] Robert Scalapino and Chong-sik Lee, *Communism in Korea,* Vol. 2, pp. 829-830.

[59] Baik Bong, *Kim Il-song* (Tokyo: Miraishi, 1969), Vol. 3, p. 377.

Politburo and was a presumptive successor until his son Kim Jong succeeded to that honor. Ideological commitment ebbs; in the 1960s, over 80 percent of North Korean foreign trade was with Communist countries, in 1975 only half.

Castro's Cuba has in the 1970s gained something economically but lost much or most of the dash and verve of the embattled years, becoming more like other Latin American countries, less the outpost of social revolution. Castro, having put on dress uniform instead of guerrilla kakhi, has given up the old style of personalism and ad hoc intervention as the state and party have become institutionalized. With less repression, there is more grumbling. Castroism, now the establishment, takes young people to task for susceptibility to U. S. music. For the new elite, there are luxury night clubs, luxury cars, beach homes, special restaurants, all in the face of considerable privation of the masses.[60] Corruption became a problem when the revolution was a decade old.[61] By 1972 it was possible for employees of a shoe factory to sell stolen shoes openly from door to door, a freedom earlier inconceivable.[62]

Yet it must be reemphasized that the Communist form is very strong. If the creed is in some ways absurd, in others it is intellectually appealing, modern-sounding, and universalistic in a world striving toward unity. Best of all, it mobilizes aggressiveness and charity together in the service of power. Marxism-Leninism enables rulers to do what they want to do with the conviction of doing good. It is because of this verbal righteousness or self-righteousness that much of the world credits Communists with the best of intentions while they effectively serve their own interests. It is no mystery—although the question is often asked—why Western intellectuals are much more inclined to become indignant at the abuses of rightist than leftist dictatorships.

Communism, both the ideology and the state, promotes discipline and order. It is admirable how the Chinese return discarded objects to travellers, how the Soviets have banished pornography (at least from view), how the streets of Communist capitals are safe at night. In the same way, Communist states are to be congratulated for offering employment to everyone, medical care, education, and opportunities to be useful. In the Communist state there is less to worry about—indeed, less drive to do anything, less competition and emulation, probably less envy. Communism can (witness East Germany) claim rationality through central guidance and modern organization. That the state may not progress economically need not be a threat to the political order; consumer luxuries may be sacrificed to goals of social or political structure. Nor is intellectual creativity necessary, since it is always possible to borrow.

[60] Roberto E. Hernandez and Carmelo Mesa-Lago, "Labor Organization and Wages," in *Revolutionary Change in Cuba,* C. Mesa-Lago, ed. (Pittsburgh: University of Pittsburgh Press, 1971), p. 231.

[61] Hugh Thomas, *Cuba: The Pursuit of Freedom* (New York: Harper & Row, 1971), p. 1486.

[62] Rene' Dumont, *Is Cuba Socialist?* (New York: Viking Press, 1974), p. 153.

The Communist state is self-sustaining at least for a considerable period. It takes and holds all the bases of power. Those with the inside track have a vested interest in keeping things as they are. They are educated only in Marxism-Leninism. To denationalize the economy is out of the question. There is no basis for competing political parties, and to admit political competition would seem an invitation to paralysis in the complexly integrated system. Probably not many persons of importance desire real change. Everyone who counts enjoys a position of superiority and probably wants to keep it that way; the system is geared for their mutual reinforcement. Thus the settled Communist state needs no enthusiasm from its citizens, only apathy; and apathy comes easily. The usefulness of the Communist system is shown by the degree to which Communist states, including those free to change, hold fast to it. Cuba, after groping for new ways, drifted into the formal structure; and China's Cultural Revolution reverted to conventional bureaucratic Communism.

But the strengths may be all undone by the central weakness of Communism, the inability to check and allocate power. It lacks means of consequential reform from within, just as it excludes reform from without. The system is designed to prevent political change. A pluralistic system can absorb change without breaking; the Communist system fears that any crack may be fatal.

There is no overt or respectable method in Communist states for choosing new leadership, no limit on tenure or definition of powers at the top. Except in the satellite countries and with Soviet assistance, the old heroes cannot be retired; a Tito or Mao, like Stalin, occupies the top post to his deathbed. The independent Communist states (other than the Soviet Union) are still run by revolutionary commanders and their comrades in battle; eventually they must be replaced by people who have risen by virtue of their connections. They will seldom be as capable as their predecessors. Among the Nazis, Albert Speer reported, "In order to avoid raising up a rival in his own household, many a minister took care not to appoint a vigorous and intelligent deputy,"[63] and there is no evidence that Communist states are exempt from this law of authoritarian decadence.

The Communist state is, beneath all ornaments, dictatorship; and there is no visible reason, except the possession of ideology, that Communists should expect to escape the decomposition which always afflicts dictatorships. The virtue of democracy is not so much that it follows the popular will—which may or may not be wise—but that it provides a morally acceptable framework within which leadership may be constrained, legitimated, and changed. Arbitrary authority ultimately means disorder.

There is no answer within the axioms of the system. Even if the leadership wished to set up a means of renewal of power at the top, sacrificing their own positions to do so, they lack means. Without centers of power outside the

[63]Albert Speer, *Inside the Third Reich* (New York: Macmillan, 1967), p. 253.

official apparatus, there is no way to assure obedience to any rules in the future. And the autocratic regime lacks a self-perspective. Its image of the world is that fed into it by its agents, who see the outside in terms of their own pre-conceptions and needs. The authoritarian government, concerned with secu-rity, probably depends most on the very security forces that magnify dangers for their own purposes.[64] Good management decisions require the kind of information that Communist systems do not allow. As Khrushchev reflected, "Only if a leadership is under public control will it be protected from actions which are incompatible with our socialist doctrine and harmful to our socialist way of life."[65] Still more is it necessary to have external inputs if leading officials are to be persuaded to surrender power for the good of the state.

In this view, the specialness of the Communist states must be impermanent. Having lost the capacity to remake themselves, they presumably must become more like existing non-Communist states. One direction in which they might go is toward the general Western model of pluralistic societies. They might grad-ually become opener, permit more autonomy to groups and people, relax economic controls, regularize authority by giving more reality to legal forms of constitutional and representative government, and become more sensitive to rights and freedoms. This seems more conceivable for states nearer the Western tradition, particularly East European countries.

Other Communist states will, in all probability, evolve in the direction of many authoritarian states of the non-Western world that have never experienced a Communist revolution. Third World states, like Communist states, usually have only a feeble constitution in terms of the allocation and limitation of power; that is, a formally democratic government probably has the option of abolishing democratic practices should the necessity arise.

Symptomatic of this trend is the evident convergence of conservative Communist and radical non-Communist movements in the Third World. The Communist states lose Marxism; the Third World nationalists find it, in simplified form, highly useful. The speeches of the Communist delegates in the United Nations sound very much like those of the impoverished majority in their generalities and philosophy. The Communists have ceased to be revolutionary except in talk, while Third World leaders, who want no more revolution once they control the government, like to use its rhetoric and base their demands on its logic. The residue of Marxism-Leninism in action is mostly anti-Westernism, nationalism, militarism, economic statism, something vaguely called socialism, and rationalization of dictatorship—the great themes of the majority of countries of the Third World.

---

[64] P. V. Burks, "Technological Political Change in Eastern Europe," in *Change in Com-munist Systems* Chalmers Johnson, ed., (Stanford: Stanford University Press, 1970), p. 294.

[65] *Khrushchev Remembers* (Boston: Little, Brown, 1970), pp. 312-313.

If the Communist states continue on the course they appear to be following toward degradation of everything the revolution once meant, either returning to a Western, pluralistic society (as in the case of some East European countries wrenched from their historic associations by Soviet power) or toward the political ways of the Third World (as in the case of most Marxist-Leninist states), it will be clear that Communism, or Marxism-Leninism as a political form, is time-bound and associated with certain circumstances in a period of historical transition—especially with the failures and errors of the Western world in this century. Lenin blamed capitalism and imperialism for World War I, and the war made possible the Russian Revolution. Japanese aggression (industrialized Japan may be counted part of the West in this connection) and the Second World War brought Communism to power in China. Hitler's brutality and folly restored a decadent Soviet system and brought Communism to Eastern Europe. U. S. short-sightedness and insensitivity made Communism possible in Cuba, and the French and American wars to sustain Western or pro-Western power in Indochina gave victory to Communism in that area.

Communism is then, in sum, a reaction of technologically less advanced states, a defensive reaction of proud but injured societies, beginning with intellectual violence of the Russian intelligentsia of the nineteenth century and ending, so far as can be seen, with the liquidation of the Western colonial holdings. It has offered, in the emergency, a means of unity, strength, and discipline to muster military force and moral strength to resist the intrusion and a means of modernization to meet the West on its own ground. It is wholly natural that the reaction should be Russian-shaped and Russian-led because Russia was and is by far the strongest non-Western power injured by the West. The non-Western reaction would in any case have to be a mixture of modernization and authoritarianism, but Russia lent a special character: universalist, because of the multinationalism of the Russian empire; pseudo-democratic, because of the long Russian tradition of borrowing of forms; pseudo-scientific because of the Russian dependence on and admiration for Western technology.

But Communism is an eccentric movement with a philosophy alien to the traditional cultures of the world, and it could begin only in the unique circumstances of semi-Westernized Russia. After it had shown success there, it could spread elsewhere only with the help of violence to raise passions and destroy alternatives. Without violence, Communism is not a viable choice. The Communist state is in effect self-limiting, because the efficacy of controls eventually causes economic and technological weakness.

The utopia of Marxism is backward-looking and essentially primitive, a promise not of mastery of contemporary problems but of escape from them. Communism does not solve any of the basic problems of social order but postpones them or ignores them. The fundamental crux of politics, the conflict between interests of individuals and of the collective, it pretends out of existence, or smothers by allowing some to consider their interests to be those of the collective. The ideology of Marxism-Leninism murders common sense (is your friend a proletarian?) and has no positive contribution to the grave questions of the latter part of the twentieth century. It is contradicted most of all by the Marxist-Leninist states themselves, which demonstrate clearly how class and exploitation can have a political rather than an economic base.

Lenin claimed to bring an answer to the world's problems. It would have been miraculous if he had done so; such miracles have not occurred in our times. But he established a political form of extraordinary effectiveness in certain circumstances. It will be fascinating for future political philosophers to chronicle the life story of Maxist-Leninist Communism.

SUMMARY

1. The key characteristics of the Communist state are a modern, universalistic, basically authoritarian and anti-Western ideology, an especially firm organization made possible by this ideology, and an exceptional degree of political control over society.

2. Communism appeals primarily to countries of authoritarian background injured by Western intrusion, military, political, economic, and/or cultural.

3. A major function of Communism is the defense of the injured society by organization, remoralization, militarization, and industrialization.

4. Communism copies outward aspects of Western politics as a defense against Western political ideas and a means of mobilization.

5. Communism serves as a basis of unity where unity is difficult, raising ideological over ethnic or other loyalties, a fact especially important for Marxism in the former Russian empire.

6. Communism is promoted by persons of partly Western background with a desire to be at once modern and independent of the West.

7. Communism gains power only in a situation of tension, conflict, and destruction of older values, particularly war against a "capitalist" power.

8. The strengths of Communism are most evident in war; it is close in spirit to the military, and it uses military organization and methods for peacetime politics.

9. The victory of Communism in a disturbed situation is the victory of the most purposeful and coherent organization and the most power-minded, the two characteristics being correlated.

10. The genesis of Communism was possible in Russia as a multinational empire with messianic directions, autocratic yet accustomed to borrowing forms as well as technology from the pluralistic Western world.

11. Non-Russian Communisms are offshoots not of Lenin's state but of Soviet Communism as modified by Stalin toward nationalism, bureaucratism, and dogmatism.

12. Communist states, taking the Soviet model, tend to similarity of patterns even under diverse conditions because they find the Leninist-Stalinist patterns useful for the support of political power.

13. Marxism-Leninism is a strong ideology because it offers persuasive, modern reasons that tell rulers they are right in the exercise of power.

14. Communism has almost absolute powers of self-perpetuation because the totality of controls offers no foothold for organized opposition.

15. The greatest task of Communist states in peacetime is to maintain the political status quo despite internal and external change, to minimize demands upon the political system and to maximize compliance with its directives.

16. Because their political essence is the concentration of power, Communist states have no means of self-reform.

17. Communist systems are subject to erosion because of recession of the revolution, cessation of conflict, aging and passing of leadership, and external influences diluting ideological conviction.

18. Communist systems become conservative, the elite self-perpetuating and self-serving.

19. Communist systems have not solved the problem of allocation of power at the center, or of securing stability by orderly change.

20. Communist states tend to become less distinctively Communistic, but are subject to contrary influences, toward Westernization and toward simple dictatorship.

21. With the enfeeblement of ideology, the effort to borrow Western technology becomes less effective and the negative aspects of controls become more apparent, partly defeating the effort to catch up with the West.

22. In reaction to erosion of the system, Communist states would tighten controls, but they are unable to do so effectively because the state loses capacity to move society, and there enters a degree of informal and irregular pluralism.

23. The revolution receding, Communist states may tend to become more like states of the non-Western world which have not had a comparable revolution.

Index

C

Vietnam *(cont.)*
  consolidation of power in, 90-93
  ethnic divisions in, 19
  French colonization of, 88
  French reoccupation of, 90-92
  Japanese invasion of, 89-90
  military men in leadership of, 41
  military prowess of, 57
  nationalism in, 89
  Nationalist Party of, 89
  reunification of, 185
  shadow parties in, 7
  Workers' Party of, *see* Communist
    Party *above*
Vietnam war
  China and, 131
  United States in, 47, 57-58

W

Walwyne, Wm., 50
Wang Hung-wen, 135
Warsaw Treaty Organization (WTO),
  145
Water Margins (Chinese novel), 138
Webb, Beatrice, 110
Webb, Sidney, 110
Weber, Max, 209
West Germany, 149-51
  Yugoslav workers in, 168
What Is to Be Done (Lenin), 67
Wilson, Woodrow, 54

X

Xoxe, Koci, 88

Y

Yao Wen-yuan, 135
Yugoslavia, 1, 2, 81, 83, 84, 163-73
  Communist Party of, 86-87
    Albanian Communist Party and,
      173-74
    expulsion by Stalin of, 164-66
    openness of, 168
    organization of, 5

Yugoslavia
  Communist Party of *(cont.)*
    power of, 7-8
    "self-management" ideology of,
      166-67
    10th Congress of, 170
    in World War II, 45
  consolidation of power in, 86-87
  decentralization in, 166-68, 170
  dissidence in, 17
  ethnic divisions in, 19
  foreign trade of, 168-69
  importance of ideology in, 23
  liberalization in, 169-73
  military men in leadership of, 41
  national development of, 39
  national republics of, 167
  private agriculture in, 165
  private business in, 11
  secrecy in, 10
  travel restrictions of, 11

Z

Zhivkov, Todor, 148
Zinoviev, Grigori, 106
  as oppositionist, 123
"Znak" group, 157
Zog, King of Albania, 87